Fair Trade

The challenges of transforming globalization

**Edited by
Laura T. Raynolds,
Douglas L. Murray, and
John Wilkinson**

 Routledge
Taylor & Francis Group

LONDON AND NEW YORK

First published 2007
by Routledge
2 Park Square, Milton Park, Abingdon, Oxon OX14 4RN

Simultaneously published in the USA and Canada
by Routledge
270 Madison Ave, New York, NY 10016

*Routledge is an imprint of the Taylor & Francis Group,
an informa business*

Typeset in Times New Roman by
Newgen Imaging Systems (P) Ltd, Chennai, India
Printed and bound in Great Britain by
Antony Rowe Ltd, Chippenham, Wiltshire

British Library Cataloguing in Publication Data
A catalogue record for this book is available
from the British Library

Library of Congress Cataloging in Publication Data
    Fair trade : the challenges of transforming globalization / edited by
Laura T. Raynolds, Douglas Murray, and John Wilkinson.
        p. cm.
    Includes bibliographical references and index.
    1. International trade. 2. Competition, Unfair.
I. Raynolds, Laura T., 1959– II. Murray, Douglas L., 1947–
III. Wilkinson, John, 1946–

    HF1379.F345 2007
    382'.104–dc22   2006034325

ISBN10: 0–415–77202–8 (hbk)
ISBN10: 0–415–77203–6 (pbk)

ISBN13: 978–0–415–77202–0 (hbk)
ISBN13: 978–0–415–77203–7 (pbk)

Fair Trade

This book explores the challenges and potential of Fair Trade, one of the world's most dynamic efforts to enhance global social justice and environmental sustainability through market-based social change.

Fair Trade links food consumers and agricultural producers across the Global North/South divide and lies at the heart of key efforts to reshape the global economy. In arenas, Fair Trade is aligned to a range of alternative globalization and trade justice efforts. In movement arenas, Fair Trade is aligned to a range of alternative globalization and trade justice efforts. This book reveals the challenges Fair Trade faces in its effort to transform globalization, emphasizing the inherent tensions in working both in, and against, the market. The volume explores Fair Trade's recent rapid growth into new production regions, market arenas, and commodity areas through case studies of Europe, North America, Africa, and Latin America undertaken by prominent scholars in each region. The authors draw on, and advance, global commodity and value chain analysis, convention, and social movement approaches through these case studies and a series of synthetic analytical chapters. Pressures for both more radical and more moderate approaches intertwine with the movement's historical vision, reshaping Fair Trade's priorities and efforts in the Global North and South.

This text will be of strong interest to students and scholars of politics, globalization, sociology, geography, economics, and business.

Laura T. Raynolds is Co-Director of the Center for Fair and Alternative Trade Studies and Professor of Sociology at Colorado State University, USA.

Douglas L. Murray is Co-Director of the Center for Fair and Alternative Trade Studies and Professor of Sociology at Colorado State University, USA.

John Wilkinson is a Senior Lecturer in Development, Agriculture and Society (CPDA) at the Rural Federal University, Rio de Janeiro, Brazil.

We dedicate this book to those near and far committed to creating a fair and just world. During the more than three years that went into this project, a number of the authors lost loved ones. They remain an inspiration to us all.

In memoriam
Joan Blackmer
Ger Conroy
Eileen Jones
Lois Murray
Donald Murray
Maretha du Toit
Annabel Ware

Contents

Illustrations

Figures

Tables

Box

Contributors

Editors

Laura T. Raynolds is Co-Director of the Center for Fair and Alternative Trade Studies and Professor of Sociology, Colorado State University. Her research focuses on fair/alternative trade, global agrofood networks, and gender and labor force restructuring particularly in the Caribbean and Latin America. She has published extensively in these areas, including recent articles in *World Development, Sociologia Ruralis, Agriculture and Human Values, Journal of International Development,* and *Gender & Society*.

Douglas L. Murray is Co-Director of the Center for Fair and Alternative Trade Studies and Professor of Sociology, Colorado State University. He has published numerous articles and two books on the unsustainable nature of development based on chemical intensive agriculture in Latin America. He has served as an advisor to various NGOs, governments, and international development institutions on pesticide hazard reduction and related issues. His recent work explores the potential for market-based progressive social change.

John Wilkinson holds a PhD in sociology from Liverpool University. He is a Senior Lecturer at the Graduate Center, Development, Agriculture and Society (CPDA), Rural Federal University, Rio de Janeiro, Brazil. He is the (Co)Author/editor of 10 books and over 70 articles/chapters on different aspects of the food system, economic sociology, and convention theory. He serves as a consultant on food related issues to EEC, OECD, FAO, ECLA, and international NGOs.

Contributors

Stephanie Barrientos is a Fellow at the Institute of Development Studies, University of Sussex. She has researched and published widely on gender and development in Africa and Latin America, globalization and informal work, corporate accountability, fair trade, ethical trade, and international labor standards. She coordinated the UK Ethical Trading Initiative Impact Assessment (2003–2005).

Zina Angelica Cáceres Benavides received her PhD at the Rural Federal University, Rio de Janeiro, Brazil. She is an Economist at the Universidad Nacional Mayor de San Marcos, Peru where she works on issues relating to traditional production systems and new quality markets.

Aurélie Carimentrand is a PhD student at the Center for Economics and Ethics for the Environment and Development (C3ED), University of Versailles-St. Quentin en Yvelines, France.

Michael E. Conroy, PhD is an economist who taught at the University of Texas (1971–1994) and Yale University (2003–2006). While at the Ford Foundation (1994–2003) he developed and managed a program supporting certification systems, including Fair Trade, as tools for poverty alleviation. He was elected to the Board of Directors of TransFair USA in 2003.

Andries du Toit is a Senior Researcher at the Programme for Land and Agrarian Studies at the University of the Western Cape. His research interests include agrofood reregulation and restructuring in the Western Cape wine and fruit industries and the political economy of chronic poverty and governmentality in South Africa more broadly.

Ann Grodnik works in public finance in the power sector at Seattle Northwest Securities in Seattle, Washington. Her interest and ambition lie in environmental finance and, more broadly, the intersection between business and environment.

Elaine Jones has worked as a practitioner in the fields of Fair and Ethical Trade for over 15 years. She is a Board member of the London-based organization Twin which was a founder of the Fair Trade movement and of CaféDirect and Divine Chocolate.

Sandra Kruger is a postgraduate student and researcher at the Programme for Land and Agrarian Studies at the University of the Western Cape. Her research interests include land and labor reform in agriculture, black economic empowerment in South Africa and international systems of private regulation.

Michael A. Long is a PhD student in the sociology department at Colorado State University, where he is also a research assistant at the Center for Fair and Alternative Trade Studies working on various aspects of fair and alternative trade and local food systems.

Gilberto Mascarenhas is a PhD student at the Rural Federal University, Rio de Janeiro, Brazil, and a researcher on issues linked to Fair Trade, family farming, and quality markets for small producer organizations.

Victor Pérez-Grovas is an agronomist with a MA in Rural Development. Since 1992 he has been Technical Advisor to La Union Majomut coffee cooperative. He is the former coordinator of the Mexican Coordination Network of Fair Trade and is the President of CLAC (Latin American and Caribbean Coordination of Fair Trade Small Producers).

Marie-Christine Renard is a Professor of Sociology at the University of Chapingo, Mexico. Her doctoral dissertation in 1996 and subsequent book were a pathbreaking inquiry into Fair Trade, and her ongoing research in Mexico has provided critical insight into understanding the global Fair Trade coffee sector.

Sally Smith is a Research Officer at the Institute of Development Studies, Sussex, UK, specializing in Fair Trade and Ethical Trade. Her portfolio of work includes several consultancy projects with fair trade organizations.

Acknowledgments

This project would not have been possible without the generous support of the Ford Foundation, which supported the research and writings of many of the authors in this book. It also fostered the ongoing networking and collaboration between scholars and practitioners linked through a series of research institutions around the world. Early support for the investigation into the potential and limits of Fair Trade was provided by the John D. and Catherine T. MacArthur Foundation. Colorado State University has provided both funding and other resources to this project, and through the creation of the Center for Fair and Alternative Trade Studies, has given considerable impetus to the future sustainability of work in this area. The Institute for Development Studies at Sussex University has also supported this project, hosting the initial planning meeting for the research that went into this book. The Federal Rural University in Rio de Janeiro hosted the follow up workshop in which the basic design of this book was developed. Michael Long was the Research Assistant to the project coordinators, and did a superb job of making sure all the pieces in the puzzle fit together at the end of the day. We owe special thanks to Michael A. Conroy, whose many years of dedication to and enthusiasm for the questions that guide this project have had a powerful impact on both the book and the broader movement it investigates. Finally we wish to acknowledge the myriad people that have worked to envision and support initiatives to increase fairness and sustainability around the world. These efforts have inspired us all.

Abbreviations

ATO	Alternative Trade Organization
CSR	Corporate Social Responsibility
EFTA	European Fair Trade Association
FAO	Food and Agriculture Organization
FINE	FLO, IFAT, NEWS!, EFTA
FLO	Fairtrade Labelling Organizations International
FtF	Fairtrade Foundation
FTF	Fair Trade Federation
IFAT	International Fair Trade Association
IFOAM	International Federation of Organic Agricultural Movements
ILO	International Labor Organization
IMF	International Monetary Fund
ISO	International Organization for Standardization
NEWS!	Network of European Worldshops
NGO	Non-Governmental Organization
SME	Small and Medium Enterprise
WTO	World Trade Organization

Part I
Introduction

1 Globalization and its antinomies

Negotiating a Fair Trade movement

Douglas L. Murray and Laura T. Raynolds

Introduction

Mainstream economists would have us believe that consumers seek out the lowest price for goods of any given quality, maximizing their individual gains. But how then do we explain why millions of consumers around the world are now choosing certified Fair Trade products instead of other often cheaper options? Are they actively "voting with their money" for a different model of global trade that is tangibly "fairer" than conventional trade? Further, traditional economic logic tells us that producers seek to maximize their competitive advantage over others in a zero sum game of winners and losers in the global marketplace. How do we then explain the systematic assistance that early participants in Fair Trade provide to subsequent entrants into this dynamic market? Are Fair Trade certified producers replacing competition with solidarity? Finally, mainstream economists also tell us that corporations will always purchase products at the lowest possible price, bargaining down their input costs where possible through competitive sourcing. Why then would an increasing number of companies, both large and small, willingly participate in a system where they must pay a price negotiated by a third party, well above the conventional price, for products that are produced under Fair Trade standards?

Far from anomalies – or the lingering inefficiencies the mainstream economists bemoan – these are but a few of the examples explored in this book that are part of the rapidly growing Fair Trade phenomenon. These examples cannot be discounted as merely the practices of an obscure and irrelevant group of progressive producers and elite consumers. Fair Trade products represent one of the fastest growing segments of the global food market, with total Fair Trade sales reaching US$ 1.6 billion annually (see Chapter 2). In the Global South, over five million farmers, farm workers, and their families across 58 countries have joined the Fair Trade movement, and many more are actively seeking access (FLO 2005).

Yet tensions are rising in conjunction with this movement's remarkable success. As Fair Trade has moved into the mainstream of international trade, it has become embroiled in a range of debates and dilemmas that threaten to divide the movement. Fair Trade is both confronting and engaging large corporate actors in the Global North and South. In the process it is being challenged by its supporters and its opponents. The following discussions reveal the difficult dilemmas and even contradictions facing the movement as it seeks to both challenge the existing global trade regime, and to transform it from within.

What is Fair Trade?

Fair Trade is perhaps the most dynamic of a range of movements, campaigns, and initiatives that have emerged in recent decades in response to the negative effects of globalization. Efforts such as the anti-sweatshop movement in garments, eco-labeling in timber, and Fair Trade certification in food products all seek to create a more sustainable and socially just future. These movements represent the constituent elements of what we describe as "the new globalization," reshaping the patterns of international trade and the very processes of corporate expansion in the global economy that have historically undermined ecological and social conditions around the world. Northern activists working with producers, laborers, and other impoverished sectors of the Global South, are using market-based strategies to mobilize consumer awareness in order to bolster incomes and empower Southern producers and workers. In so doing, Fair Trade seeks to redirect globalization's transformative powers toward the creation of greater social equity on a global scale (Brown 1993; Ransom 2001; Raynolds 2000).

The moral appeal of Fair Trade and associated movements is demonstrated by the widespread adoption of their logic and terminology by varied groups. The term "fair trade" is currently used extensively, sometimes to support efforts which stand in stark contrast to the vision of the Fair Trade movement. Most strikingly, neoliberal politicians are increasingly utilizing the concept of "fair trade" as a synonym for "free trade" to give moral weight to their arguments for abolishing trade restrictions, even if these changes would undermine national social and environmental conditions. In recent political debates in the United States, "fair trade" has been used to refer to trade that results in fewer US job losses, while opening up export markets overseas without regard for the impacts on jobs in those countries. In its more progressive sense, the term "fair trade" is used by social activists to refer to a broad array of efforts which share at least some common ground with the Fair Trade movement. For example, direct local farmer-to-consumer food networks or initiatives promoted in the World Social Forum have described themselves as "fair trade" efforts.[1]

The Fair Trade movement is comprised of a set of groups which are linked through their membership associations – the Fairtrade Labelling Organizations International (FLO), the International Federation of Alternative Trade (IFAT), the Network of European Worldshops (NEWS!), and the European Fair Trade Association (EFTA). Together these organizations are identified as the FINE network, a name created from the first letter of each of the four association's names. We include in this definition of the Fair Trade movement the associates of the Fair Trade Federation, the North American equivalent to the European-based FINE.

According to the Fair Trade movement's joint statement, their goals are ambitious, yet straightforward:

1   to improve the livelihoods and well-being of producers by improving market access, strengthening producer organizations, paying a better price, and providing continuity in the trading relationship;
2   to promote development opportunities for disadvantaged producers, especially women and indigenous people and to protect children from exploitation in the production process;
3   to raise awareness among consumers of the negative effects on producers of international trade so that they exercise their purchasing power positively;
4   to set an example of partnership in trade through dialogue, transparency, and respect;
5   to campaign for changes in the rules and practice of conventional international trade;
6   to protect human rights by promoting social justice, sound environmental practices, and economic security.

Certified Fair Trade benefits marginalized producers and workers in the Global South in four critical ways. First, it provides producers with guaranteed prices that are higher than conventional world market prices, particularly in volatile tropical commodity markets. Second, it supports organizational capacity building for the democratic groups that are required to represent small-scale producers (via cooperatives) and workers (via unions). Third, it enhances production and marketing skills for participants and their families which extend beyond Fair Trade production. Fourth, it provides a social premium to finance broader community projects such as health clinics, schools, better roads and sanitation, and other social services.

Fair Trade's success has indeed been remarkable. In less than two decades it has grown from an obscure *niche* market to a globally recognized phenomenon. Fair Trade has evolved from a small church and Third World solidarity movement appealing to a conscience-motivated consumer minority, to a movement with expanded conventional market-bases, directed toward the mainstream consumer majority. Within the past several years Fair Trade has entered into a new phase characterized by changes in Northern markets and supporting Non-Governmental Organization (NGO) movements, in the relationships between Northern activists and Southern producer groups, and in the nature and functioning of Southern producer groups and movements.

With Fair Trade's growth and transformation have come new pressures simultaneously pulling the movement in multiple directions. The challenges that are emerging for Fair Trade raise serious questions about the nature and future direction of Fair Trade. Where is the movement headed? As it becomes increasingly subject to the disciplining forces of global trade and development, is it maturing into a less dynamic phenomenon than it once was? Or is it becoming part of a broader-based and more sustainable challenge to the neoliberal globalization regime? While the answers to these questions are critical to the future of Fair Trade, they are also important for other initiatives pursuing market-based strategies for social change.

Globalization...

Fair Trade is best understood as an emerging response to the negative effects of contemporary globalization, and particularly to the often unjust and inequitable nature of contemporary international trade. As such it is not an "antiglobalization" movement, but instead it is part of what we describe as a "new globalization," being developed through counter-hegemonic networks (Evans 2005) pursuing a strategy of reframing globalization from below (Falk 1997).

To understand globalization in its current form and the potential of one of its emerging challenges, Fair Trade, we need to look back over the past 50 years. In the post World War II era (and most dramatically since the 1980s) the ties linking national and regional economies to the global economy were significantly deepened, subordinating many aspects of social life to global realities (Dicken 1998; Hoogvelt 1997). Technological advances, particularly in transportation and communication, fueled processes of globalization in economic, political, and cultural arenas. With the globalization of production and consumption, people in the Global North became increasingly accustomed to ever-cheaper and ever more-available food, apparel, appliances, and other products. Wealth, in gross material terms, increased to previously unimaginable levels in some parts of the world, but so too did income inequalities within and between countries.

These processes of globalization have led to a "race to the bottom" where corporations compete globally to exploit the lowest cost human and environmental inputs. Workers and producers, first in the Global South but then also in parts of the North, saw real wages, incomes, and standards of living stagnate or decline, sometimes precipitously. Entire communities have been uprooted and swept aside by the social, economic, and political forces of postwar globalization. Land and water resources have been so affected that biodiversity around the world has been declining at an unprecedented rate (Millenium Ecosystem Assessment 2005).

The rise of transnational corporations has been at the heart of accelerating globalization, sourcing, and marketing in an increasingly unfettered fashion. Powerful private enterprises have exploited the emerging international trade regime and gained increasing influence over not only economic, but political (Held et al. 1999) and cultural (Appadurai 1990) realities around the world. The ability of these corporations to reap the benefits of globalization has been fostered by institutional and political changes in the postwar era. Global financial institutions, most importantly the International Monetary Fund (IMF) and World Bank, have become primary vehicles for promoting neoliberal economic policies forcing the deregulation of national economies. Import substitution regimes and important national economic development policies were dismantled in the 1980s. These policy changes undermined national protections for workers, producers, and consumers. The creation of the World Trade Organization (WTO) in 1995 cemented the hegemony of the neoliberal orthodoxy and the free trade vision of world development.

...and its antinomies

Over recent decades we have also seen dramatic changes in popular pressures for social change in both the industrialized North and the developing South. During the 1970s and 1980s the civil rights movement in the United States and the anti-war and organized labor movements in the United States and Europe faded. The collapse of the Soviet Union and the failure of Third World revolutions gave credence to the emerging dominance of neoliberal capitalism. At the same time, it became apparent that the grinding hardships and poverty long associated with authoritarian and totalitarian regimes were increasingly being imposed by the global market itself. Rather than focusing their efforts at the national level, social movements in this context shifted their strategies to global arenas and new movement goals.

Particularly striking has been the emergence of market-based approaches to challenging conventional globalization and its negative effects. Consumer boycotts, such as the grape boycott launched by the United Farm Workers Union in 1965 to address labor conditions, and the international Nestlé's boycott begun in 1977 to challenge the marketing of baby formula in the developing world, were two early examples. The international divesture movement that sought to end financial ties with companies in South Africa and thus challenge the Apartheid regime was yet another. What is novel about these initiatives is that they were primarily market-based, often transnational in nature, and their actions were directed at corporations rather than nation states.

The Fair Trade movement emerged from this milieu. After World War II, church organizations began marketing handicrafts from the recovering war-ravaged communities of Europe. These direct marketing links became central to a number of religious group solidarity efforts with impoverished regions of the developing world, and shaped the early principles of social justice and equity in commercial relations that came to be the defining features of the Fair Trade movement. By the 1960s the principles of the movement were refined to highlight the injustices facing the world's poor and the unequal trading relations that maintained this poverty. Sales through "World Shops" maintained by Alternative Trade Organizations (ATOs) gave conscience-motivated consumers an opportunity to purchase commodities in dedicated shops. These marketing initiatives promised to return a greater portion of the market price to Third World producers by eliminating intermediaries and providing a more direct route into Northern markets. The movement gradually branched out from handicrafts to include a few food commodities such as tea, coffee, and cocoa.

By the late 1980s new certification and labeling initiatives were seeking to capture growing consumer interest. In the United States, the soaring sales of organic foods most clearly highlights the rising market power of certified goods (Guthman 2004). In Europe, similar interest in organic products was accompanied by a rise in cause related labeling and purchasing linked to environmental and social concerns (Zadek et al. 1998). Numerous overlapping and sometimes competing social and environmental certification and labeling initiatives have recently emerged (Barrientos and Dolan 2006; Raynolds et al. forthcoming; Taylor 2005).

These consumption-based pressures gave impetus to the founding of Fair Trade organizations like Max Havelaar, the Fairtrade Foundation and Transfair USA, which pursued certifying and labeling of Fair Trade items for sale in mainstream retail outlets, rather than direct marketing. New labeling efforts focused attention on creating more precise indicators of how poor Third World producers benefit from Fair Trade and on substantiating labeling claims. As more Fair Trade organizations developed throughout the industrialized North, the need for coordination became apparent. In 1997 FLO was created, with its headquarters in Germany, to harmonize national labeling efforts. FLO's central goal has been to take Fair Trade beyond its historical alternative trade roots and move "Fairtrade into the supermarket where most people do their shopping" (FLO 2006). As FLO and its member organizations argue, expanding Northern markets offers the possibility of providing Fair Trade benefits to a greatly increased number of marginalized producers and workers around the world.

Europe and North America now have important markets for a growing number of Fair Trade certified products. This market success is predicated on the rising engagement of large-scale retailers, branders, and other corporations bringing Fair Trade to the mainstream public. On both sides of the Atlantic we see widespread and growing public support for the Fair Trade concept and Fair Trade products. This support is propelling the move of Fair Trade from the market margins to the mainstream, increasing the involvement of dominant corporate brands, like Procter & Gamble and Nestlé, and major supermarket chains like Tesco, Carrefour, and Sam's Club.

In the global South a growing number of producers have turned to Fair Trade in search of higher fixed prices, a more reliable link to markets, and greater access to financing or more reliable payments (Murray et al. 2003). But producers and workers also have been drawn to Fair Trade's promise of broader social benefits, including the support for rural livelihoods and rural communities, for local autonomy, and in some cases for the promotion of indigenous rights. A variety of local movement groups have increased their engagement with Fair Trade to complement their multiple economic, political, and social agendas.

Fair Trade has grown into a significant force in the global economy with annual sales of over US$ 1.6 billion and growth continuing apace. As *Time* magazine recently noted, "Fair Trade is taking off" (Roosevelt 2004). One analyst looking at the US food industry suggested:

> Fair trade goods represent 0.01 percent of the total food and beverage industry, which makes them look really minuscule and irrelevant...But a 50 percent growth rate at the $131 million level is outstanding and uncommon...If fair trade can successfully move its brand to other categories besides coffee,

as it should, then it will have the growth potential to become significant in the food and beverage industry.

(Rogers cited in Van Loo 2003)

Coffee is the second largest traded commodity after oil, so Fair Trade's remarkable growth in this area alone is significant. But Fair Trade is making inroads into other commodities as well. Fair Trade bananas (the world's sixth largest traded commodity) are just entering the large US market, but have already captured major portions of European markets, with Switzerland in the lead, where Fair Trade accounts for roughly 50 percent of total national banana sales (COOP Swiss and AgroFair 2004). Fair Trade certified commodities now include not only coffee and bananas, but tea, cocoa, sugar, honey, fresh fruits and vegetables, dried fruit, fruit juices, rice, wine, nuts and oilseeds, cut flowers, ornamental plants, cotton, and sports balls, with plans for certifying many other products under way.

The Fair Trade movement is rapidly becoming one of the most dynamic dimensions of the new globalization. Mass protests against the negative consequences of globalization (from Seattle to Cancun, Durbin to Edinburgh) have accelerated the search for new approaches to globalization. Trade- and market-based strategies for social change have become a central feature of contemporary popular struggles for social justice. But as we will demonstrate in the ensuing chapters, in its ascendancy Fair Trade is being drawn into ever more complex dilemmas, some of which raise difficult challenges for this movement as well as for its relationship to the broader struggles within which it is located.

The challenges facing the Fair Trade movement

There are a number of complicated and overlapping challenges facing the Fair Trade movement whose resolution will chart its course for the future. In this book we will identify analytically distinct yet related challenges and associated questions.

1   The first challenge relates to Fair Trade's increasing pursuit of large-volume markets and business partnerships involving large-scale traders, distributors, supermarkets, and other retailers. While alternative trade organizations helped found the movement, there is a clear limit to their direct sales strategy. ATOs have been, and continue to be, very successful at educating consumers and demonstrating that new ways of organizing trade are possible, but they are perhaps necessarily sidelined to the margins of the mainstream market. Seeking to maximize the positive benefits of Fair Trade has meant engaging transnational corporations and other unlikely partners, a strategy that is causing considerable concern and debate within the movement.

• Will working within conventional markets erode the movement's historical mission of challenging the unjust and inequitable nature of conventional international trade?

- Will capturing market share overshadow the moral purpose of Fair Trade?
- Is transnational corporate Fair Trade an oxymoron?
- Are the alternative market and conventional market strategies of Fair Trade in fundamental opposition, or is there a path on which the movement can tread that reaps the returns of one while maintaining the ethics of the other?

2   A second, but related challenge grows out of the integration of large-scale estates or plantations into certified Fair Trade production. Expanding the Fair Trade market through conventional outlets greatly increases the scale of market impact and consumer product availability, yet it also necessitates the production of unprecedented volumes of certified goods and the integration of larger numbers of producers and workers. The Fair Trade movement initially had a strong commitment to working with small-scale producers organized into cooperatives. But commodities produced through large-scale production systems have increasingly joined the Fair Trade fold.

- Can the movement maintain and advance Fair Trade principles working with large-scale plantations as well as small-scale producers?
- Can large numbers of workers as well as producers come to reap the benefits of Fair Trade individually and collectively?
- Will sourcing Fair Trade commodities from larger enterprises push out small-scale Fair Trade producers due to entrenched economies of scale?

3   The third challenge relates to the changing nature of the Fair Trade movement itself. Fair Trade was traditionally defined by the vision of Northern NGOs working on behalf of Southern producers and workers. As the success of these efforts has become apparent, Southern producer and NGO groups are now seeking a more active role in shaping the debates over the future of Fair Trade. As Fair Trade becomes a more central element in global movements for social justice, it must respond to new movement pressures in both the North and South.

- Will Fair Trade be able to maintain its traditional principles as it becomes engaged with other social movements emerging in the Global South and Southern governments seeking to advance the interests of disadvantaged populations?
- Can Fair Trade be adapted to differing national conditions, allowing national Fair Trade initiatives to develop in the Global South as well as the North?
- Can FLO adapt to the increasingly diverse interests in Fair Trade and still maintain the moral vision of the movement, or will particular and relatively narrow sets of interests come to dominate?

4   A final challenge grows out of the shifting consumer base of the Fair Trade movement. Conscientious consumers have been the foundation of Fair Trade and other initiatives to bring social justice and greater equity to international trade

and globalization. But as Fair Trade extends into broader mainstream markets, it must connect with this broader mainstream consumer sector.

- Can Fair Trade maintain and communicate its unique message in the face of the growing number of competing corporate and NGO standards and certifications?
- Can Fair Trade successfully fuel consumer consciousness in mainstream as well as dedicated markets and promote broader citizen action in support of social justice as well as conscientious consumption?
- Will Fair Trade be able to maintain its place as part of a movement for an alternative vision of trade, development, and globalization, or will it be reduced over time to just another set of standards?

The organization of the book

The 13 chapters of this book are arranged both thematically and regionally, leading to the concluding chapter that redefines our understanding of the character and future potential of Fair Trade. Individual chapters will raise and revisit the history and issues central to understanding the future prospects of this movement for social change. Each chapter provides a different perspective on the major dilemmas facing Fair Trade moving from the Global North to the Global South, from the movement's insider views to those of outside observers. As the chapters progress, our understanding of Fair Trade grows richer, allowing the reader to triangulate on the factual record and the differing interpretations of events provided by the analysts.

Part I of this book identifies the key dynamics of Fair Trade and the challenges it faces. This first chapter has sought to locate Fair Trade broadly in its historical and global context and to outline the current tendencies emerging in this rapidly growing movement. Murray and Raynolds argue here that to understand the future of Fair Trade we must first explore the challenges it currently faces. Chapter 2 analyzes the historical foundations and current empirical dimensions of Fair Trade, focusing on this initiative's institutional base, consumption and market dynamics, and production and trade patterns. This chapter provides the most complete and up to date data available on the parameters of Fair Trade. Raynolds and Long identify key tensions which have shaped Fair Trade movements and markets around the world and their current dynamics within divergent regions and commodities.

Chapter 3 then outlines the analytical dimensions of Fair Trade within the global agriculture and food sector. Raynolds and Wilkinson explore a range of theoretical traditions that help inform an analysis of Fair Trade within the rapidly changing global context. As they demonstrate, analyses of global commodity/value chains, shifting public/private quality standards, and new social movement dynamics provide constructive avenues for exploring Fair Trade's current character and future potential. This theoretical discussion helps position the cases presented in the ensuing chapters.

Chapter 4 introduces Part II with a comparative discussion of the rise and current characteristics of Fair Trade in the Northern industrialized world.

Barrientos, Conroy, and Jones explore the social movement origins of Fair Trade in Europe and North America and argue that while significant regional differences still exist, Fair Trade is in both contexts being refashioned by the increasing engagement of large-scale enterprises and commercial market venues. They outline a series of new challenges raised by this process of mainstreaming.

In Chapter 5, Raynolds analyzes the development of Fair Trade in the United States as it moves beyond its initial base in the coffee sector into its first fresh produce area, bananas. The recent launch of Fair Trade certified bananas has fueled heated debates over the role of transnational corporate distributors in Fair Trade, given their dominance in the US banana market. The chapter asks: Would a Fair Trade/TNC label be a symbol of success or an oxymoron? Exploring this question reveals the challenges arising from the heightened role of large corporations in Fair Trade and how movement actors are working to defend core Fair Trade values, practices, and institutions.

Chapter 6 examines the growth of Fair Trade coffee in the United States and why different types of companies are turning to certification. Grodnik and Conroy focus on the case of Green Mountain Coffee Roasters, demonstrating how certification is being used to communicate corporate commitment and create brand identity within the specialty coffee industry. This case demonstrates the tensions facing corporations at the forefront of the mainstreaming process, questioning the opportunities and limits of engaging corporations in the Fair Trade movement.

In Chapter 7, Barrientos and Smith shift to the United Kingdom and the challenges of mainstreaming Fair Trade in some of the world's largest supermarkets. UK Fair Trade sales are growing most rapidly in newly introduced supermarket own-brand product lines. This chapter compares the sourcing and marketing of own-brand Fair Trade chocolate produced by small-scale farmers and fresh fruit produced by large estates. The authors question whether this process of mainstreaming represents an expansion of Fair Trade's benefits or a watering down of its positive impacts.

Chapter 8 opens Part III by exploring the dynamic changes occurring in the Global South where large social movements, at times interacting with progressive government programs, set a very different context for the expansion of Fair Trade than in the Global North. Wilkinson and Mascarenhas outline the engagement of diverse Southern actors in shaping Fair Trade and their particular concerns related to increasing participation in Northern markets, developing Fair Trade markets in the Global South, and adapting, FLO policies to a shifting multilateral context.

In Chapter 9, Renard and Pérez-Grovas explore the shifting nature of Fair Trade from the point of view of small-scale coffee producers in Mexico. This chapter identifies the challenges being faced by the pioneering Fair Trade coffee producer groups as they confront, and shape, the new realities of the movement. The authors analyze small farmer resistance to the increasing incorporation of plantation producers and new FLO rules and fees, efforts to organize Fair Trade cooperatives on a national and regional basis, and the efforts of coffee cooperatives to engage new market opportunities to ensure sales and solid prices.

Chapter 10 focuses on the recent establishment and growth of Fair Trade in Brazil. Wilkinson and Mascarenhas argue that Fair Trade is burgeoning as a result of global NGO activities, established ATO initiatives, FLO interest, and Brazilian government and social movement programs. In this context key debates center around the creation of a Brazilian Fair Trade label, the development of South/South Fair Trade circuits, the role of the State, and FLO's control over certification procedures. As these authors show, corporate mainstreaming of Fair Trade in export markets and the parallel processes in Brazilian national markets are restricting producer participation.

Chapter 11 explores the expansion of Fair Trade beyond traditional Southern export crops (such as coffee or bananas) into quinoa, a traditional Andean staple food. Cáceres, Carimentrand, and Wilkinson argue that the integration of quinoa into Fair Trade circuits represents both an opportunity to revitalize Bolivia's domestic producer sector and a challenge to Andean food security. This chapter explores the redefinition of the qualities by which quinoa is evaluated in international markets and the standards developed within the FLO certification system as well as competing ATO and supermarket labels.

In Chapter 12, Kruger and du Toit explore the expansion of Fair Trade into fruits produced on South African estates. They tell a complex story of how FLO has negotiated with farmers, farm workers, and their allies and adapted South African government policies to create national Fair Trade standards specific to post-Apartheid South Africa. The chapter considers the negotiations and networks established between national and international stakeholders focusing on how power has been differentially manifested in the setting of these new conventions.

Chapter 13 concludes the volume, returning to the key question, Whither Fair Trade? Drawing on the insights provided in prior chapters, Raynolds and Murray analyze to what degree Fair Trade is moving beyond its origins as a social movement defined by organizations in the Global North to assist disadvantaged producers in the Global South to become a truly Global movement able to incorporate diverse interests in the Global South. This transition requires coming to terms with Fair Trade's divergent goals as a movement seeking to fundamentally alter conventional trade practices and as a market seeking to improve social and ecological conditions through maximizing certified sales. Raynolds and Murray conclude that Fair Trade will need to address a series of key challenges if it is to realize its potential as a force for progressive global social change.

Note

1 While there are important commonalities between some of these progressive initiatives, to avoid confusion in this book we utilize the lower case "fair trade" to refer to these broader engagements. We then capitalize "Fair Trade" to distinguish efforts that are linked directly to the Fair Trade movement. We discuss Fair Trade efforts organized by alternative trade organizations as distinct from "certified" or "labeled" Fair Trade which refers to Fair Trade circuits certified by FLO and its national affiliates.

References

Appadurai, A. (1990) "Disjuncture and difference in the global cultural economy," *Theory, Culture and Society*, 7: 295–310.

Barrientos, S. and Dolan, C. (eds) (2006) *Ethical Sourcing in the Global Food Chain*, London: Earthscan.

Brown, M.B. (1993) *Fair Trade*, London: Zed Press.

COOP Swiss and AgroFair. (2004) "The coop in Switzerland goes for 100% fairtrade bananas," Press Release: COOP Swiss and AgroFair.

Dicken, P. (1998) *Global Shift: Transforming the World Economy*, 3rd edition, New York: Guilford Press.

Evans, P. (2005) "Counter-hegemonic globalization: transnational social movements in the contemporary global political economy," in T. Janoski, A. Hicks, and M. Schwartz (eds), *Handbook of Political Sociology*, London: Cambridge University Press.

Falk, R. (1997) "Resisting 'globalisation-from-above' through globalisation-from-below," *New Political Economy*, 2: 17–24.

FLO (Fairtrade Labelling Organizations International). (2005) *2004/2005 FLO Annual Report*, Online. Available at: www.fairtrade.net (accessed May 17, 2006).

—— (2006) *About FLO*, Online. Available at: www.fairtrade.net/sites/aboutflo (accessed May 17, 2006).

Guthman, J. (2004) *Agrarian Dreams: The Paradox of Organic Farming in California*, Berkeley, CA: University of California Press.

Held, D., McGrew, A., Goldblatt, D., and Perraton, J. (1999) *Global Transformations: Politics, Economics, and Culture*, Stanford, CA: Stanford University Press.

Hoogvelt, A. (1997) *Globalization and the Postcolonial World: The New Political Economy of Development*, Baltimore, MD: Johns Hopkins University Press.

Millenium Ecosystem Assessment. (2005). *Living Beyond our Means: Natural Assets and Human Well-Being*, Online. Available at: www.millenniumassessment.org/en/products.aspx (accessed August 22, 2006).

Murray, D., Raynolds, L.T., and Taylor, P.L. (2003) "One cup at a time: poverty alleviation and fair trade coffee in Latin America," Fort Collins: Colorado State University, Online. Available at: www.colostate.edu/Depts/Sociology/FairTradeResearchGroup/index.html (accessed August 10, 2006).

Ransom, D. (2001) *The No-Nonsense Guide to Fair Trade*, London and Oxford: New Interrnationalist Publications Ltd.

Raynolds, L.T. (2000) "Re-embedding global agriculture: the international organic and fair trade movements," *Agriculture and Human Values*, 17: 297–309.

Raynolds, L.T., Murray, D., and Heller, A. (forthcoming) "Regulating sustainability in the coffee sector: a comparative analysis of third-party environmental and social certification initiatives," *Agriculture and Human Values*, 24.

Roosevelt, M. (2004) "The coffee clash: many firms see a marketing advantage in selling politically correct beans. Will Starbucks get hurt?" *Time*, March 8, Online. Available at: www.time.com (accessed March 10, 2004).

Taylor, P.L. (2005) "In the market but not of it: fair trade coffee and forest stewardship council certification as market-based social change," *World Development*, 33: 129–147.

Van Loo, R. (2003) "Coming to the grocery shelf: fair-trade food," *Christian Science Monitor*, September 29, Online. Available at: www.csmonitor.com (accessed June 4, 2004).

Zadek, S., Lingayah, S., and Forstater, M. (1998) *Social Labels: Tools for Ethical Trade – Executive Summary*, Luxemburg: Office for Official Publications of the European Communities.

2 Fair/Alternative Trade

Historical and empirical dimensions

Laura T. Raynolds and Michael A. Long

Introduction

Fair Trade seeks to challenge historically unequal international market relations and transform North/South trade from a vehicle of exploitation to a means of empowerment. Fair Trade works to alleviate poverty in the global South through a strategy of "trade, not aid," improving farmer and worker livelihoods through direct sales, better prices, and stable market links as well as support for producer organizations and communities. This movement also works to educate Northern consumers about the negative consequences of conventional trade, offer fairly traded alternative products, and promote the selection of more ethical purchases. Fair Trade thus creates concrete alternative commodity networks while at the same time promoting alternative norms and practices in conventional trade arenas. While Fair Trade's basic goals are increasingly well understood, the past and present experiences of the Fair Trade movement and market are less well known.

This chapter analyzes the historical and empirical dimensions of Fair Trade, laying the groundwork for subsequent chapters and facilitating an understanding of Fair Trade's future. First we explore the characteristics of Fair Trade networks, institutions, and standards, revealing the historical and contemporary roles of Alternative Trade Organization (ATO) and Fair Trade labeled segments of the movement and market. The chapter next considers Fair Trade's recent rapid growth, highlighting the expanding range of commodities, increasing mainstream supermarket sales, and growing popularity of Fair Trade consumption. We next explore the increasing scale and scope of Fair Trade production, documenting the geographic and organizational implications of this expansion. We conclude by discussing key tensions within the Fair Trade movement and market which, as will be seen in later chapters, repeatedly emerge, thus shaping Fair Trade's current and future prospects.

Networks, institutions, and standards

The Fair Trade movement grows out of a variety of North American and European initiatives which have since the 1940s sought to help disadvantaged groups by creating alternative trade networks. Pioneer organizations like Sales Exchange for

Refugee Rehabilitation and Vocation (SERRV) and Oxfam,[1] and later other faith and development groups, began purchasing handicrafts from poor producers in the Global South at above-market prices, selling them directly to conscientious consumers. During the 1960s and 1970s, these types of ATOs and their direct sales networks expanded significantly. ATOs proliferated in Europe, establishing thousands of popular handicraft stores known as "World Shops." Smaller ATO initiatives developed in North America, selling through catalogues and small shops. By the 1980s these diverse efforts had shaped the beginning of a common Fair Trade movement, with shared norms based on ideas of "fairness," common practices involving direct importing and sales, and an institutional framework of ATOs (EFTA 2002; Grimes and Milgram 2000; IFAT 2005; LeClair 2002; Littrell and Dickson 1999; NEWS! 2005).

In the late 1980s and early 1990s, ATOs consolidated their efforts within four major associations (see Table 2.1). The Network of European World Shops (NEWS!) and the European Fair Trade Association (EFTA) represent national world shop associations and ATOs across Europe. The Fair Trade Federation (FTF) represents ATOs in the United States and Canada as well as producer organizations found largely in Asia. The International Fair Trade Association (IFAT) has emerged as the most international and largest umbrella group, including 65 ATO members from Europe (including NEWS! and EFTA); 23 ATO members from North America; seven ATO members from the Pacific region; 150 producer organizations from Asia, Africa, and Latin America; and 34 individual members (IFAT 2005).

Table 2.1 Major Fair Trade associations

Associations	Established	Type of members	Number of members/number of countries[a]	Major regions of operation
Fairtrade Labelling Organizations International (FLO)	1997	National labeling	20 members in 21 countries	Europe; North America
International Fair Trade Association (IFAT)	1989	Alternative trading	280 members in 62 countries	Europe; North America; Asia; Africa; Latin America
Network of European World Shops (NEWS!)	1994	National world shops	15 members in 13 countries	Europe
European Fair Trade Association (EFTA)	1987	Alternative trading	11 members in 9 countries	Europe
Fair Trade Federation (FTF)	1994	Alternative trading	106 members in 8 countries	North America; Asia

Sources: FINE (2003); FTF (2005).

Note

a These data are not fully comparable: IFAT and FTF membership includes producer groups; NEWS! and EFTA membership includes only distributors, though producer groups are identified as partners; and only national labeling initiatives are formal FLO members.

A distinctive new strand of the Fair Trade movement was established in the late 1980s with the introduction of product certification and labeling. European ATOs and their allies in the Global North and South initiated labeling to expand sales by moving beyond the handicraft sector and solidarity shop outlets to sell major food commodities like coffee in conventional supermarkets (EFTA 2002). This certification and labeling strategy[2] has been highly successful in increasing Fair Trade availability and sales for these products. European Fair Trade labeling groups harmonized and consolidated their activities, forming the Fairtrade Labelling Organizations International (FLO) umbrella group in 1997 (see Table 2.1). FLO represents 20 national initiatives – 15 in Europe, three in North America, and two in the Pacific region – and continues to grow. Commercio Justo in Mexico and the Fair Trade Association of Australia and New Zealand are some of the newest FLO members; national initiatives from Brazil and South Africa are currently negotiating FLO membership (FLO 2006a). Though only national initiatives are considered to be FLO members, other stakeholders also participate. The FLO Board of Directors is comprised of representatives of five national initiatives, four producer groups, two importers, and two consumer groups.[3]

Fair Trade's history can be seen in some ways in stages, with a shift in the 1980s from an ATO dominated to a certification/labeling dominated movement (Roozen and van der Hoof 2001). Yet the continued vitality of ATOs should not be overlooked, for while ATO sales have in most regions lagged behind labeled commodities due to the historical focus on the low-growth handicraft sector and low-volume alternative shops, this is not true everywhere (Solagral 2002). For example Italy's CTM Altromercato (2005), the world's second largest ATO, continues to increase sales of a range of food and nonfood items promoted through movement and mainstream channels. There are also key organizations that integrate the ATO and labeling approaches: groups like Equal Exchange in the United States and Café Direct in the United Kingdom were founded as ATOs, but currently sell substantial volumes of certified commodities. The ATO model remains particularly strong in Europe and Japan, is resilient in North America, and appears to have strong growth potential in Latin America.[4] Understanding the similarities as well as differences between the ATO and the labeling strands is central to understanding the current tensions within Fair Trade (Moore 2004; Raynolds 2002; Renard 1999, 2003).

Since 1998, major ATO and labeling groups have worked to find common ground and pursue joint interests through an informal alliance called FINE, an acronym made up of the first letter of the member group names: FLO, IFAT, NEWS!, and EFTA.[5] FINE seeks to promote member activities by sharing information, harmonizing Fair Trade guidelines, and maintaining a joint Fair Trade Advocacy Office in Brussels. FINE (2003) has developed a common definition of Fair Trade which is referenced across the movement.

> Fair Trade is a trading partnership, based on dialogue, transparency and respect, that seeks greater equity in international trade. It contributes to sustainable development by offering better trading conditions to, and securing

the rights of, marginalized producers and workers – especially in the South. Fair Trade organizations (backed by consumers) are engaged actively in supporting producers, awareness raising and in campaigning for changes in the rules and practice of conventional international trade.

As this statement suggests, Fair Trade has two quite distinct goals: (1) to foster egalitarian trade links between Northern consumers and Southern producers and (2) to campaign for changes in conventional (unequal) trade practices.

While Fair Trade groups voice a common commitment to these key goals, ATO and labeling strands of the movement pursue these goals differently. ATOs create new channels of commodity exchange and are typically involved directly in importing and retailing. These groups are thus positioned to promote egalitarian norms in their face-to-face relations with producers and consumers. ATOs can promote the flow of information as well as commodities within their relatively autonomous networks, forging "dense networks of connectivity" through which Southern producers learn about the lives of consumers as well as the characteristics of markets and Northern consumers learn about the lives of producers as well as the attributes of products (Whatmore and Thorne 1997). To the extent that ATOs can successfully promote alternative values and practices of fairness, partnership, and respect, they can "shorten the distance" between consumption and production in global arenas (Raynolds 2002). ATOs have historically provided critical information and support to consumers and producers. Yet egalitarian ideals are easier to maintain in theory than practice (Tallontire 2002).

The ATO model assumes that the integrity of alternative exchange networks and the credibility of fairness claims can be upheld through relations of trust. This approach was well suited to the early retail strategy of selling to socially conscious consumers in small dedicated outlets, where ATOs could explain their activities and rely on their reputations for consumer assurance. This informal model continues to be effective in smaller networks, with more face-to-face contact, and more intensive networks like those in the solidarity economy (Solagral 2002). But as ATOs have increased in size and number and non-ATO businesses have sought to enter the ethical trade market, it has become increasingly difficult to explain ATO procedures and maintain public trust. To boost ATO credibility, IFAT launched a Fair Trade Organization Mark in 2003. Members using the mark are expected to meet standards regarding working conditions, wages, child labor, and the environment with these criteria upheld through self-assessment, mutual review, and external verifications (IFAT 2005). The IFAT mark exemplifies the growing bureaucratic rationalization of the ATO system, though it remains much less formalized and strict than FLO's product certification system.[6]

While FLO and its member organizations are in principle committed to the same goals of fairness in trade as the ATO wing of the movement, this commitment is institutionalized differently. The labeling model of Fair Trade hinges on independent certification, where interactions between producers and consumers are mediated by increasingly formalized rules, standards, and product labeling procedures (Raynolds 2002).[7] In the certified Fair Trade model (unlike the

ATO model) importing and sales are handled largely by mainstream commercial enterprises. Labeling organizations communicate with producers largely indirectly through the implementation of certification standards and procedures; communication with consumers is similarly indirect and is essentially reduced to a small product sticker. Creating a meaningful partnership between producers and consumers under these conditions is clearly a challenge.

Fairness within the FLO-based labeling system is largely institutionalized through standards regarding "fair" prices and exchange relations. FLO regulates certification standards; activities in major markets are overseen by national initiatives like TransFair USA and the UK Fairtrade Foundation. FLO has developed formal standards for traders and producers. Traders licensed by FLO must pay a fee for use of the Fair Trade label and must: (1) buy from approved grower organizations using long-term contracts; (2) guarantee payment of the FLO minimum price (including a set premium for certified organic items) established to cover the costs of sustainable production and living; (3) pay an additional social premium to be invested in community development; and (4) provide partial prepayment, upon request, at the time of purchase rather than waiting until the commodity is sold to retailers (FLO 2005a). Within this framework, FLO details price and premium calculations as well as contract and payment conditions for each of its 18 certified items (FLO 2005b).

Fair Trade producer standards further institutionalize norms of "fairness" by requiring that benefits be shared democratically. There are generic standards for small producers and hired labor situations, though in coffee and cocoa only small producers are certified (FLO 2005b). Small farmer standards require that producers be organized into associations, often cooperatives, which can fuel development through the democratically determined investment of the Fair Trade premium and other resources. Hired labor standards involve similar requirements regarding democratic associations, in this case typically unions, as well as adherence to key International Labor Organization (ILO) conventions related to freedom of association, forced and child labor, freedom from discrimination, minimum work, occupational health, and safety conditions.[8] FLO product-specific standards identify minimum entry, and progress criteria ensuring continued improvements.[9] Once free, certification fees are being introduced for Fair Trade producers.

Over recent years, the bureaucratic and industrial nature of the Fair Trade certified system has been greatly heightened (Raynolds 2002). Initially, FLO's small staff both developed standards and certified compliance. To accomodate its rapid growth and avoid potential conflicts of interest, FLO has spun off its certification unit. FLO e.V. continues to develop standards and provide support to producers. An independent organization, FLO-Cert is now responsible for monitoring and certifying the compliance of producer groups as well as importers (and, if separate, exporters) with established standards (FLO 2006a). This division of labor bolsters FLO's legitmacy in international regulatory circles, positioning FLO in line with the International Organization for Standardization (ISO) Standards.[10] Yet the imposition of conventional regulatory practices may simultaneously render more difficult the creation of alternative norms, rules, and institutions within Fair Trade.

Fair Trade's recent expansion has involved significant institutional development in the ATO and certification/labeling strands of the movement. The original and moderately growing ATO strand continues to pursue an integrated alternative network approach. In contrast, the newer and much more rapidly expanding FLO certified commodity strand involves a more formalized labeling system operating within mainstream markets. While some facets of the divide between the ATO and labeling approaches have grown, joint advocacy efforts and the shared tendency to increase bureaucratic oversight speak to the commonality of movement interests and market pressures across Fair Trade.

Distribution and consumption

The total world market for Fair Trade, including ATO and labeled products, is valued at US$ 1.6 billion. Though this represents a minor share of global trade, sales are expanding very rapidly, particularly in the food sector. As outlined in Table 2.2, ATO and labeled sales are substantial and growing. It is possible

Table 2.2 Fair Trade sales 2004/2005 (US$ 1,000)

	FLO certified sales[a]	ATO sales[b]	Total Fair Trade sales
Europe	942,000	90,000[c]	1,020,300
UK	345,000	7,400	351,500
Switzerland	178,000	1,400	179,200
France	136,000	6,700	141,800
Germany	88,000	14,300	100,400
Netherlands	45,000	21,700	63,900
Italy	34,000	n/a	34,000[d]
North America	472,000	87,400	547,800
US	428,000	79,800[e]	507,800
Canada	43,000	6,600[e]	49,600
Pacific	7,000	15,600	22,600
Japan	4,000	n/a	4,000[d]
Australia/New Zealand	3,000	n/a	3,000[d]
Total	1,421,000	193,000	1,614,000

Sources: Compiled by authors based on FLO (2006a); FTF (2005); Krier (2005).

Notes
a FLO certified sales figures are for 2005; figures are converted from Euros with the 2005 yearly conversion rate of US$ 1.245 = 1 Euro.
b ATO sales figures for 2005 are not yet available, so they were estimated using FTF (2005) base figures for 2004 projected forward according to that year's growth rates (15 percent for North America and Europe and 5 percent for the Pacific).
c Estimated based on world shop sales of 50 percent labeled and 50 percent ATO products (US$ 1.245 = Euro 1).
d Includes only FLO certified sales.
e Estimated based on the ATO share of all North American sales in 2005.

to sketch the basic contours of the two wings of Fair Trade, though detailed comparisons are hindered by the scarcity of data.[11] Labeled items account for the lion's share of Fair Trade sales and growth in major markets, with these commodities accounting for roughly 88 percent of all earnings. Sales of Fair Trade certified product volumes grew 483 percent between 1998 and 2005; fully 23 percent between 2004 and 2005. Quantifying growth across more dispersed ATO ventures is hard, but it is clearly more modest. Europe maintains its historical prominence in both ATO and labeled Fair Trade markets, with the United Kingdom in the lead with US$ 345 million in FLO certified sales and US$ 7.5 million in ATO sales. Yet it is the United States that now has the largest national Fair Trade market with roughly US$ 428 million in certified and US$ 80 million in ATO sales.

The Fair Trade boom is linked to a broader increase in conscientious consumption across the Global North. Rising numbers of consumers express concern over environmental and social sustainability and consider these issues in their purchases. Fueled by mounting distrust of the industrial agrofood system, conscientious consumption is most clearly evident in the food sector, where Fair Trade, organic, local, and slow food segments are growing exponentially. Conscientious consumption is increasing rapidly across Europe (Leatherhead Food International 2003). In the United Kingdom, 65 percent of residents identify themselves as "green or ethical consumers." The UK ethical market is valued at US$ 5.6 billion, with food accounting for US$ 3.2 billion. Half of UK consumers report avoiding brands associated with negative social and environmental characteristics and most support the Fair Trade concept, even if they do not purchase these items (Co-operative Bank 2003). Recognition of the Fair Trade label is increasing rapidly among UK shoppers, jumping from 16 to 39 percent between 2001 and 2004 (Fairtrade Foundation 2005a).[12]

We see a parallel rise in conscientious consumption in the much larger US market. The US consumer segment identified as "Lohas" (lifestyles of health and sustainability) includes 68 million people with purchases of US$ 230 billion per year (Cortese 2003). Though Americans are notoriously brand conscious, 81 percent of consumers say they will switch brands to support a cause (Cone/Roper 2002 cited TransFair USA 2005a) and 70–80 percent of consumers report a willingness to pay more for items made under good working conditions (Prasad et al. 2004). While stated preferences are not always translated into action, a recent study finds that 26 percent of US consumers will purchase items produced under good working conditions even if they cost more.[13] Only 20 percent of US consumers are aware of Fair Trade products, but almost half of these people report buying them (TransFair USA 2005b).

The most reliable figures available to track the growth of Fair Trade are those related to FLO certified items as measured by volume.[14] As Table 2.3 shows, sales of all certified commodities are concentrated in Europe. Two groups of countries lead the European market. The first includes Switzerland, the Netherlands, and Germany, where long running campaigns have captured significant market shares and growth has slowed. Switzerland is a longstanding certified Fair Trade leader – it has the second largest market in Europe and sales continue to grow. The Swiss

Table 2.3 Core Fair Trade labeled commodity sales volumes by country (2003)

	Coffee volume metric tons	Tea volume metric tons	Cocoa volume metric tons	Bananas volume metric tons	Total volume metric tons[a]	Total volume growth rate 2002–2003 (%)
Europe						
UK	2,889	1,090	903	18,177	24,212	61
Switzerland	1,550	36	275	19,002	23,336	26
Netherlands	3,096	60	147	2,610	5,998	11
Germany	2,865	156	343	116	4,217	−2
France	2,368	52	227	829	4,059	81
Italy	230	10	346	2,038	3,330	405
North America						
US	3,574	52	92	—	3,718	163
Canada	648	6	54	—	738	52
Pacific						
Japan	22	8	—	—	30	72
Total[b]	19,895	1,990	3,473	51,336	83,297	42

Source: FLO (2005d).

Notes
a Includes sales for all labeled commodities, not just the listed core commodities.
b Includes all, not just listed, countries.

lead the world in per capita Fair Trade spending (Leatherhead Food International 2003). The Netherlands, the original labeling pioneer, has Europe's third largest market. Germany is the next largest, but here sales are declining. The second set of countries includes the United Kingdom, France, and Italy, which have less well established, but very rapidly growing markets propelled by mounting consumer and movement interest. The United Kingdom has become the leading European Fair Trade market, with sales of 24,000 tons and annual growth rates of 61 percent. France has a much smaller Fair Trade market, but sales are rising 81 percent per year. Astonishingly, in Italy labeled sales are growing at 405 percent annually. In France and Italy, nonlabeled ATO sales are also growing impressively (Solagral 2002).

North American sales of Fair Trade labeled products are booming, with expansion also in ATO sales. FLO affiliates were only established in Canada in 1997 and the United States in 1999 and there are still only a few labeled commodities available, but markets are developing rapidly. Canada has a solid and growing Fair Trade market. Though the United States has the world's most valuable certified Fair Trade market (see Table 2.2), sales volumes are lower than in some European countries due to the more limited product range (see Table 2.3). Growth in the US Fair Trade market has been astounding: certified volumes rose by 163 percent and earnings by 53 percent in 2003. Given mounting consumer interest and strong movement initiatives, US Fair Trade sales are likely to keep soaring.

Fair Trade market expansion is fueled by the proliferation in the number of FLO certified commodities as well as broadening availability. The top-labeled product areas are coffee (the founding item); other early core items, including tea, cocoa, and sugar; the fresh produce pioneer, bananas; and recently added fresh fruits and juices. FLO also now certifies honey, cotton, dried fruit, nuts and oil, seeds, quinoa, rice, herbs and spices, wine, fresh vegetables, cut flowers, ornamental plants, and even sports balls. FLO plans to continue to expand their product range in response to the growing demand. Table 2.4 outlines the rapid rise in key Fair Trade commodity areas, complementing the commodity sales by country data presented in Table 2.3. As these tables suggest, sales of FLO certified items vary significantly by region based on traditional consumption patterns and the history of product launches.

Coffee represents the core of the certified Fair Trade system at global and national levels. Coffee generates roughly a quarter of all earnings, making it by far the most valuable certified commodity (FLO 2005c). Fair Trade certified coffee sales continue to grow impressively due to renewed interest in established markets as well as growth in newer markets. Europe accounts for 82 percent of Fair Trade coffee consumption, with the Netherlands, United Kingdom, and Germany at the forefront. Fair Trade coffee sales have leveled off in much of Europe at about 1.2 percent of the total market. But UK labeled coffee sales continue to escalate despite already having a 3 percent market share (Fairtrade Foundation 2005b). The United States has the world's largest national market for certified coffee, with annual consumption over 3,500 tons (see Chapter 6). US sales are skyrocketing, increasing at 80 percent per year (TransFair USA 2005a).

Sales of other core Fair Trade certified items – tea, cocoa, and sugar – are also expanding, though markets remain significantly smaller than for coffee (see Table 2.4). Fair Trade cocoa has long been the most important of this group and certified sales continue to rise at roughly 35 percent per year. The market for Fair Trade certified tea is substantial and sales are also rising at close to 30 percent annually. Sugar has until recently been a less important Fair Trade product,

Table 2.4 Sales volumes of top Fair Trade labeled commodities 1998–2005 (metric tons)

Commodities	1998	2001	2004	2005	Annual growth rate 2004–2005 (%)	Growth rate 1998–2005 (%)
Coffee	11,664	14,388	24,222	33,992	40	191
Tea	665	1,085	1,965	2,614	33	293
Cocoa	806	1,453	4,201	5,657	35	602
Sugar	282	468	1,960	3,613	84	1,181
Bananas (fresh)	14,656	29,072	80,641	103,877	29	793
Other fresh fruit/juice	—	966	9,699	13,145	36	1,749[a]
Total[b]	28,913	48,506	125,596	168,476	34	483

Sources: FLO (2005c, 2006a).

Notes
a Growth 2000–2005.
b Includes other labeled commodities measured in tons, but not those measured in other units.

but sales have recently taken off with growth reaching 80 percent per year. As noted in Table 2.3, sales of these certified commodities are largely concentrated in the United Kingdom.

Bananas are now the second most valuable Fair Trade labeled product, though FLO certification only became available in 1996 in Europe and even more recently in North America. Table 2.4 reports sales of over 103,000 tons of certified Fair Trade bananas in 2005. Switzerland has the highest sales, with Fair Trade bananas now holding 50 percent of the market (COOP Swiss 2004). Certified bananas have only been recently introduced in the United States, but they are gaining significant ground (see Chapter 5). Building on the success of bananas, FLO has recently launched a number of additional labeled fresh fruits and juices. Certified citrus, grapes, and deciduous fruits are still only available in select markets, but sales growth is impressive.

The rapid growth of Fair Trade certified markets across Europe, especially the United Kingdom, and North America, especially the United States, is being fueled in large measure by the integration of these items into mainstream corporate and retail circuits. Fair Trade coffee in the United States has moved increasingly from the core activity of ATOs, to the minor lines of major corporations like Starbucks and Procter & Gamble. In the United Kingdom there is a parallel shift as Fair Trade food items move out of the hands of ATOs into the brand name lines of major supermarkets like Tesco (see Chapter 7). Those operating from a business perspective laud these trends, arguing that "Fair Trade labeling has moved from being a radical solidarity movement to a mainstream trend in retail" (Nicholls and Opal 2005: 142). Those operating from a social movement base are concerned that these trends may represent a pattern of corporate "clean washing" where Fair Trade is essentially "put up for sale" (Ransom 2005). The chapters in Part II will address these opposing positions through detailed case studies in the United Kingdom and the United States.

Production and trade

Over the past decade, Fair Trade production has grown dramatically throughout the Global South. Bourgeoning Northern demand has fueled the rise and diversification of Fair Trade exports. This growth has been simultaneously fostered by the widespread adoption of neoliberal policies across the Global South, which have undercut traditional sectors and promoted nontraditional exports, and by rising interest among a broad range of Southern producers in pursuing alternative markets. Though data are incomplete, production of items for sale in ATO circuits appears to be rising significantly in Latin America, Africa, and Asia along with a rising number of ATO affiliates from these regions (EFTA 2002; FTF 2005; IFAT 2005). Expanding production within the FLO system is more clearly documented, though data remain incomplete.[15]

Fair Trade labeling was launched in one item, coffee, produced in one country, Mexico. As noted in Table 2.5, the number of FLO certified commodities was up to 18 by 2004. The expanding range of labeled products is associated with

Table 2.5 Growth of FLO 1998–2004

	1998	2002	2004
Certified commodities[a]	7	12	18
Certified producer groups	211	302	433
Producer countries	40	45	53[b]
National initiatives	17	18	20
Certified traders	—	253	406
Labeled Fair Trade sales (MT)	28,902	58,809	125,595
Fair Trade benefit to producers (US$ million)	—	38	50

Sources: Compiled by authors based on FLO (1999, 2005e, 2006b).

Notes
a These figures understate commodity expansion because some are grouped (i.e. fresh fruit and juice included 1 item in 2002 and 10 in 2004).
b As of the start of 2005.

an extension in the geographic base of production, with labeled commodities now originating in 53 countries across Latin America, Africa, and Asia. The extension of the FLO system has involved a dramatic growth in the number of certified producer groups. FLO certified producer groups doubled from 211 to 433 between 1988 and 2004. FLO's Strategic Plan projects continued rapid growth: 650 groups, 30 certified commodities, and 210,000 tons of certified commodities are expected by 2008. Hundreds of thousands of small-scale growers and workers around the world are now producing certified Fair Trade items and their numbers appear poised to increase.

Table 2.6 outlines the production geography of the top six certified Fair Trade commodity areas – coffee, bananas, cocoa, tea, sugar, and other fruits and juices – specifying both production volumes and estimated values.[16] Latin America represents the hub of certified Fair Trade production. This region exports about US$ 95 million in labeled commodities per year (77 percent of the total). Latin America produces 83 percent of all Fair Trade certified coffee, 98 percent of all bananas, 48 percent of all cocoa, and 68 percent of all sugar. Coffee is by far the region's lead Fair Trade export, generating US$ 61 million, followed by bananas which generate US$ 21 million annually.

As noted in Table 2.7, there are 314 producer organizations involved in Fair Trade production across Latin America (58 percent of FLO's total registry). Most Latin American groups produce certified coffee. Mexico remains the regional and world leader with 39 out of 55 registered groups producing coffee for the export and nascent national markets (see Chapter 9). Colombia, Honduras, Bolivia, Guatemala, and Nicaragua are also important Fair Trade coffee producers. Peru has 46 FLO certified groups; most grow coffee, but some produce cocoa, sugar, bananas, or other fruits and juices, and a few produce newly certified quinoa (see Chapter 11). Ecuador is a major producer of certified bananas; Costa Rica of sugar. The Dominican Republic is the world's top producer of Fair Trade cocoa. Brazil is an important producer of Fair Trade citrus and processed fruit juices (see Chapter 10).

Table 2.6 Fair Trade certified production by region and commodity (2004)

	Coffee	Banana	Cocoa	Tea	Sugar	Other fruit and juices	Other[a]	Total
Latin America								
Production volume (metric tons)	24,932	64,670	1,889	0	5,778	4,052	1,351	102,672
Estimated FOB value (US$ 1,000)	60,600	21,390	3,306	0	3,005	4,491	2,613	95,405
Africa								
Production volume (metric tons)	4,386	1,317	2,073	1,620	2,027	5,976	13,180	30,395
Estimated FOB value (US$ 1,000)	10,660	436	3,628	3,239	1,054	3,592	1,183	23,792
Asia								
Production volume (metric tons)	764	0	0	766	714	11	12	2,267
Estimated FOB value (US$ 1,000)	1,858	0	0	1,532	371	14	546	4,321
Total								
Production volume (metric tons)	30,082	65,987	3,962	2,386	8,519	10,039	14,543	135,334
Estimated FOB value (US$ 1,000)	73,118	21,826	6,934	4,771	4,430	8,097	4,342	123,518

Source: Compiled by authors based on FLO (2005d).

Note
a Includes honey, rice, wine, nuts, flowers, spices, and sport balls (some are not measured in tons).

Certified Fair Trade production is currently expanding most rapidly in Africa, with exports valued at US$ 24 million in 2004 (see Table 2.6). Africa is the leading exporter of certified tea, fruits (other than bananas) and juices, and newly certified items like flowers and wine. Africa also exports certified coffee, bananas, cocoa, and sugar. The number of FLO certified groups in Africa is rising dramatically, increasing from 78 to 152 between 2004 and 2005 (see Table 2.7). Certified groups in Africa have in the past largely produced coffee or tea. But Ghana is a major exporter of FLO certified cocoa. South Africa has recently emerged as the region's Fair Trade leader with 52 FLO registered groups and is now the world's largest exporter of certified fresh and processed fruits, juices, and wine (see Chapter 12). Asia exports a more modest US$ 4 million in certified Fair Trade products annually. The region has 78 FLO affiliated producer groups, most

Table 2.7 Number of Fair Trade certified producer groups by commodity and country (2005)[a]

	Coffee groups	Banana groups	Cocoa groups	Tea groups	Sugar groups	Other fruit/ juice/wine groups	Other commodity groups[b]	Total
Latin America/ Caribbean[c]	187	19	15	1	10	43	29	314
Mexico	39	—	—	—	—	3	13	55
Peru	25	1	6	1	1	5	7	46
Guatemala	22	—	—	—	—	—	5	27
Bolivia	19	—	1	—	—	1	2	23
Colombia	19	1	—	—	—	—	—	20
Honduras	19	—	—	—	—	—	—	19
Nicaragua	13	—	1	—	—	—	3	17
Brazil	6	—	—	—	—	10	1	17
Costa Rica	6	1	1	—	3	4	—	15
Ecuador	1	4	1	—	1	4	2	13
Dom. Republic	3	6	2	—	—	—	—	11
Chile	—	—	—	—	—	5	4	9
Haiti	7	—	1	—	—	—	—	8
El Salvador	7	—	—	—	—	—	1	8
Asia[c]	8	—	—	48	2	1	19	78
India	—	—	—	29	—	1	6	36
Sri Lanka	—	—	—	14	—	—	1	15
Thailand	1	—	—	—	—	—	8	9
Africa[c]	33	1	4	17	1	69	27	152
South Africa	—	—	—	5	—	47	—	52
Uganda	12	—	—	4	—	—	1	17
Tanzania	7	—	—	6	—	—	2	15
Kenya	—	—	—	1	—	—	11	12
Ghana	—	1	1	—	—	8	—	10
Total[c]	228	20	19	66	13	113	85	544

Source: FLO (2006b).

Notes

a This chart includes the top six certified commodity areas and all those countries with eight or more producer organizations.

b Includes rice, honey, sportballs, nuts, nut seed oil, seed, cotton, quinoa, flowers, and spices.

c Includes all regional producer groups, not just those in the listed countries.

located in India and Sri Lanka. Asia is an important source of Fair Trade tea, but is a minor supplier of other certified items.

The historical expansion of certified Fair Trade production has involved a broadening not just of commodities and regions, but also types of production enterprises. Fair Trade certification was initially developed in cooperation with small-scale coffee producers in Mexico. There are now 228 FLO registered coffee cooperatives, representing 670,000 small-scale farmers around the world, and their numbers continue to rise (FLO 2005c).[17] Certification in cocoa, another early and core Fair Trade commodity, has maintained FLO's small farmer base, with growth augmenting the number of registered cooperatives. But the expansion of certification into sugar and tea propelled Fair Trade into the plantation sector, introducing FLO certification to enterprises dependent largely on hired, as opposed to family, labor. Though Fair Trade's mandate to help "disadvantaged producers" was originally seen as securing markets for peasant farmers, the movement has had to confront that (1) in most of the Global South, landless workers are the most severely disadvantaged and that (2) many key export commodities are rarely produced on a small scale. FLO certification of sugar and tea required the establishment of new standards of "fairness" based on democratic worker representation and good labor conditions in large-scale production enterprises. Over the years the importance of large-scale enterprises in certified Fair Trade production has risen dramatically.

The move of Fair Trade certification into the fresh produce sector has increased the engagement of large enterprises in both production and distribution. FLO certification of bananas and rising exports in this commodity area has expanded certified production across small- and large-scale enterprises. The perishability of bananas makes shipping and handling of this commodity much more demanding than in most Fair Trade commodities, increasing technical and capital requirements and limiting the participation of small-scale enterprises.[18] FLO's recent certification of other fresh fruits and processed fruit juices which have even greater scale economies, reinforces the role of large production and distribution enterprises and the erosion of the small farmer basis of Fair Trade.

For small-scale producers, the most direct benefits from certified Fair Trade come from the higher guaranteed prices set by FLO. The importance of these price guarantees for small farmers has been most evident in coffee, where the FLO minimum has far exceeded the world market price for most of the past six years. Certified Fair Trade also guarantees a social premium to be invested in small farmer production and community education, health, nutrition, housing, and transportation services (Murray et al. 2003). For larger enterprises, the FLO price floor helps provide economic stability. But it is the Fair Trade social premium that most directly enhances worker welfare through investments in training, equipment, and ownership shares and broader community welfare through the provision of various social services. The FLO price advantage and the social premium together transferred roughly US$ 50 million to producers in 2004 (FLO 2005c). Yet for both producers and workers, the most important benefits of Fair Trade engagement appear in the long run to come from the multifaceted support provided for individual and organizational capacity building (Raynolds et al. 2004).

Though the potential benefits of Fair Trade for producers and workers in the global South are quite significant, the increased geographic spread, product diversification, and enterprise variation within certified networks makes realizing those benefits much more difficult. The spread of certified Fair Trade production across dozens of countries requires adjusting this model to varied local political economic circumstances and to varied local producer and worker organizations. Expansion into minor food items (like quinoa), perishable fruits and vegetables (like bananas and horticultural crops), and processed commodities (like orange juice and wine) alters the nature of certified markets. In perishable and processed goods, the technical and capital requirements of production challenge the historical primacy of small-scale producers in Fair Trade. The growth of large-scale production raises questions about the ability of Fair Trade to empower workers and build capacity within these new organizational frameworks. The chapters in Part III will address these issues through case studies in Mexico, Brazil, South Africa, and Bolivia.

Conclusions

This chapter has outlined the historical and empirical parameters of Fair Trade, laying the groundwork for subsequent more detailed analyses of the initiative's current and future trajectory. We identify three key arenas of ongoing negotiation. First, in the realm of network politics, we find that while Fair Trade is dominated by Fair Trade certified commodity circuits, institutions, and standards, distinct ATO strands of the movement and market remain important. Second, in the realm of consumption politics, we see that rising Fair Trade sales are linked to mounting consumer interest in bolstering the ethical and environmental conditions of food production, yet is simultaneously associated with the mainstreaming of Fair Trade into conventional corporate and retail sectors. And third, in the realm of production politics, we find that increasing Fair Trade production involves a broadening of geographic, commodity, and enterprise participation which is eroding the movement's historical small-farmer base, though it may widen the potential distribution of benefits. As later chapters will demonstrate, these arenas of negotiation are shaping Fair Trade's current and future prospects.

Notes

1 SERRV was established to aid European World War II refugees, selling crafts through dedicated US venues (www.agreatergift.org).
2 Certification and labeling together define this Fair Trade strategy. We use the two terms interchangeably in distinguishing this from the ATO strand of the Fair Trade movement.
3 The FLO Board's composition has shifted significantly over recent years. Initially comprised of national initiatives it has grown to include producer and buyer, and most recently consumer group representatives.
4 See Part II for the importance of ATOs in the Global North; Part III for their importance in the South.
5 Though FTF is not represented in FINE this reflects the distance between this North American group and its European counterparts, not a major strategic divide. FINE is a working group with no decision-making power.
6 IFAT states that its mark is an organizational seal not a product label, but consumers may not understand the difference.
7 For a parallel argument regarding organic certification see Mutersbaugh (2002) and Raynolds (2004).
8 FLO (2006a) recently strengthened standards for hired labor situations.
9 Entry standards are set low enough to include poor marginalized producers; progress standards foster improvements.

10 The ISO IEC Guide 65 outlines general requirements for bodies operating certification systems. Though ISO standards are technically voluntary, guidelines established by this public/private institution are increasingly expected in international markets.
11 Labeled commodity data are collected by FLO and its national affiliates in the certification process and thus are more readily available than ATO figures which are compiled from incomplete surveys. This chapter draws on the more extensive FLO data, but points where possible to ATO trends.
12 Continental European consumer awareness of Fair Trade is close to 40 percent (Leatherhead Food International 2003).
13 This study placed socks labeled as being produced "under good working conditions" for sale alongside identical, though cheaper, nonlabeled socks. Preferential purchases of these items suggests broader consumer preferences (Prasad et al. 2004).
14 See note 11 for ATO data issues. FLO only recently began calculating sales values.
15 FLO production data are not as extensive as market data.
16 While volume figures are likely to be more accurate within and across regions, value estimates highlight important differences between commodities.
17 In coffee only small-scale growers (not estates) may be FLO certified.
18 Where Fair Trade coffee networks successfully eliminate exporters and other middlemen, banana networks continue to rely on these intermediaries due to their important technical skills and equipment.

References

Co-operative Bank. (2003) *The Ethical Consumerism Report*, London: Cooperative Bank.
COOP Swiss. (2004) "The co-op in Switzerland goes for 100% fairtrade bananas," Press Release: COOP Swiss and AgroFair.
Cortese, A. (2003) "They care about the world (and they shop, too)," *New York Times*, July 20, Online. Available at: www.nytimes.com (accessed June 4, 2004).
CTM Altromercato. (2005) *Ctm Altromercato*, Online. Available at: www.altromercato.it/ (accessed May 17, 2006).
EFTA (European Fair Trade Association). (2002) *EFTA Yearbook: Challenges of Fair Trade 2001–2003*, Maastricht: EFTA.
Fairtrade Foundation. (2005a) *MORI Poll Shows Leap in Public Recognition of Fairtrade Mark*, Online. Available at: www.fairtrade.org.uk/pr150504.htm (accessed May 17, 2006).
—— (2005b) *Sales of Fairtrade Products in the UK*, Online. Available at: www.fairtrade. org.uk/about_sales.htm (accessed May 17, 2006).
FINE. (2003) *What is FINE?* Online. Available at: www.rafiusa.org/programs/ Bangkok%20proceedings/12What%20is%20FINE.pdf (accessed May 17, 2006).
FLO (Fairtrade Labelling Organizations International). (1999) Internal Documents.
—— (2005a) *Certification*, Online. Available at: www.fairtrade.net/sites/certification/ certification.html (accessed May 17, 2006).
—— (2005b) *Standards*, Online. Available at: www.fairtrade.net/sites/standards/ standards.html (accessed May 17, 2006).
—— (2005c) *Products*, Online. Available at: www.fairtrade.net/sites/products/ products_02.html (accessed May 17, 2006).
—— (2005d) *Fair Trade Statistics*, unpublished data.
—— (2005e) *2004/2005 FLO Annual Report*, Online. Available at: www.fairtrade.net (accessed May 17, 2006).

—— (2006a) *FLO 2005/2006 Annual Report: Building Trust*, Online. Available at: www.fairtrade.net (accessed July 10, 2006).

—— (2006b) *FLO News Bulletin, January*, Online. Available at: www.fairtrade.net (accessed January 15, 2006).

FTF (Fair Trade Federation). (2005) *2005 Report: Fair Trade Trends in North America and the Pacific Rim*, Washington, DC: FTF.

Grimes, K.M. and Milgram, B.L. (2000) *Artisans and Cooperatives: Developing Alternative Trade for the Global Economy*, Tucson, AZ: University of Arizona Press.

IFAT (International Federation for Alternative Trade). (2005) *Annual Report 2004*, Culemborg, Netherlands: IFAT.

Krier, J.M. (2005) *Fair Trade in Europe 2005: Facts and Figures on Fair Trade in 25 European Countries*, Brussels: FINE.

Leatherhead Food International. (2003) *Fairtrade Foods – Market Prospects for the Ethical Option*, Online. Available at: www.lfra.co.uk/ (accessed May 17, 2006).

LeClair, M.S. (2002) "Fighting the tide: alternative trade organizations in the era of global free trade," *World Development*, 30: 949–958.

Littrell, M.A. and Dickson, M.A. (1999) *Social Responsibility in the Global Market: Fair Trade of Cultural Products*, Thousand Oaks, CA: Sage Publications.

Moore, G. (2004) "The fair trade movement: parameters, issues, and future research," *Journal of Business Ethics*, 53: 73–86.

Murray, D., Raynolds, L.T., and Taylor, P.L. (2003) "One cup at a time: poverty alleviation and fair trade coffee in Latin America," Fort Collins: Colorado State University, Online. Available at: www.colostate.edu/Depts/Sociology/FairTradeResearchGroup/index.html (accessed August 10, 2006).

Mutersbaugh, T. (2002) "The number is the beast: a political economy of organic coffee certification and producer unionism," *Environment and Planning A*, 34: 1165–1184.

NEWS! (2005) *NEWS! – The Network of World Shops*, Online. Available at: www. worldshops.org/index.html (accessed May 17, 2006).

Nicholls, A. and Opal, C. (2005) *Fair Trade: Market-Driven Ethical Consumption*, New York: Sage.

Prasad, M., Kimeldorf, H., Meyer, R., and Robinson, I. (2004) "Consumers of the world unite: a market-based response to sweatshops," *Labor Studies Journal*, 29: 57–80.

Ransom, D. (2005) "Fair trade for sale," *New Internationalist*, 377 (April): 34–35.

Raynolds, L.T. (2002) "Consumer/producer links in fair trade coffee networks," *Sociologia Ruralis*, 42: 404–424.

—— (2004) "The globalization of organic agro-food networks," *World Development*, 32: 725–743.

Raynolds, L.T., Murray, D., and Taylor, P. (2004) "Fair trade coffee: building producer capacity via global networks," *Journal of International Development*, 16: 1109–1121.

Renard, M.-C. (1999) "The interstices of globalization: the example of fair coffee," *Sociologia Ruralis*, 39: 484–500.

—— (2003) "Fair trade: quality, market and conventions," *Journal of Rural Studies*, 19: 87–96.

Roozen, N. and van der Hoff, F. (2001) *Fair Trade*, Amsterdam: Uitgeverij Van Gennep.

SOLAGRAL. (2002) *Etat des Lieux et Enjeux du Changement D'Echelle du Commerce Equitable*. Nogent Sur Marne Cedex, France: SOLAGRAL.

Tallontire, A. (2002) "Challenges facing fair trade: which way now?," *Small Enterprise Development*, 13: 12–24.

TransFair USA. (2005a) *Coffee Program*, Online. Available at: www.transfairusa.org/content/certification/coffee_program.php (accessed May 17, 2006).

—— (2005b) "Fair trade certified produce – everyone profits when you choose fair trade," paper presented at the International Banana Conference, North American Preparatory Meeting, Washington, DC, February 2005.

Whatmore, S. and Thorne, L. (1997) "Nourishing networks: alternative geographies of food," in M. Watts and D. Goodman (eds), *Globalising Food: Agrarian and Global Restructuring*, New York: Routledge.

3 Fair Trade in the agriculture and food sector

Analytical dimensions

Laura T. Raynolds and John Wilkinson

Introduction

Over the past decade, the agriculture and food sector has emerged at the forefront of prevailing processes of economic, political, and cultural globalization as well as proliferating alternative globalization efforts. Transformations in this sector illuminate changing Global North/South relations. Agriculture and food products represent some of the earliest and the most important internationally traded commodities and some of the first to experience the widening and deepening of market ties that define globalization today. The agrofood sector lies at the heart of current efforts to regulate international trade under the auspices of the World Trade Organization (WTO) and other multilateral agencies. Yet at the same time, the agrofood sector forms a central terrain for contesting globalization within the World Social Forum and various other alternative globalization initiatives (Delgado and Romano 2005). In recent years, Fair Trade has emerged as one of the key challenges promoted by alternative globalization efforts within and beyond the agrofood sector.

This chapter locates Fair Trade as a manifestation of, and response to, shifting international trade and North/South relations. Fair Trade certification emerged and expanded most rapidly within the coffee sector, a tropical export arena defined by the history of colonialism. The historical polarization of the world along a North/South axis has profoundly shaped both conventional trade relations and alternative global visions like Fair Trade. Yet in the current era, Fair Trade markets and movements are being repositioned within the context of a new global architecture. As elaborated in this book, Fair Trade has grown to incorporate an increasingly complex array of commodities, production/consumption relations, and local and global politics.

We identify three major interconnected transformations that define Fair Trade's market and movement dynamics and guide our analysis. First, we analyze the nature of global changes within the agrofood sector which alter the market referents both for dominant trading practices and Fair Trade alternatives. Second, we situate Fair Trade within broader struggles over the regulation of global markets, involving new public/private rules and standards which frame the renegotiation of power and resources in global trade. And third, we consider how Fair

Trade has been caught up in the shifting strategies of new social movements which target global corporations and the market, rather than the State, as the nexus of progressive change. As we argue, Fair Trade has emerged as a constituent component of the new forces of market construction, coordination, and regulation which link social movements, commodities, and policies in new global networks.

Globalization and Agrofood restructuring

In the post World War II period, agro-industrial development based on the increasing appropriation of nature, intensified use of chemical and technical inputs, corporate concentration, and standardization of products underwrote the Fordist system of mass production for mass consumption (Goodman et al. 1987). This system was upheld in national arenas through Keynesian State policies and in international arenas through a food regime rooted in Northern food surplus exports and Southern tropical commodity exports (Friedmann and McMichael 1989). Fair Trade emerged within this context, envisioned as a way to support marginalized peasants in the Global South producing goods purchased by consumers in the Global North. The growth of Fair Trade has centered on coffee, a commodity which illustrates shifting international market dynamics, including the historical problems of market volatility and downward price slides and the rise of new upscale market niches (Daviron and Ponte 2005).

Over the past 25 years, neoliberalism has undermined Fordism in agrofood and other sectors. We have seen the deregulation of States and national agrofood systems, the deterritorialization of agricultural production and food consumption, and the rise of flexible production of differentiated food items (Goodman 1997; Higgins and Lawrence 2005). Traditional exports like coffee, bananas, cocoa, tea, and sugar remain central for many countries in the Global South. Yet mounting competition and declining prices in these arenas has fueled the growth of nontraditional exports (Raynolds 1997). In recent years, the fastest growing agroexports from the Global South are semiprocessed and nontraditional food items such as processed fruits and vegetables, counterseasonal and exotic fresh produce, animal feed, meat, and fish products. Export diversification has reshaped the dominant international agrofood trade. The diversification and differentiation of agrofood exports has also fomented the rapid rise of the South to North trade in organic and Fair Trade products (Raynolds 2002, 2004).

Global agrofood trends are associated with fundamental changes in foreign direct investment as well as trade. Foreign direct investment in agrofood sectors in the global South has increased markedly in recent years, especially but not exclusively in middle-income countries (Gopinath 2000; Wilkinson 2006). Investment is rising in agrofood production for new product markets in the Global North and expanding regional and domestic markets in the Global South. Shifting global investment patterns are promoting South to South trade and domestic markets in the South in both dominant commodity arenas and alternative arenas like Fair Trade.

The French regulation school (Aglietta 1976; Boyer 1990) provides key insights into these macro-political, economic, and social configurations in the agrofood sector. In both political economy and mainstream research, a commodity approach has been adopted to analyze agriculture/industry relations (Davis and Goldberg 1987; Friedland 1984). The Latin American (Vigorito 1978) and French filière (Lauret 1983) traditions emphasize the institutional regulation of commodity circuits. A regulation framework provides an analytical window into the organizational dynamics of agrofood chains and agro-industrial complexes, illuminating how economic power is exercised by lead actors over distinct links in the production chain without resorting to vertical integration (Wilkinson 1997).

Gereffi's (1994) global commodity chain approach provides an insightful associated framework for analyzing the social organization of transnational production, trade, and consumption networks. This approach challenges traditional inter-national notions of trade, demonstrating how trade is now largely within transnational corporations or global networks governed by dominant firms. Commodity chain analysis investigates the interlinking of products and services, organizational and spatial configuration of enterprises, and governance systems determining the distribution of profits and other resources in manufacturing (see Gereffi and Kaplinsky 2001; Henderson et al. 2002). The global commodity chain approach is often now referred to as the global value chain approach.[1] A vibrant literature extends the global commodity/value chain analysis into the agrofood sector (Daviron and Ponte 2005; Gibbon and Ponte 2005; Raynolds 1994).

Studies of commodity/value chain governance analyze how lead firms set and enforce production processes and schedules, product quantities and specifications, and firm participation (Humphrey and Schmitz 2001). Gereffi (1994) argues that globalization has eroded traditional producer-driven chains, where producers dominate due to their control over capital and proprietary knowledge, and fostered buyer-driven chains, where distributors dominate through their control over design, brands, and market access. Studies in the agrofood sector confirm that powerful buyers are increasingly governing commodity networks. Food retailing is undergoing rapid concentration particularly in Europe, but also elsewhere in the world. The top supermarkets, French-based Carrefour, Dutch-based Ahold, US-based Wal-Mart, and UK-based Tesco dominate sales in many markets and now operate in 30, 28, 11, and 10 countries respectively (Coe 2004). UK supermarkets exert especially tight control over their international supply chains (Dolan and Humphrey 2000; Marsden et al. 2000). Dominant retailers are reconfiguring agroexports from the Global South as well as setting conditions in domestic food sectors in both the North and the South (Farina et al. 2005; Henson and Reardon 2005).

Despite its strengths, the commodity/value chain tradition understates the variability of global market coordination (Raikes et al. 2000; Smith et al. 2002). The producer versus buyer-driven dichotomy ignores lead firm variability and persistent tensions between powerful firms. In key commodities – like coffee, bananas, and cocoa – global processors and traders remain critical (Fold 2002; Ponte 2002). There is substantial difference between the types of control exerted by retailer, processor, and trader firms which often goes unanalyzed (Sverrison 2004).

The agrofood sector has areas that are largely producer-driven, like the agricultural input industry, and others that are largely buyer-driven, like the retail and to a lesser extent the final food industries (Wilkinson 2002).

Gereffi and his colleagues (2005) have recently developed a typology of commodity/value chain governance based on the complexity of transactions, ability to codify transactions, and capabilities of suppliers.[2] They identify three forms of firm coordination between the extremes of open market transactions and vertical integration. (1) In the modular case, codification allows for production chain segmentation with frequent transactions and relative supplier independence. (2) In the relational mode, solidarity and cooperation prevail, balancing power across the network. (3) In the captive mode, producers are firmly controlled by processors and retailers often through contracts.[3] This typology illuminates the dynamics of Fair Trade networks. Fair Trade provides a prototype for "relational chains," where transactions are primarily based on trust. Yet Fair Trade networks may move toward "captive chains," if power asymmetry and Northern market control is heightened, or "modular chains," if standardization, certification, and market diversification loosens supplier networks.

Though commodity chain/value chain analytics are instructive, the case of Fair Trade demands a view of chain coordination that goes beyond the strategies of lead firms. New standards and certifications have become central in coordinating the activities both of the dominant agrofood sector and Fair Trade networks. Market coordination is shaped not just by economic firms, but also by social and political actors. Recent research on national production networks points to the emergence of innovative forms of market coordination shaped by social groups, public authorities, and producer associations.[4] These institutional innovations appear also in global networks as in the case of Fair Trade, which is simultaneously a mainstream niche, an alternative network, and a social movement.

While drawing on the insightful work in the global commodity/value chain tradition, this book highlights the rise of innovative forms of economic coordination and the interface between economic and noneconomic actors. To signal this more complex understanding, we move from the language of "chains" to "networks" (see Henderson et al. 2002). Commodity/value chain analysis acknowledges social network theory and sometimes uses the term network. We argue for a more systematic application of the network concept to portray the complex web of material and nonmaterial relationships embedded within commodities and to highlight the importance of social and political as well as economic dynamics in commodity relations (see Busch and Juska 1997).

Quality and standards

Agrofood production, trade, and consumption are being reorganized around the social redefinition of "quality" and the standards and processes by which quality is judged. The mass production of industrial food has given way to market segmentation and product differentiation. The rise in specialized food production for niche markets has been identified by some as a move away from price competition and a turn toward a "quality economy" (Thévenot 1995). As Busch (2000) argues, however, the notion of a new "quality economy" may be a misnomer since it overlooks how industrial foods are defined by quality attributes upheld by dominant firms and regions. Agro-industrial standards – based on product criteria such as size, color, and appearance – have become minimum requirements for market participation with market transactions then mediated by prices.

Studies of the rise of new qualities within the agrofood sector take two somewhat divergent approaches to analyze alternative and mainstream commodity networks. The first focuses on the social distinctiveness of nonmainstream agro-food production and consumption. This literature analyzes Fair Trade and other alternative food networks such as organic foods, regional geographic appellations, and local foods and emphasizes how new quality attributes are created and rein-forced (Barham 2003; Marsden et al. 2000; Murdoch et al. 2000; Raynolds 2002, 2004; Wilkinson 2002). This research points to the centrality of new social, environmental, and place-based attributes in the re-valuation and differentiation of food items. Social movement and consumer concerns over issues of health, ethics, environment, and animal welfare focus attention on qualities associated with production processes, rather than qualities inherent in the product itself. These new quality criteria reassert contextual values stripped from food items under the agro-industrial system. In the consumption arena, these new quality attributes are linked to ethical, health, and environmental concerns, while in the production arena, they involve a relocation of value upstream to the point of agricultural production. The quality turn thus engages different but converging interests on the part of food consumers and farm producers.

Analyses of alternative food networks often draw on convention theory approaches to the social construction and institutionalization of quality. This tradition analyzes the constellation of ideas and practices which comprise quality assessments and the ways in which these qualifications are integrated into production, exchange, and consumption (Allaire and Boyer 1995; Boltanski and Thévenot 1991; Eymard-Duvernay 1995). Paralleling key concerns in economic sociology (Granovetter 1985; Polanyi 1957), convention theory highlights the socially embedded nature of economic activity. Research suggests that while the dominant agrofood system is characterized by *industrial* and *market* norms defined by corporate enterprises on the basis of cost/scale efficiency, alternative food networks involve *civic* and *domestic* norms (related to trust, place attachment, and social benefits) upheld by new producer consumer networks and organizations (Ponte 2002; Raynolds 2002; Wilkinson 1997).

Convention theory provides an avenue for analyzing how divergent norms and values are negotiated within and between commodity networks. Dominant agro-industries were, at the height of the Fordist period, able to simply assert the superiority of *industrial/market* values and institutions (Wilkinson 2002). Given the current consumer mistrust of these norms, corporations now present their values in light of *civic/domestic* norms appropriated in industrial form (DuPuis 2000; Hughes 2005). Similarly, although Fair Trade, organic, and other alterna-tive food systems are rooted in *civic/domestic* ideas and practices, they encounter significant pressure to adapt to dominant *industrial/market* conventions if they increase sales, enter mainstream retail venues, or sell to mainstream consumers (Murdoch et al. 2000; Murray and Raynolds 2000; Raynolds 2004).

The second major approach to the re-definition of quality within the agro-food sector focuses on the rise of new standards in mainstream markets. This approach analyzes the new rules and technologies established largely by dominant retailers to measure, regulate, and enforce agrofood grades and standards (Busch 2000; Busch and Bain 2004; Henson and Reardon 2005; Reardon et al. 2001). Research documents how supermarket chains, either independently, or in alliance with governments, are redesigning (1) food quality standards in response to rising consumer demands for freshness, convenience, and consistent availability and (2) food safety standards in response to mounting consumer distrust of agro-industrial foods. Outbreaks of "mad cow" disease and other food contamination scares, particularly in Europe, call into question the division of public and private responsibilities and the distinctions between quality and safety attributes.[5] To shore up consumer trust and bolster their competitive positions, dominant retailers are instituting new food and traceability requirements. The shift to private quality regulation is propelled by the acceleration of product innovation and the globalization of supply chains, both of which erode public regulation. Retailer regulations shift the focus from measurable product attributes, to the auditable attributes of production and exchange relations (Hughes 2001). New retailer rules point to ethical, environmental, and health concerns, but their substantive and redistributive impacts may be neutralized. In some cases, quality redefinitions represent nothing more than a "new packaging model" (Freidberg 2003: 29); in other cases, we may see environmental and health benefits, yet increased social exclusion in agriculture (Dolan and Humphrey 2000).

Several authors argue that we are seeing a fundamental shift from the public/ State regulation to the private regulation of national and international food supplies (Busch and Bain 2004; Marsden et al. 2000). Studying the rise of super-market standards, Henson and Reardon conclude that "it is private rather than public standards that are becoming the predominant drivers of agri-food systems" (2005: 242). This supermarket-driven conceptualization of food standards under-states the centrality of global branders and processors in some commodities and the variation in retail concentration in major markets.[6] Yet this research points to important new food quality and safety standards promoted by corporate retailers, processors, and traders. In Europe, an alliance of large-scale supermarkets has developed industrywide production and management standards related to qual-ity, safety, environment, and labor under EurepGAP, the Euro-Retailer Produce Association Good Agricultural Practices (Dankers 2003). Transnational super-market chains are generating global standards that homogenize markets, while creating new patterns of exclusion in agrofood production and consumption.

Though corporate redefinition of food standards is important, strong public regulatory activities continue. In Europe, EU traceability requirements are being consolidated in all major commodities. In the United States, the Food and Drug Administration still establishes food safety standards. At the global level, the reinforcement of the WTO Codex Alimentarius can be seen as a similar move to strengthen public regulation. Even in countries where the privatization of quality standards is most advanced, emerging certification systems are accredited by the State. In England the uncertainty and mistrust provoked by food scares has increased the involvement of the State in the eradication of foot and mouth disease. Even global retailers are seeking public support for their quality claims, as does Carrefour in relying on an official French certification in guaranteeing its meat products (Ménard and Valceschini 2005).

As quality and safety become barely distinguishable, the roles of private and public regulation become increasingly enmeshed. In organic foods, national regulations codify what were previously private market rules (Guthman 2004; Raynolds 2004). Fair Trade is also facing increased State regulatory pressure. FLO has been pressured to align its procedures to uphold ISO 65 verification and auditing rules; in France, State regulation of Fair Trade is being contemplated based on traceability concerns. While the private (particularly retail) corporate sector is taking the lead in the global regulation of quality standards, the tight links between quality and increasingly uncertain safety issues, reassert questions regarding the nature and extent of public regulation.

Research on the corporate-led regulation of quality typically understates the role of noncorporate private actors, particularly consumer and producer groups, in creating and enforcing new standards. The fact that social, environmental, and ethical issues are integrated into new private standards speaks to the power of consumers and consumer-based groups in shaping prevailing expectations in the agrofood sector (DuPuis 2000; Giovannucci and Ponte 2005; Wilkinson 2005). Producer groups have also been critical in creating alternative quality standards in areas like organic and regional appellation systems (Barham 2002, 2003; Guthman 2004). While the retailer-driven view of private food regulation assumes the oligopolistic power of supermarkets, producer organizations are often central to these quality redefinitions and implementing new standards requires public endorsement and government support.

Social movements, non-governmental organizations, and certification

In recent years a number of social initiatives have emerged broadly aligned under the Global Social Justice umbrella. These initiatives challenge dominate processes of corporate globalization fueled by neoliberal global regulation and forge a counter-hegemonic globalization based on embedded, territorially specific, social and ecological rights and values (de Sousa Santos 2004). The Global Social Justice effort combines traditional movement interests defined around labor and citizen demands with new movement concerns focused on social, cultural, and ecological rights (Buttel and Gould 2004). Food sovereignty and rural resource issues are central to the alternative globalization agenda promoted by increasingly powerful international voices like that of the Via Campesina Movement founded in Latin America and the Solidarity Economy Movement founded in Europe. A key feature of these new movement efforts is the novel ways in which they span North/South and producer/consumer divides in promoting social justice.

The Global Social Justice movement includes an ensemble of social movement unions, new political parties, civil society groups, and perhaps most importantly NGOs (Clawson 2003; Evans 2005). NGOs have proved central to these new movement constellations. Oxfam International for example, which has a long history of engagement in Fair Trade, recently launched a global campaign to "make trade fair." Such NGO campaigns gain their strength from transnational advocacy networks that link local and global constituents via exchanges of material and rhetorical resources (Keck and Sikkink 1998). As Evans (2000) argues transnational advocacy networks represent a critical avenue for challenging the destructive aspects of corporate globalization, fighting marginalization, and forging a "counter-hegemonic" pattern of globalization.

New global movements mobilize protest against key multilateral institutions, particularly the WTO, while transnational NGOs work to develop concrete alternatives. NGOs have traditionally focused on lobbying for changes in State policies to further their social and environmental goals, but many now focus on pressuring corporations directly to improve their practices (Winston 2002). This strategic shift is grounded in an understanding that neoliberal policies have undermined the power of nation states to regulate production, and institutions like the WTO have largely ceded regulation to the open market. As NGOs have found, highly visible brand names create key pressure points for large corporations. To the degree that the symbolic and financial value of global brands has risen over recent years (Klein 2000; Lury 2004), so too has corporate vulnerability to image damage. Seizing this opening, movement groups pursue a powerful strategy of "naming and shaming" – publicizing poor corporate practices to propel social and environmental improvements. This strategy is often combined with consumer "boycotts" that punish negligent corporations by avoiding their products and rewarding better performers by promoting their products. These new strategies have proved particularly effective in branded product areas with high identity content like food and fashion (Barrientos 2000; Esbenshade 2004; Jenkins et al. 2002).

Social movement initiatives converge with political and economic interests in fueling the recent proliferation of codes of conduct, certifications, and labels, producing new regulatory frameworks which are altering production relations across national and international commodity networks (Gereffi et al. 2001). These initiatives incorporate a range of ethical, social, and environmental concerns, acknowledging the importance of production conditions in the quality of the final product. Since these quality attributes are typically not visible in the products themselves, they are communicated through corporate advertising or product labels. Given rising concerns about agrofood production conditions, these new regulatory efforts are growing particularly rapidly in food and other natural resource products like flowers, timber, and fibers (Barrientos and Dolan 2006; Cashore et al. 2004; Hughes 2001). Thus, the technical package of the green revolution is now being replaced by an institutional package for the global monitoring of the quality food economy.

Major corporations around the world also now address issues of corporate social responsibility. Given extensive consumer concern over food quality and safety issues, large food retailers and traders have been at the forefront of this move, establishing internal codes of conduct and product seals (Busch and Bain 2004; Hughes 2005). These self-regulatory efforts, or first-party certifications, leave standard setting and monitoring up to individual firms. Corporations rely on their own brand reputations in assuring consumers of the validity of their quality claims. While most large food retailers and traders now have policies addressing food safety and quality, and often other social and environmental conditions, the self-interested nature of these claims limits their credibility.

To bolster the legitimacy of their quality claims, many corporations pursue second-party certifications that shift standard setting and monitoring responsibilities to an industry group (Gereffi et al. 2001). There are numerous agrofood industry standards and certifications, some that operate in a specific commodity (like the Common Code for the Coffee Community), some across the retail sector (like EurepGAP), and some that include food and manufacturing companies (like the Ethical Trade Initiative) (Barrientos and Dolan 2006). While outside pressure from consumers and social movement groups has propelled these industry measures, they are now integral to corporate business. The ethical, environmental, and health values previously associated with social movement groups have thus been transformed into key facets of corporate profitability, branding, and marketing.

Third-party certifications that have non-industry nonstate coordinating bodies appear to be growing most rapidly due to their greater legitimacy and credibility (Gereffi et al. 2001). NGOs play a key role in these certification systems, developing standards, monitoring procedures, and labels. NGOs are central in promoting the values undergirding third-party systems, though monitoring and certification is increasingly handled by separate agencies. Fair Trade certification in the food sector joins others, like Forest Stewardship Council certification in timber, among the ranks of the major NGO certification and labeling initiatives (Cashore et al. 2004). These third-party systems address a broad range of social, cultural, labor, and environmental concerns. In the agrofood sector certification standards may specify farm locations, inputs, and methods, environmental protection measures, employment terms and conditions, and processing, trade, and retail criteria. While organic and Fair Trade certifications are the most well known, there are dozens more. In coffee for example, there are five key third-party certifications, each with their own standards and procedures (Raynolds et al. forthcoming). Some corporations have sought third-party certification for their products in response to consumer or movement pressures or as an inexpensive way to bolster their quality claims.[7]

Third-party certification systems face a number of challenges arising from the inherent tensions between the alternative conventions these efforts seek to promote and dominant industrial and market forces. These certifications are costly and often these costs exclude limited resource producers or consumers. In many initiatives, such as organics, certification costs are borne by producers, limiting the participation of small-scale farmers (Guthman 2004; Raynolds 2004). The introduction of certification fees in Fair Trade in 2004 raises similar concerns about exclusionary pressures in production. Most third-party certified items, including Fair Trade products, are sold at higher retail prices potentially excluding poorer consumers.

A second related problem is that the bureaucratic industrial standards and monitoring procedures involved in certification may undermine the values NGO sponsors seek to promote. Again these problems are clearly evidenced in organic certification, where complex ecological concerns may be reduced to input bans and ecosystem monitoring may resemble a uniform audit (Mutersbaugh 2002). The challenges raised by bureaucratic industrial procedures may be even greater for Fair Trade, since alternative social relations based on trust and partnership are fundamental to movement values (Raynolds 2002). Significant tensions are emerging in both the North and the South between the social values promoted by the Fair Trade movement and the industrial market values promoted in the bureaucratic certification process.

Fair Trade and other NGO certification initiatives have emerged from a social movement base, and while their alternative values may be appropriated, these values tend to reemerge and fuel new social movement interests. Callon (1998) suggests that however far the market goes to absorb alternative movement issues, competition will create new forms of exclusion of particular values, actors, and spaces. This process may be best understood within a cyclical process of corporate appropriation and social movement outflanking (Brunori 1999). Fair Trade and related initiatives may become appropriated into conventional circuits with alternative products transformed into new consumer goods. But this process may in turn fuel new social initiatives that outflank market interests. Our analysis suggests that an appropriation of Fair Trade may shift symbolic and material resources downstream, away from rural actors and spaces toward large-scale urban actors, particularly supermarkets, with values attaching to the corporate brand. But to counteract this trend and outflank corporate takeover, new social movement initiatives are likely to up the stakes in the reformulation of alternative values and networks.

Conclusions

Social movements pursuing social justice and environmental sustainability values no longer direct their demands exclusively to governments or against global corporations. Instead, they focus increasingly on reshaping the parameters of economic activity itself to accommodate movement values. Business, in its turn, no longer dismisses these values as externalities to be ignored or relegated to the public sector. The terrain of social movements has now become the terrain of competing market growth strategies. The cost of the neoliberal dream of transforming market economies into market societies has thus become an unimagined expansion of market responsibility and accountability.

The distinction between economic and noneconomic actors and activities has blurred as social and environmental quality attributes become internalized within strategies of corporate competition. In this context, NGOs advance from critique to the co-construction of economic frontiers and governing rules, and firms accept triple-bottom-line auditing and monitoring based on social, environmental, and economic criteria. Social movements and alternative networks negotiate and contest the global production/consumption relations of the mainstream agrofood system. Yet processes of mainstreaming dilute the "alternative" component of these movement efforts, internalizing the fault line which previously separated the movement from the mainstream. The current tensions within Fair Trade thus arise from the merging of markets, networks, and social movements.

While necessarily schematic, we suggest that the analytical framework developed here can illuminate the issues and debates elaborated in this book's later chapters. Fair Trade is currently being shaped by the changing nature of the global agrofood system, new patterns of regulation based on governance by quality standards and certification systems, and a merging of the frontiers between markets and social forces. Yet this is a reciprocal and dynamic process, for Fair Trade is in turn contributing to the reshaping of the agrofood system, quality standards and certification, and the market and social interface. The analysis of Fair Trade ideas and practices is thus important, not just for understanding the alternative globalization agenda, but for understanding prevailing processes of globalization in the agrofood sector and beyond.

Notes

1 While the "commodity chain" tradition has its roots in world systems theory and "value chain" analysis grows out of the business literature, recent studies merge the two traditions, with Gereffi still at the forefront (e.g. Gereffi et al. 2005). For further discussion regarding these and related conceptualizations see Raikes et al. (2000), Raynolds (2002), and Wilkinson (1997).

2 Gereffi and colleagues' reformulated framework combines transaction costs, social network theory, and resource/competence theories of the firm. But their key questions fall mostly within the "new" transaction cost domain in analyzing how intermediary coordination can supplant the make or buy dualism (see Ménard and Valceschini 2005).

3 This form of coordination characterizes many agrofood commodities where growers receive technological and capital inputs from buyers and are required to sell to these buyers under contracted conditions (e.g. Dixon 2002).

4 Sauvée and Valceschini (2004) analyze the emergence of innovative forms of coordination in pork and meat production in Holland and Spain. The pork filière is jointly coordinated by consumer and environmental associations, public authorities, and a producer association. Production norms are defined by an autonomous foundation that owns the brand; monitoring is done by an independent firm. In the meat filière, the brand is the property of the region and is overseen by a committee of different sector representatives.

5 As does the more recent global threat of avian flu.

6 Much of the literature focuses on the United Kingdom where the top five supermarkets control 80 percent of sales, ignoring cases like the United States where the top five supermarkets control less than 40 of the market (see Busch and Bain 2004: 330).

7 Supermarkets for instance can relieve themselves of the costs of monitoring special quality claims by requiring that suppliers gain third-party certification.

44   *L.T. Raynolds and J. Wilkinson*

References

Aglietta, M. (1976) *La Théorie de la Régulation: Une Analyse Critique*, Paris: La Découverte.

Allaire, G. and Boyer, R. (1995) *La Grande Transformation*, Paris: INRA.

Barham, E. (2002) "Towards a theory of values-based labeling," *Agriculture and Human Values*, 19: 349–360.

—— (2003) "Translating terroir: the global challenge of French AOC labeling," *Journal of Rural Studies*, 19: 127–138.

Barrientos, S. (2000) "Globalization and ethical trade: assessing the implications for development," *Journal of International Development*, 12: 559–570.

Barrientos, S. and Dolan, C. (eds) (2006) *Ethical Sourcing in the Global Food Chain*, London: Earthscan.

Boltanski, L. and Thévenot, L. (1991) *De la Justification: Les Économies de la Grandeur*, Paris: Gallimard.

Boyer, R. (1990) *The Regulation School: A Critical Introduction*, Translated by C. Charney, New York: Columbia University Press.

Brunori, G. (1999) "Alternative trade or market fragmentation? Food circuits and social movements," University of Pisa, Italy, unpublished.

Busch, L. (2000) "The moral economy of grades and standards," *Journal of Rural Studies*, 16: 273–283.

Busch, L. and Bain, C. (2004) "New! Improved? The transformation of the global agrifood system," *Rural Sociology*, 69: 321–346.

Busch, L. and Juska, A. (1997) "Beyond political economy: actor networks and the globalization of agriculture," *Review of International Political Economy*, 4: 668–708.

Buttel, F. and Gould, K. (2004) "Global social movement(s) at the crossroads: some observations on the trajectory of the anti-corporate globalization movement," *Journal of World-Systems Research*, 10: 36–66.

Callon, M. (1998) *The Laws of the Market*, Oxford and Malden, MA: Blackwell Publishers.

Cashore, B., Auld, G., and Newsom, D. (2004) *Governing Through Markets: Forest Certification and the Emergence of Non-State Authority*, New Haven, CT: Yale University Press.

Clawson, D. (2003) *The Next Upsurge: Labor and the New Social Movements*, Ithaca, NY: Cornell University Press.

Coe, N.M. (2003) "The internationalisation/globalisation of retailing: towards a geographical research agenda?" GPN, Working Paper 8, Manchester University.

—— (2004) "The internationalisation/globalisation of retailing: towards an economic – geographical research agenda," *Environment and Planning A*, 36: 1571–1594.

Dankers, C. (2003) *Environmental and Social Standards, Certification and Labelling for Cash Crops*, Rome: Food and Agriculture Organization.

Daviron, B. and Ponte, S. (2005) *The Coffee Paradox: Commodity Trade and the Elusive Promise of Development*, London: Zed.

Davis, J.H. and Goldberg, R. (1987) *A Concept of Agribusiness*, Boston, MA: Harvard University Press.

Delgado, N.G. and Romano, J.O. (2005) "The world social forum: a space for the translation of diversity in social mobilization," in S. De Paula and G.A. Dymski (eds), *Reimagining Growth: Towards a Renewal of Development Theory*, London and New York: Zed Books.

de Sousa Santos, B. (2004) "The world social forum: toward a counter-hegemonic globalisation (Part 1)," in J. Sen, A. Anand, A. Escobar, and P. Waterman (eds), *Promise of Development*, London: Zed.

Dixon, J. (2002) *The Changing Chicken: Chooks, Cooks, and Culinary Cultures*, Sydney: University of New South Wales Press.

Dolan, C. and Humphrey, J. (2000) "Governance and trade in fresh vegetables: the impact of UK supermarkets on the African horticulture industry," *The Journal of Development Studies*, 37: 145–176.

DuPuis, E.M. (2000) "Not in my body: rBGH and the rise of organic milk," *Agriculture and Human Values*, 17: 285–295.

Esbenshade, J. (2004) *Monitoring Sweatshops*, Philadelphia, PA: Temple University Press.

Evans, P. (2000) "Fighting marginalization with transnational networks: counter hegemonic globalization," *Contemporary Sociology*, 29: 230–241.

—— (2005) "Counter-hegemonic globalization: transnational social movements in the contemporary global political economy," in T. Janoski, A. Hicks, and M. Schwartz (eds), *Handbook of Political Sociology*, London: Cambridge University Press.

Eymard-Duvernay, F. (1995) "La négociation de la qualité," in F. Nicolas and E. Valceschini (eds), *Agro-Alimentaire: Une Economie de la Qualité*, Paris: INRA.

Farina, E.M.M.Q., Gutman, G.E., Lavarello, P.J., Nunes, R., and Reardon, T. (2005) "Private and public milk standards in Argentina and Brazil," *Food Policy*, 30: 302–315.

Fold, N. (2002) "Lead firms and competition in 'bi-polar' commodity chains: grinders and branders in the global cocoa-chocolate industry," *Journal of Agrarian Change*, 2: 228–247.

Freidberg, S. (2003) "Cleaning up down south: supermarkets, ethical trade and African horticulture," *Social & Cultural Geography*, 4: 27–43.

Friedland, W. (1984) "Commodity systems analysis: an approach to the sociology of agriculture," in H.K. Schwarzweller (ed.), *Research in Rural Sociology and Development*, Greenwich, CT: JAI Press Inc.

Friedmann, H. and McMichael, P. (1989) "Agriculture and the state system: the rise and decline of national agricultures, 1870 to the present," *Sociologia Ruralis*, 24: 93–117.

Gereffi, G. (1994) "The organization of buyer-driven global commodity chains," in G. Gereffi and M. Korzeniewicz (eds), *Commodity Chains and Global Capitalism*, Westport, CT: Praeger.

Gereffi, G. and Kaplinsky, R. (eds) (2001) "The value of value chains," *Special Issue, IDS Bulletin*, 32.

Gereffi, G., Garcia-Johnson, R., and Sasser, E. (2001) "The NGO-industrial complex," *Foreign Policy*, July/August: 56–65.

Gereffi, G., Humphrey, J., and Sturgeon, J. (2005) "The governance of global value chains," *Review of International Political Economy*, 12: 78–104.

Gibbon, P. and Ponte, S. (2005) *Trading Down: Africa, Value Chains, and the Global Economy*, Philadelphia, PA: Temple.

Giovannucci, D. and Ponte, S. (2005) "Standards as a new form of social contract? Sustainability initiatives in the coffee industry," *Food Policy*, 30: 284–301.

Goodman, D. (1997) "World-scale processes and agro-food systems: critique and research needs," *Review of International Political Economy*, 4: 663–687.

Goodman, D., Sorj, B., and Wilkinson, J. (1987) *From Farming to Biotechnology: A Theory of Agro-Industrial Development*, Oxford: Basil Blackwell.

Gopinath, M. (2000) *Foreign Direct Investment in Food and Agricultural Sectors*, Online. Available at: http:/oregonstate.edu/dept/IIFET/2000/papers/gopinath.pdf (accessed May 15, 2006).

Granovetter, M. (1985) "Economic action and social structure: the problem of embeddedness," *American Journal of Sociology*, 91: 481–510.

Guthman, J. (2004) *Agrarian Dreams: The Paradox of Organic Farming in California*, Berkeley, CA: University of California Press.

Henderson, J., Dicken, P., Hess, M., Coe, N., and Yeung, H.W.-C. (2002) "Global production networks and the analysis of economic development," *Review of International Political Economy*, 9: 436–464.

Henson, S. and Reardon, T. (2005) "Private agri-food standards: implications for food policy and the agri-food system," *Food Policy*, 30: 241–253.

Higgins, V. and Lawrence, G. (2005) "Globalization and agricultural governance," in V. Higgins and G. Lawrence (eds), *Agricultural Governance: Globalization and the New Politics of Regulation*, London and New York: Routledge.

Hughes, A. (2001) "Global commodity networks, ethical trade and governmentality: organizing business responsibility in the Kenyan cut flower industry," *Transactions of the Institute of British Geographers*, 26: 390–406.

—— (2005) "Corporate strategy and the management of ethical trade: the case of the UK food and clothing retailers," *Environment and Planning A*, 37: 1145–1163.

Humphrey, J. and Schmitz, H. (2001) "Governance in global value chains," *IDS Bulletin* 32: 19–29.

Jenkins, R., Pearson, R., and Seyfang, G. (eds) (2002) *Corporate Responsibility and Labour Rights*, London: Earthscan.

Keck, M. and Sikkink, K. (1998) *Activists Beyond Borders: Advocacy Networks in International Politics*, Ithaca, NY: Cornell University Press.

Klein, N. (2000) *No Logo: Taking Aim at the Brand Bullies*, New York: Picador USA.

Lauret, F. (1983) "Sur les etudes de filières agro-alimentaires," *Economies et Sociétés Cahiers de l'ISMEA*, 17: 721–740.

Lury, C. (2004) *Brands: The Logos of the Global Economy*, New York: Routledge.

Marsden, T., Banks, J., and Bristow, G. (2000) "Food supply chain approaches: exploring their role in rural development," *Sociologia Ruralis*, 40: 424–438.

Ménard, C. and Valceschini, E. (2005) "New institutions for governing the agri-food industry," *European Review of Agricultural Economics*, 32: 421–440.

Murdoch, J., Marsden, T., and Banks, J. (2000) "Quality, nature, and embeddedness: some theoretical considerations in the context of the food sector," *Economic Geography*, 76: 107–125.

Murray, D. and Raynolds, L. (2000) "Alternative trade in bananas: obstacles and opportunities for progressive social change in the global economy," *Agriculture and Human Values*, 17: 65–74.

Mutersbaugh, T. (2002) "The number is the beast: a political economy of organic coffee certification and producer unionism," *Environment and Planning A*, 34: 1165–1184.

Polanyi, K. (1957) *The Great Transformation: The Political and Economic Origins of Our Time*, Boston, MA: Beacon Press.

Ponte, S. (2002) "The 'latte revolution?' Regulation, markets and consumption in the global coffee chain," *World Development*, 30: 1099–1122.

Raikes, P., Jensen, M., and Ponte, S. (2000) "Global commodity chain analysis and the French filière approach: comparison and critique," *Economy and Society*, 29: 390–417.

Raynolds, L.T. (1994) "Institutionalizing flexibility: a comparative analysis of Fordist and post-Fordist models of Third World agro-export production," in G. Gereffi and M. Korzeniewicz (eds), *Commodity Chains and Global Capitalism*, Westport, CT: Praeger.

—— (1997) "Restructuring national agriculture, agro-food trade, and agrarian livelihoods in the Caribbean," in D. Goodman and M. Watts (eds), *Globalising Food: Agrarian Questions and Global Restructuring*, London: Routledge.

—— (2002) "Consumer/producer links in fair trade coffee networks," *Sociologia Ruralis*, 42: 404–424.

—— (2004) "The globalization of organic agro-food networks," *World Development*, 32: 725–743.

Raynolds, L.T., Murray, D., and Heller, A. (forthcoming) "Regulating sustainability in the coffee sector: a comparative analysis of environmental and social certification and labeling initiatives," *Agriculture and Human Values*, 24.

Reardon, T., Codron, J., Busch, L., Bingen, J., and Harris, C. (2001) "Global change in agrifood grades and standards," *International Food and Agribusiness Management*, 2: 421–435.

Sauvée, L. and Valceschini, E. (2004) "Agro-alimentaire: la qualité au coeur des relations entre agriculteurs, industriels et distributeurs," in A. Colin (ed.), *Déméter 2004: Economie et stratégies agricoles*, Paris: Armand Colin.

Smith, A., Rainnie, A., Dunford, M., Hardy, J., Hudson, R., and Sadler, D. (2002) "Networks of value, commodities and regions: reworking divisions of labour in macro-regional economies," *Progress in Human Geography*, 26: 41–63.

Sverrison, Á. (2004) "Local and global commodity chains," in C. Pietrobelli and Á. Sverrison (eds), *Linking Local and Global Economies: The Ties that Bind*, London: Routledge.

Thévenot, L. (1995) "Des marchés aux normes," in G. Allaire and R. Boyer (eds), *Régulation et Conventions dans L'Agriculture et L'Agro-Alimentaire*, Paris: INRA.

Vigorito, R. (1978) *Criterios Metodológicos para el Estúdio de Complejos Agroindustriales*, Mexico: ILET.

Wilkinson, J. (1997) "A new paradigm for economic analysis," *Economy and Society*, 26: 305–339.

—— (2002) "Genetically modified organisms, organics, and the contested construction of demand in the agrofood system," *International Journal of Sociology of Agriculture and Food*, 10: 1–8.

—— (2005) "Consumer society: what opportunities for new expressions of citizenship and control?" in S. de Paula and G. Dymsky (eds), *Reimagining Growth*, London: Zed Books.

—— (2006) "Network theories and political economy. From attrition to convergence?," in T.K. Mardsen and J. Murdoch (eds), *Research in Rural Sociology and Development, Vol 12, Between the Local and the Global: Confronting Complexity in the Contemporary Agri-Food Sector*, London: Elsevier.

Winston, M. (2002) "NGO strategies for promoting corporate social responsibility," *Ethics and International Affairs*, 16: 71–87.

Part II
Fair Trade in the Global North

4 Northern social movements and Fair Trade

Stephanie Barrientos, Michael E. Conroy, and Elaine Jones

Introduction

Europe and North America have seen significant growth in Fair Trade and provide rich insights into the dynamics of Fair Trade occurring in the Global North. This chapter introduces the second part of the book by exploring the social movement origins of Fair Trade and the emerging tensions as Fair Trade moves further into the commercial mainstream. At issue is the relation between the social principles of Fair Trade, and the commercial imperatives of the trading environment in which it operates. These tensions are playing out in a context where diverse elements have come together in a social movement that has successfully driven the expansion of Fair Trade, with increasingly positive responses by both retailers and consumers. The diversity of this movement is reflected both in its origins and in the different channels through which Fair Trade has evolved.

The underlying tensions between the social and commercial principles of Fair Trade are being sharpened by the success of Fair Trade in the mainstream market. These tensions are playing out in different ways in Europe and North America, but the challenges are the same. The key questions are how these tensions are being managed in the face of different perspectives on Fair Trade, and, ultimately, how this process will determine the future trajectory of Fair Trade. This chapter lays the background for subsequent chapters which analyze these tensions in more depth in a set of detailed cases. Here, we look first at the social movement origins of Fair Trade and the different perspectives within it, as they evolved in Europe and North America. Next we examine the mainstreaming of Fair Trade in a more ethically aware consumer market, often dominated by large mainstream commercial companies. Finally we consider how these tensions are playing out in different contexts in the chapters that follow.

From alternative trade to Fair Trade labeling in Europe

Fair Trade in Europe has seen phenomenal growth over the past five years, as demonstrated in Chapter 2. It is one of the fastest growing markets on the continent, and currently accounts for an estimated 60–70 percent of all global Fair Trade sales (Krier 2005). Yet, the successful growth of Fair Trade in Europe has brought both fresh challenges and potential divisions among its advocates. The Fair Trade movement in Europe is not a homogenous group. It emerged out of two broad perspectives: first the "political" influences which emerged from progressive social movements and solidarity campaigns whose primary purpose is to fundamentally change the terms of world trade; and second the faith-based influences which emerged through organizations whose starting point was more of a philanthropic mission for a better world. Both had a vision of greater social justice and fairer trade, but from different origins. Cutting across both groups are those who maintain a "pure" commitment to their principles, and those who take a more pragmatic approach to extending the reach of Fair Trade within the commercial mainstream. Though simplified, this characterization of the broad influences that initiated the Fair Trade movement in Europe highlights the fact that the Fair Trade movement has always contained an amalgam of diverse and overlapping perspectives and groups.

Links between Fair Trade and progressive social movements are reflected in the strong relationship in some European countries between the Cooperative and the Fair Trade movements.[1] For example, in the United Kingdom there is synergy between Fair Trade and the mission of the Co-operative Retail Group which has been instrumental in recent years in blazing the trail for the national mainstreaming of Fair Trade. In Italy, the Fair Trade movement also has close links with the cooperative movement which, in turn, has close links with progressive socialist parties. The largest Fair Trade organization in Italy, CTM (Cooperazione Terzo Mondo), is a cooperative which maintains international synergistic relations with Fair Trade producers in the global South who are themselves organized as cooperatives. The links between cooperative and Fair Trade principles are underlined by the fact that there are 300,000 Co-ops in Europe with an estimated 83.5 million members who subscribe to the cooperative values and principles as laid down by the International Cooperative Alliance, many of which parallel the values underpinning Fair Trade (ICA 2006).

Fair Trade in Europe can also trace its roots to its origins in faith-based organizations and Non-Governmental Organizations (NGOs). In the United Kingdom these include Traidcraft and Christian Aid , as well as Oxfam-UK which originates in the Quaker movement (Barratt Brown 1993). Many of these organizations established "alternative" trade through so-called World Shops as a way of supporting Southern producer groups. These shops were established in the 1960s and 1970s, initially selling handicrafts and later "solidarity" or "campaign" coffee from countries such as Nicaragua in support of the Sandinista movement. World Shops acted as both an outlet for Fair Trade products and a source of educational and campaigning materials on the "unfairness" of the world trade system. Given the constituency-based nature of these membership organizations, their supporters made up a large percentage of the activists of the nascent Fair Trade movement.

The 1970s saw an increasing awareness among campaigners, student groups, trade unions, and activists from a variety of causes regarding the wider economic and social issues, including the global injustices facing poor producers in a commercial world dominated by large corporations and unequal trading relations. This was given further impetus by the solidarity movement which grew in tandem with the spread of military takeovers in Latin America in the 1960s and 1970s. With the emergence of Alternative Trade Organizations (ATOs) and World Shops, small producer groups found routes into export markets based on principles of commercial transparency, social justice, and community support. This further strengthened the connections between Southern producers and Northern consumers. The ideological paradigm which gave birth to a movement for Fair Trade thus began to take shape.

By the late 1980s, a thriving network of ATOs had been established across Europe. This network now forms the basis of the rapid growth of Fair Trade in many European countries, particularly the United Kingdom, Switzerland, and the Netherlands (Krier 2005). The movement has grown, as described in Chapter 2, into a broad group of overlapping efforts, loosely coordinated through the FINE network. FINE's working definition of Fair Trade has two basic components: the first is to provide a working model of international trade that makes a difference to the producers and consumers that engage in it, and to do so in such a way that social objectives are met and the second, and more radical component, is to challenge orthodoxy in business practice and to encourage business toward more social ends (Moore et al. 2006). This two-faceted working definition reflects the diversity of Fair Trade's origins and contemporary profile. In Europe, the NGOs and ATOs supporting the expansion of Fair Trade collaborated to advance an *alternative* to mainstream trade, but increasingly within them there was also pressure to advance Fair Trade *within* the mainstream of commercial retailing.

European ATOs evolved from different origins and coalitions of groups. One of the pioneers of the Fair Trade movement in the United Kingdom was Twin and Twin Trading. Founded from the ashes of the disbanded Greater London Council, Twin sought to forge trade links and create trade agreements with countries excluded from the world trade arena, such as Vietnam, Cuba, Nicaragua, and Mozambique. Twin's founding conference in 1985 was attended by delegates from 20 Southern countries, British local councils, cooperatives, trade unions, and ATOs. The main aim of Twin and Twin Trading was to develop new forms of economic relations between the South and the North based on the principles of mutual advantage and independence of partners, and countering exploitative relations. Twin took an overtly political stance by declaring that the intention was to trade on "non-capitalist principles" with the intention of creating jobs, improving the quality of work, and reinforcing the labor movement.[2] The emphasis on trading with cooperatives was particularly significant and was influential in shaping the subsequent Fair Trade labeling standards which initially focused on collective and cooperative forms of ownership in producer organizations. Twin went on to collaborate with other UK groups (Oxfam, Traidcraft, and Equal Exchange) to set up CaféDirect – the first Fair Trade brand in the United Kingdom. Twin also later collaborated with The Body Shop and Christian Aid to support Kuapa Kokoo (the Ghanaian cooperative of small cocoa farmers) setting up the Day Chocolate Company – the first producer-owned Fair Trade brand (Barratt Brown 1993; Nicholls and Opal 2005; Tiffen et al. 2004).

The advance into mainstream commercial channels was galvanized through the introduction of Fair Trade labeling. Labeling was initiated by the Max Havelaar group in the Netherlands in 1987 and later in 13 European countries. The Netherlands remains a key European Fair Trade market, joined now by the United Kingdom and Switzerland. While World Shops and other ATO outlets effectively "certified" the Fair Trade nature of all their products by selling only products that were, in one way or another, more beneficial for producers (though without strict standards), one of the main aims of Fair Trade labeling was to provide a vehicle to advance Fair Trade goods within mainstream shops and supermarkets, side by side with conventional products. The different national labeling schemes were harmonized in 1997 through the Fairtrade Labelling Organizations International (FLO).

As noted in Chapter 2, the original focus of Fair Trade labeling was on food products produced by small producers, particularly coffee, tea, and chocolate. This was followed by Fair Trade bananas sourced from both small-scale producers and some plantations. Handicraft products continued to be sold through ATOs based on their reputation rather than an accredited label, linked through the International Fair Trade Association (IFAT). IFAT has since developed a self-assessment scheme as a basis for allowing its members to use an IFAT trademark, which it insists is *not* a consumer label, although some companies are using it to that end. IFAT and FLO have begun to discuss ways in which their standards can be harmonized.

Increasing harmonization has not altered the fact that diverse perspectives form the basis of Fair Trade. The social movement behind the expansion of Fair Trade was driven in part by adherence to an alternative to mainstream trade based on a vision of equity and justice in trade for marginalized producers. Yet the paradox of growth was that Fair Trade was increasingly being anchored within the same mainstream commercial sector many sought to avoid. As noted in Chapter 2, the net retail value of Fair Trade products in Europe (both labeled and nonlabeled) reached US$ 819 million in 2004, an increase of 154 percent over the preceding five years. Of these European sales only one-third derives from World Shops; the majority occur in some 55,000 supermarkets, largely associated with major retailer chains (Krier 2005). For many, this growth pattern has proven that Fair Trade can and has broken out of its "niche market" tradition. But as demonstrated in the subsequent chapters on the UK and US Fair Trade experience, it has also generated tensions as the dual goals of Fair Trade are played out.

Origins and growth of Fair Trade in North America

In North America, the Fair Trade movement developed according to a different tempo than in Europe, although along parallel lines. Fair Trade's recent dramatic growth, particularly in the United States, has greatly accentuated underlying differences across the movement. In this context tensions between movement-based ATO-led Fair Trade, and certified Fair Trade in mainstream outlets are, if anything, more acute than in Europe.

After World War II the US faith-based organization SERRV began working with European refugees.[3] Other ATOs were established in the United States and Canada, including Ten Thousand Villages started by the Mennonite Central Committee. Ten Thousand Villages provides "vital, fair income to Third World people by marketing their handicrafts and telling their stories in North America" and has grown to include more than 160 nonprofit retail stores.[4] Reflecting common core ATO principles, Ten Thousand Villages seeks to bring justice and hope to the poor, trade with artisan groups who pay fair wages and demonstrate concern for their members' welfare, and provide consistent purchases, advances, and prompt final payments.[5] SERRV and Ten Thousand Villages were among the founding members of IFAT in 1989.

In the 1990s Oxfam America and Oxfam Canada developed a large and relatively successful catalog-sales operation for handicrafts sourced directly from village level producers around the world. Other stand-alone efforts, such as "Pueblo to People" (now defunct) attempted to expand the market and build direct sale supply chains from impoverished handicraft producers to ethically motivated final consumers. The definitions of Fair Trade varied, although in most cases producers received higher prices than they would have received through normal commercial handicraft channels.

In the United States the work of these and other ATOs led to the creation of the Fair Trade Federation (FTF) in 1994, set up as "an association of Fair Trade wholesalers, retailers, and producers whose members are committed to provide fair wages and good employment opportunities to economically disadvantaged artisans and farmers worldwide."[6] The FTF also sees its role as educational and policy-oriented, fostering "a more equitable and sustainable system of production and trade that benefits people and their communities."

In the mid-1990s, a more formalized certified Fair Trade model developed around coffee, and that model has become a dominant force in US Fair Trade. Certified Fair Trade coffee was the initiative of a small group of NGOs that had been in contact with Max Havelaar and other European initiatives and a small group of ATO-like, but often for-profit, coffee roasters and retailers who had been developing their own models of fairer pricing and trade relations with small-scale coffee producers. The founding meeting of Transfair USA, the FLO-affiliated national Fair Trade certifying organization, was held in 1995. This meeting was hosted by an NGO, Institute for Agriculture and Trade Policy, which was interested in developing alternative, fairer models for global agricultural commodity trade and in launching a line of certified Fair Trade coffee. After a brief hiatus for early organizational efforts, TransFair USA and certified Fair Trade sales took off.

US Fair Trade coffee sales leapt from virtually nothing in 1998 to over 3,500 tons in 2003 as noted in Chapter 2. The rapid growth of Fair Trade coffee in the United States can be attributed to three principal factors:

1   the organization of successful "market campaigns" by advocacy NGOs designed to put pressure on companies to adopt lines of Fair Trade coffee and other products;

2   the adoption of Fair Trade products by a number of coffee roasters and retailers as a distinguishing characteristic for marketing purposes; and

3   the creation of a sophisticated business-oriented service structure by Transfair USA for Fair Trade licensees.

Each of these factors has limitations and each has contributed in important ways to ongoing struggles within the Fair Trade movement, in the United States and elsewhere.

Self-certified "fair trade" coffee has been sold in the United States since 1986 by Equal Exchange, a Massachusetts-based for-profit worker owned firm that began selling "fairly priced" coffees through solidarity networks.[7] Equal Exchange draws its name, and principles, from the theoretically based assertion that historical relations of "unequal exchange" must be challenged in order to reduce global inequalities.[8] Though not initially affiliated in a formal way with its European Fair Trade counterparts, Equal Exchange adopted parallel principles to those articulated by Max Havelaar and other European groups, which it saw as providing a more equitable distribution of production risk across farmers, intermediate traders, roasters, and retailers (Berman and Rozyne circa 1992). Today Equal Exchange views its mission as: "building long-term trade partnerships that are economically just and environmentally sound, to foster mutually beneficial relations between farmers and consumers and to demonstrate, through our success, the viability of worker cooperatives and Fair Trade."[9] Equal Exchange was one of TransFair USA's first licensees and has grown rapidly in recent years to become one of the country's largest vendors of Fair Trade certified products in the US. Equal Exchange remains a leader of the set of ATO coffee roasters committed to selling only Fair Trade products (the "100-percenters").

The "breakthrough" moment for certified Fair Trade in "mainstream" markets came on April 13, 2000, when Starbucks, the world's largest chain of specialty coffee houses, signed a letter of intent with TransFair USA to offer certified coffee in all 2,700 US Starbucks cafes. This deal was fostered in large part by the social activist organization Global Exchange which had carried out a yearlong campaign to promote this move and had organized simultaneous demonstrations against Starbucks coffee shops in 30 US cities that was to happen on the following day (April 14, 2000). In response to the signing, Global Exchange turned the planned demonstrations into high-profile celebrations of Starbucks' commitment to purchase Fair Trade coffee. A few months later, certified Fair Trade coffee began to be sold in Starbucks stores nationwide.

Peet's Coffee, Tully's Coffee, and a host of other competing specialty coffee companies soon followed suit in initiating sales of Fair Trade certified coffee. None of these major vendors was willing to commit to selling solely Fair Trade coffees. Motivated more by NGO pressure than by either internal corporate culture or consumer demand, the participation of these companies nevertheless resulted in the dramatic increase in 2001 and 2002 of Fair Trade certified coffee sales.

Over recent years other NGOs and faith-based groups have played key roles in campaigning to promote Fair Trade products in the United States. The NGO

Co-op America has focused on convincing more mainstream coffee companies, such as Procter & Gamble, to introduce a line of Fair Trade coffees (which they have done). Oxfam America has been central in training student leaders to develop campus campaigns to shift college and university institutional coffee to Fair Trade and has assisted the launch of a United Students for Fair Trade organization. Lutheran World Relief (LWR) has created an Interfaith Fair Trade Initiative to encourage congregations of many faiths to purchase and serve Fair Trade coffee and tea in their institutions and to encourage members to purchase Fair Trade products for their homes. The initial goal of the Interfaith Fair Trade Initiative was to secure adoption of Fair Trade coffee in "at least 1000 congregations of differing religious denominations across the nation." In less than three years, the campaign reached no fewer than 15,000 congregations, where Fair Trade coffee is served after services, and members of the congregations commit to campaigning locally to get Fair Trade coffee placed in local stores.[10] Most of the coffee sold through this campaign comes from Equal Exchange.[11]

Another factor influencing the rapid growth of certified Fair Trade in the United States, both within the coffee market and across newly introduced products such as cocoa and chocolate products, tea, and bananas, is the unusual business focus of TransFair USA. Perhaps symbolic of the more general evolution of Fair Trade, TransFair USA was founded by a former Central American solidarity activist who later obtained an MBA degree. Under his leadership, TransFair USA has pursued a strict business model to expand sales of Fair Trade certified products. With a current staff of 40 and an annual budget in excess of US$ 2 million, TransFair USA has become a primary force in the mainstreaming of Fair Trade. For example in 2005, TransFair USA succeeded in converting all private label coffee sold by Costco, the giant big-box retailer, to certified Fair Trade; in introducing a line of Fair Trade coffee at Sam's Clubs, the warehouse branch of Wal-Mart; and in launching Fair Trade coffees regionally in McDonald's.

Challenges to mainstreaming Fair Trade in Europe and North America

Efforts to mainstream Fair Trade in Europe and North America have brought new challenges to the fundamental model of Fair Trade that emerged from ATOs. Some in the Fair Trade movement have bemoaned what they see as a vision of Fair Trade that is becoming less and less distinguishable from a traditional market vision. Fair Trade advocacy NGOs question in particular whether the basic concept of Fair Trade is being "bastardized" by its mainstreaming in shops and restaurants where most of the products sold are not ethically certified and where there are major ethical questions being raised about other aspects of the firms' business practices.

It is clear that the recent rapid growth of Fair Trade in both Europe and North America is largely attributable to the mainstreaming of Fair Trade in venues associated with large-scale corporate retailing. The move to supermarket own-brand retailing of Fair Trade certified items is largely responsible for the

United Kingdom's recent rapid market growth (see Chapter 7). In the United States, recent escalating Fair Trade certified sales can be accounted for largely by the increased adoption of Fair Trade lines by large specialty coffee roasters and food retailers (see Chapter 6), while the planned expansion within mainstream transnational corporate brands stands poised to fuel the next boom in Fair Trade markets (see Chapter 5). These developments have severely heightened tensions across the Global North over Fair Trade's future direction. Some believe that mainstreaming through supermarket and dominant corporate brands and large-scale retail sales provides an important opportunity for growth and reaches a consumer base outside of Fair Trade's traditional niche. They also argue that if one focuses on the objective of generating greater benefits for Fair Trade producers in developing countries, limitation of Fair Trade sales to "politically correct" outlets would have eliminated most of the significant increase in benefits for producers generated in recent years. Others believe that the focus should remain on Fair Trade's roots in cooperative principles and support for small producers, which may be compromised and subverted by the entry of large corporations.

The ATO challenges to Fair Trade mainstreaming involve four major dimensions largely consistent with the dilemmas laid out in Chapter 1. In the first place, they argue that mainstream vendors of Fair Trade products benefit from subsidies provided to the movement by the ATOs themselves and from advocacy NGOs who have invested heavily in support for Fair Trade producer groups and the development of the Fair Trade "social brand." Second, they argue that a distinction should be made between vendors who commit to selling only Fair Trade, the "100-percenters," and those who may sell only a small proportion of their total sales under labeled Fair Trade conditions. Third, there is great concern that filling the demand of the major mainstream companies will force Fair Trade into accepting estate or plantation-based products where only small-farmer and cooperative-based production has been acceptable in the past. And, finally, there are challenges posed by the fundamental ability of the certified Fair Trade system to audit and monitor the rapidly rising volume of product required to fill the demand from the mainstream vendors. Some have even asked whether small NGOs like Transfair USA and FLO are capable of maintaining their edge in dealings with the mammoth firms they serve, or are at risk of being swept up in their adverse mainstream commercial practices (Barrientos and Dolan 2006; Nicholls and Opal 2005).

The chapters in this part of the book point to the rapid growth of supermarket retailing of Fair Trade products in Europe and North America. Supermarket sales are important in nonperishable commodities like coffee and chocolate; they are even more critical in perishable products like bananas and other fruits which require rapid turnover. Large-scale corporate brands provide the supply chains for bringing large Fair Trade volumes to market, while large-scale retailers provide the shelf space for selling these products. These large-scale corporate enterprises give Fair Trade entry into mass markets, but they are simultaneously profiting from a "social brand" built up through long years of activity by a "core" of Fair Trade supporters and consumers. The current and past engagement of this cadre of dedicated individuals is central to the success of Fair Trade and essentially subsidizes mainstream actors now selling Fair Trade items. In Europe for example there are 100,000 volunteers helping to run World Shops which remain important outlets for Fair Trade products. In North America dedicated volunteers also contribute significantly to Fair Trade education, retailing, and activism.

Major investments over the years by numerous organizations, including Fair Trade organizations, ATOs, Fair Trade brands, solidarity and development NGOs, and church groups, have also subsidized the growth and current vitality of Fair Trade. Pioneer Fair Trade retailers and brands, such as Café Direct and Divine Chocolate in the United Kingdom and Equal Exchange in the United States, play a key role in consumer education, public relations, and marketing. It is no accident that the second fastest growing Fair Trade market in the world is in the United Kingdom, where ATOs have spent an estimated US$ 22.7 million annually in recent years on public relations and awareness raising.[12] Of even more significance are the investments of ATOs and other NGOs in assisting Southern producer organization capacity building to ensure they can meet required market standards. Many Northern-based ATOs and marketing organizations have producer programs which extend technical and organizational support funded from their own margins. It is important to recognize the value of these interventions and how these activities have fostered the social capital of Fair Trade. From this vantage point it is clear why ATOs might argue that current mainstream entrants to Fair Trade are profiting from investments by others. It is also clear why these ATOs and other groups selling only Fair Trade products feel that their dedication should be acknowledged and rewarded differently from mainstream corporations with lesser commitment to Fair Trade.

The market-led expansion of Fair Trade and the demand for more products has put the FLO system under pressure to increase the number and volume of certified products and sources. The volume requirements of major retailers and brand name corporations have put pressure on FLO to increase rapidly the integration of estate and plantation suppliers of fresh produce as demonstrated in Chapters 5 and 7, raising questions about the future of Fair Trade's small-producer base. The recent incursion of mega players into Fair Trade has compounded the fears of those critical of plantation certification and has unsettled the small-scale farmers who have traditionally produced the bulk of Fair Trade items. We have seen certified Fair Trade products move beyond traditional food items like coffee and cocoa into a range of fresh fruits and more recently into cut flowers and sports balls. Supply chains for these commodities are very different from that of coffee, and FLO has had to revise its certification standards to accommodate the commercial arrangements found in plantations and factory-based production. With this expansion the FLO system is increasingly turning to the types of minimum labor standards enshrined in ethical trade and antisweatshop auditing systems, raising questions about FLO's capacity to oversee these diverse standards and ensure that they are upheld by large commercial firms.

The growth of Fair Trade has formed an important part of a wider movement aimed at achieving greater social justice and equity in trade. Over the past decade in Europe there has been a rapid growth of ethical trade which focuses on employment conditions of workers within global value chains, as distinct from Fair Trade which focuses primarily on producer prices and trading relationships. Fair Trade provided the environment for the emergence of ethical trade. Indeed, many Fair Trade organizations were involved in the UK founding of the Ethical Trade Initiative. Ethical trade involves the application of codes of labor practice by brands and retailers to their international suppliers. European supermarkets and food retailers have played a key role in the growth of ethical trade, along with other companies, trade unions, and NGOs. Within ethical trade, like Fair Trade, tensions exist among civil society actors over how to address social justice and equity in a trading environment dominated by large corporations and commercial retailers. An interesting dialectical relationship is emerging between Fair Trade and ethical trade. Yet for the general consumer, the emergence of competing "ethical" labels makes the picture increasingly confusing (Barrientos and Dolan 2006; Jenkins et al. 2002; Redfern and Snedker 2002).

In North America, Fair Trade has also emerged within and formed part of a broader set of global social justice initiatives. Activist groups have pursued a range of efforts to bolster corporate accountability for their worldwide activities. In the US manufacturing sector these efforts have coalesced within the anti-sweatshop movement, which like ethical trade, focuses on brand and retail firm responsibility for monitoring the labor practice of their international suppliers. As suggested in Chapter 6, while most major US corporations have now established internal codes of conduct, many have gone on to seek either industry certifications or third-party certifications like Fair Trade. Though numerous groups have helped foster demands for corporate accountability there are significant differences of opinion among these groups regarding the depth of corporate commitment and the role of voluntary certifications. Rising interest in corporate accountability clearly bolsters the prospects of Fair Trade, yet the proliferation of competing social and environmental labels and certifications presents an often understated challenge to Fair Trade's future (Conroy 2006; Raynolds et al. forthcoming).

Conclusions

The subsequent chapters explore the key tensions elaborated above in the United States and the United Kingdom, the centers of current Fair Trade growth in the global North. Chapter 5 shows how Fair Trade certified bananas are greatly expanding the US Fair Trade market but simultaneously raising serious questions about the role of plantations and transnational corporations in Fair Trade. Chapter 6 explores why US companies are turning to Fair Trade and the potential for synergistic relations between Fair Trade certification and socially committed companies. Chapter 7 examines the growth and dynamics of UK supermarket "own-brand" Fair Trade retailing in chocolate and fresh fruit and considers whether the shift toward sourcing from larger commercial enterprises and application of minimum labor standards represents a watering down of key Fair Trade movement demands – a "Fair Trade revisionism." Together these chapters explore the current growth, corporate engagement, and mainstreaming in Fair Trade, analyzing whether these current trends are strengthening Fair Trade or weakening the prospects for achieving greater social justice and equity in trade.

This brings us back to the basic question of the book: Where is Fair Trade going in the future? One critical point is to ensure that the success of Fair Trade does not lead to the undermining of the core values which have underpinned the movement and which lend it its legitimacy. Yet it is also important to the continued rapid expansion of the movement, especially as measured by benefits to Fair Trade producers, that the model evolve in ways that make it consistent with continued expansion in mainstream markets. The Fair Trade movement was founded on diverse perspectives. Part of its strength, and ultimately its success, has been its ability to combine visionary social goals with practical commercial engagement. Tensions within Fair Trade as a social movement have often provided the energy to drive it forward, but they could also provide the seeds of its own demise. The key for the Fair Trade movement is to ensure that those in the driving seat remember to carry the road map to their final destination – and are not diverted by the same commercial actors they set out to combat.

Notes

1 Early social movements influenced the collective consciousness of modern-day consumerism and laid the foundations for concern with the social conditions under which products are grown and manufactured. In the 1780s John Ruskin and the Abolitionist Movement called on consumers to boycott sugar grown in slave plantations. During the same period, the Christian Social Union and the Trade Unions drew up a "white list" of products which were made under decent labor conditions in the United Kingdom – possibly the first ever "ethical" label. According to research coordinated by the Cooperative College, Manchester, Co-operation, Social Responsibility and Fair Trade, early cooperative movements in Europe and the Cooperative Movement founded by Robert Owen in the United Kingdom established some of the principles that were later to inspire the development of Fair Trade.
2 See www.twin.org.uk/about.html for further information.
3 Created by the evangelical Church of the Brethren in 1949, SERRV International continues to function as an independent nonprofit organization. By 2004, it was selling US$ 6 million per year of handicrafts from some 30 countries, mostly through Internet sales. See www.cob-net.org/serrv.htm
4 See www.tenthousandvillages.com/php/about.us/mission.principles.php (accessed May 27, 2006).
5 See www.tenthousandvillages.com/php/about.us/mission.principles.php (accessed February 15, 2006).
6 See www.fairtradefederation.org/index.html (accessed February 17, 2006).
7 The US-based Equal Exchange and the UK-based Equal Exchange mentioned earlier are not organizationally related though they share many of the same principles as well as the same name.
8 Theories of unequal exchange form part of political economy-based dependency and world systems theories' challenges to neoclassical economic theories of modernization.
9 See www.equalexchange.com (accessed May 27, 2006).
10 Personal communication, Sarah Ford, coordinator of the LWR Interfaith Fair Trade Coalition.
11 Catholic Relief Services has pursued a rather strange parallel policy of introducing its own line of Fair Trade coffees, using its own proprietary seal, presumably contributing

S. Barrientos, M.E. Conroy, and E. Jones is the header.

to the Fair Trade label confusion among consumers. See www.crsfairtrade.org/ coffee_project/index.htm (accessed February 15, 2006).

12 See www.crsfairtrade.org/coffee_project/index.htm (accessed February 15, 2006).

References

Barratt Brown, M. (1993) *Fair Trade, Reform and Realities in the International Trading System*, London: Zed Press.

Barrientos, S. and Dolan, C. (eds) (2006) *Ethical Sourcing in the Global Food System*, London: Earthscan.

Berman, V. and Rozyne, M. (circa 1992) "Never underestimate hope: the impact of fair trade on coffee farmers," Equal Exchange Research Report.

Conroy, M.E. (2006) "Transnational social movements linking North and South: the struggle for fair trade," paper presented at Alternative Visions of Development: Rural Social Movements in Latin America, Center for Latin American Studies, University of Florida, Gainsville, February 2006.

ICA (International Cooperative Alliance). (2006) *The International Cooperative Alliance*, Online. Available at: www.ica.coop (accessed July 24, 2006).

Jenkins, R., Pearson, R., and Seyfang, G. (2002) *Corporate Responsibility and Labour Rights: Codes of Conduct in the Global Economy*, London: Earthscan.

Krier, J.M. (2005) *Fair Trade in Europe 2005: Facts and Figures on Fair Trade in 25 European Countries*, Brussels: FINE.

Moore, G., Gibbon, J., and Slack, R. (2006) "The mainstreaming of Fair Trade: a macro-marketing perspective," *Journal of Strategic Marketing*, 14: 329–352.

Nicholls, A. and Opal, C. (2005) *Fair Trade: Market-Driven Ethical Consumption*, London: Sage.

Raynolds, L.T., Murray, D., and Heller, A. (forthcoming) "Regulating sustainability in the coffee sector: a comparative analysis of environmental and social certification and labeling initiatives," *Agriculture and Human Values*, 24.

Redfern, A. and Snedker, P. (2002) "Creating market opportunities for small enterprises: experiences of the fair trade movement," Seeds Working Paper No. 30, Geneva: ILO.

Tiffen, P., MacDonald, J., Maamah, H., and Osei-Opare, F. (eds) (2004) *From Tree-Minders to Global Players: Cocoa Farmers in Ghana*. London: Commonwealth Secretariat.

5 Fair Trade bananas

Broadening the movement and market in the United States

Laura T. Raynolds

Introduction

Fair Trade in the United States is booming. Though Fair Trade certification was initiated within the decade and there are still only a few labeled commodities, the United States is now the world's largest Fair Trade market. Sales are worth US$ 428 million and are growing at an astonishing 60 percent per year (FLO 2006a). The US Fair Trade market and movement were built around coffee, and to a lesser extent cocoa and tea. Yet it is bananas that are propelling the next wave of expansion. The recent launch of certification in the US banana sector holds the promise of significantly broadening Fair Trade, yet this expansion simultaneously heightens inherent tensions between market and movement forces.

Fair Trade certified bananas have huge potential and are at the forefront of the move of labeling into the US fresh produce sector. In market terms the opportunities are clear: bananas are Americans' favorite fruit with purchases totaling 3.9 million tons a year (FAO 2006). In movement terms bananas are also critical since they are the most salient symbol of US neocolonialism (Striffler and Moberg 2003). Yet, the introduction of Fair Trade certified bananas in the United States has been challenging. For the first time in the experience of the growing US Fair Trade market, after a prominent launch, imports of this commodity actually fell from 3,660 tons (8.2 million pounds) in 2004, their first year, to 3,210 tons (7.2 million pounds) in 2005. The tumultuous US introduction of labeled bananas highlights the contested nature of Fair Trade's current expansion. My analysis of the tensions surrounding this launch draws on the framework elaborated in Chapter 3 (see also Raynolds 2002, 2004). A global commodity chain/value chain perspective (e.g. Gereffi 1994; Gereffi et al. 2005) illuminates the new production, distribution, and consumption relations encountered in Fair Trade's move from coffee into the highly perishable and corporate-dominated banana sector. This case demonstrates the role of powerful buyers – including retailers, but more importantly transnational corporation (TNC) branders – and Fair Trade certifiers in regulating producer participation, product qualities and quantities, and market access (see also Raynolds 2004). Yet the conflicts over certified bananas also demonstrate the centrality of Non-Governmental Organizations (NGOs), Alternative Trade Organizations (ATOs), student groups, and consumers in shaping Fair Trade in the United States.

This chapter begins with a brief overview of the movement and market forces shaping Fair Trade in the United States. It outlines the conventional and Fair Trade banana commodity chains and explores the social, political, and economic dimensions of the US introduction of certified bananas. The chapter then identifies the problems which emerged in the networks connecting producers in Latin America with consumers in the United States. It analyzes TransFair USA's plan to revive the stalled market by certifying TNC plantation bananas and the social movement opposition to this strategy. The chapter goes on to show how movement groups have challenged TransFair's market-led approach and the increasing role of plantations and dominant corporations in Fair Trade. As I conclude, this case reveals the continued importance of market and movement forces in negotiating Fair Trade ideas, practices, and institutions.

The growth of the US Fair Trade movement and market

The recent growth of Fair Trade in the United States is linked to a broad rise in conscious consumption. Over recent decades concern among US consumers over the social and environmental implications of their purchases has grown, particularly in the food sector (Raynolds 2000). Mounting organic food sales reflect this trend, with purchases spreading from the counterculture minority to a much larger, more mainstream, population concerned about ecological, farmer, and health issues (Raynolds 2004). The US organic market was valued at US\$ 12 billion in 2002, with annual increases hitting 20 percent (Kortbech-Olesen 2003: 24). While organic shoppers may be at the forefront of the trend in US conscious consumption, they are part of a much larger pool of 68 million people – the lifestyles of health and sustainability (Lohas) shoppers who prefer to make purchases that reflect their values (Cortese 2003).

The US Fair Trade market and movement have been consolidated over the past decade in junction with this rising social and environmental consciousness (Raynolds 2002). Though US ATOs began selling handicrafts in the 1940s, the first ATO specializing in food items did not appear until the 1980s with the founding of the coffee company, Equal Exchange. American ATOs are strongly mission-driven and have focused as much on educating consumers, supporting producers, and lobbying for changes in US trade policies as on sales. To spur the Fair Trade market, TransFair USA (the national Fairtrade Labelling Organizations International (FLO) affiliate) was founded in 1998, initially certifying only coffee. Equal Exchange was the first to carry its logo, followed by other small progressive coffee roasters. A number of key allied groups helped insure the success of Fair Trade labeling in the United States. ATOs began stocking certified coffee and teaching customers about the labeling concept. Church and community groups began serving Fair Trade certified coffee at their meetings. Consumer, development, and solidarity NGOs began Fair Trade public awareness campaigns.

At the outset, allied groups and TransFair USA worked closely together to promote the Fair Trade concept and encourage coffee roasters to join the Fair Trade fold (Raynolds 2002). But a number of NGOs soon turned to stronger tactics.

Oxfam America began supporting student efforts, bolstering ultimately quite successful campaigns to demand that Fair Trade coffee be served on university campuses (Oxfam America 2006). Global Exchange, a solidarity NGO and ATO, launched an ultimately successful campaign to get Starbucks to carry Fair Trade certified coffee (Global Exchange 2006). Advocacy efforts by movement groups and dedicated consumers pressured a number of major companies to offer certified coffee. With this stimulus, US Fair Trade certified coffee imports have grown 75 percent annually; reaching almost 15,000 tons in 2004 (see Table 5.1).

TransFair USA began certifying tea in 2001 and cocoa in 2002 (items which, like coffee, had already been introduced by ATOs). Fair Trade tea has grown impressively, with average annual imports up 43 percent annually. The cocoa market has expanded even more dramatically, with annual certified imports increasing at over 1,000 percent. Fair Trade's success in tea and cocoa has been fueled by the same movement groups that fostered coffee in the United States. Religious and student groups have gotten their institutions to offer certified tea and cocoa; ATOs have stocked these items; and solidarity groups have educated consumers about the plight of tea and cocoa producers. Advocacy NGOs have focused particularly on cocoa given recent findings of widespread child labor abuse in conventional production. These groups have publicly shamed major chocolate companies for buying cocoa produced by child labor and demanded that they purchase Fair Trade cocoa. Since movement groups view Fair Trade as a mechanism for revealing existing trade inequalities and promoting global social justice, they have been willing to use strong pressure tactics, including demonstrations, negative campaigns, and boycotts, to engage these issues.

TransFair USA has developed a decidedly more business friendly approach. When Starbucks was threatened with nationwide demonstrations in 2000, TransFair promised to reverse the bad press in exchange for a certification agreement covering a small share of Starbucks' coffee. Based on that experience, TransFair started promoting Fair Trade to companies based on the capacity of certification to reduce activist pressure and enhance a corporation's image.

Table 5.1 US Fair Trade certified import volumes (metric tons)[a]

	1999	2000	2001	2002	2003	2004	Average annual increase (%)
Coffee	915	1,897	2,978	4,353	8,330	14,674	75
Tea			27	40	45	76	43
Cocoa				4	80	250	1,056
Bananas						3,661	
Total	915	1,897	3,005	4,397	8,455	18,661	85

Source: TransFair USA (2006a).

Note

a These figures refer to unprocessed (i.e. unripened, unroasted) imports certified by TransFair USA as upholding Fair Trade standards. They are substantially higher than FLO figures that refer to processed/packaged volumes sold with the Fair Trade label, but both reflect the same general trends.

Since TransFair USA sees the growth of Fair Trade certified commodity sales as an end in itself, it has worked hard to create business partnerships and carefully avoid alienating large market players.

The combination of the pressure from movement groups, the demand by concerned consumers, the enticement by TransFair USA, and the promise of lucrative market shares have significantly increased Fair Trade certification among mainstream corporations as well as small progressive enterprises. As *Time Magazine* reports, "Fair Trade is taking off in the US" (Roosevelt 2004). To take advantage of and build this market momentum, TransFair has begun to widen its commodity offer. Bananas are the most important of the newly launched commodities and are at the forefront of the move of Fair Trade labeling into the US fresh produce sector. TransFair USA introduced certification for bananas, mangos, pineapples, and grapes in 2004, though the latter items are only available seasonally and in small quantities. Newly certified Fair Trade commodities encounter a broad and receptive consumer base: 20 percent of Americans are aware of Fair Trade certified products and almost half of these people report purchasing them. Yet most consumers do not fully understand what Fair Trade means and 26 percent say that lack of availability limits their purchases (TransFair USA 2005a).

Conventional and Fair Trade banana commodity chains

Bananas, like other major Fair Trade commodities, are a colonial crop produced almost exclusively in impoverished regions of the Global South for consumption in the Global North. Bananas reveal the legacy of colonial and neocolonial ties perhaps more than any other commodity (Striffler and Moberg 2003). The world banana trade today most clearly reflects the legacy of US neocolonial relations in Latin America. In the mid-1900s, the United States and the US banana company, United Fruit, intervened so extensively in promoting banana exports from Latin America that some countries came to be referred to as "Banana Republics" (Raynolds 2003). The heir to United Fruit, Chiquita, and related US transnational corporations, Dole and Del Monte, dominate the banana trade to this day. These three companies control 60 percent of the global banana market and fully 79 percent of the US market (van de Kasteele and van der Stichele 2005: 15). Though bananas are one of the world's most valuable internationally traded commodities, prices are highly volatile and in the past 15 years the world banana price has fallen sharply due to overproduction and eroding international trade agreements (EUROBAN 2005).

Most of the world's bananas still come from Latin America and corporate dominance in the region remains strong. For example, 87 percent of Costa Rica's bananas are exported under the Chiquita, Dole, or Del Monte label (Banana Link 1999). Most Latin American bananas are grown on plantations which are either owned directly by the top three corporations or have contracts to supply these corporations (Raynolds 2003). These plantations are typically characterized by their low wages, required overtime, lack of freedom of association, and poor health and safety conditions (US Leap 2005). Banana plantations in Ecuador were cited in 2002 by international human rights groups for their abuse of child labor, dismal working conditions, and retaliations against workers seeking to unionize (Forero 2002). Banana plantations are also notorious for their destructive environmental impacts, including intensive pesticide and agrochemical contamination, soil erosion, deforestation, and water pollution (EUROBAN 2005).

European solidarity groups encouraged the extension of Fair Trade into the banana sector to support remaining small-scale production, particularly in the Caribbean, and to counter the negative impacts of large-scale banana production. The certification of bananas required the refinement of Fair Trade plantation standards. Building on standards already drafted for tea, FLO consolidated a set of generic standards for hired labor situations in 1997. FLO's (2005a) certification system for bananas encompasses small and large producers. Small-scale banana producers must be organized into politically independent democratic cooperatives. Large-scale enterprises must have both a democratic joint body which represents workers and a demonstrated adherence to high labor standards (including rights to association and collective bargaining, freedom from discrimination, equal pay, safe and healthy work conditions, and the absence of forced and child labor). FLO (2006b) banana standards itemize commodity-specific trade and production criteria. Banana trade standards require distributors to purchase as directly as possible from FLO registered producers using long-term agreements and guaranteed prices, including a minimum price of US$ 5.50 farm gate or US$ 6.75 FOB for a 40 lb box, an organic premium if applicable, and a social premium of US$ 1.00 per box to be used for collective social programs.[1] FLO certified banana producers must follow environmental development guidelines enhancing agricultural sustainability and restricting agrochemical use.

Fair Trade certified bananas are produced largely in Latin America and the Caribbean as outlined in Table 5.2. Like other Fair Trade commodities, a significant

Table 5.2 Major suppliers of Fair Trade certified bananas (2003)

	FLO certified producer groups	*FLO certified sales (metric tons)*	*Share of FLO organic sales (%)*	*Share of FLO nonorganic sales (%)*	*Share of total FLO certified market (%)*
Ecuador	4	20,020	46	37	42
Dominican Republic	5	17,197	27	5	16
Windward Islands	1	5,134	—	29	14
Colombia	1	4,620	—	16	8
Costa Rica	2	2,310	—	12	6
Peru	3	1,540	27	—	14
Total[a]	18	51,336	100	100	100

Sources: FLO (2005b,c).

Note
a Total includes nonlisted countries.

portion of Fair Trade bananas are also certified organic. Ecuador is the world's leading banana exporter and is the major supplier of Fair Trade bananas, producing 42 percent of total volume. Colombia and Costa Rica are also major world market suppliers which have become important producers of Fair Trade bananas. Despite their modest roles in global banana markets, the Dominican Republic, the Windward Islands, and Peru are also major Fair Trade producers. The Dominican Republic and Peru are particularly important in supplying Fair Trade organic bananas. The Windward Islands have historically been a key supplier of UK bananas, supplies which are now largely Fair Trade certified (Reefer Trends 2005).

Max Havelaar, the Fair Trade labeling coffee pioneer, launched certified bananas in the Netherlands in 1996. Certified bananas sales increased over 100 percent a year between 1998 and 2005, outpacing growth in more well-established coffee, cocoa, and tea. Sales of Fair Trade labeled bananas neared 104,000 metric tons in 2005, representing 62 percent of FLO's total certified volume (FLO 2006a). Bananas are now the second most valuable Fair Trade commodity. As outlined in Table 5.3 Fair Trade certified banana sales remain concentrated in Europe. Switzerland leads the world with 37 percent of all certified banana sales, and Fair Trade bananas now hold an astonishing 47 percent of the Swiss market. Though Fair Trade bananas were only introduced in 2000, the United Kingdom now has the second largest market. Fair Trade sales are projected to grow to encompass about 10 percent of the European banana market (TransFair USA 2006b).

The United States offers a potentially huge new market for Fair Trade certified bananas. The country imports 3.9 million tons of bananas a year (26 percent of the world's total) valued at US$ 1.2 billion (FAO 2006). Bananas are Americans' favorite fruit: the average consumer eats over 26 pounds of bananas a year, nearly twice that of any other fruit. Ninety-six percent of Americans buy bananas on a weekly basis (TransFair USA 2006a). The potential for Fair Trade certification is often measured in reference to the certified organic market since the two markets are tightly linked. Currently about 4.5 percent of US produce sales are certified organic with this share projected to reach 10 percent over the

Table 5.3 Top markets for Fair Trade bananas (2003)

	Fair Trade banana sales (metric tons)	Share of total Fair Trade banana market (%)	Fair Trade bananas' share of national market (%)
Switzerland	19,002	37.0	47
United Kingdom	18,177	35.4	6
Netherlands	2,610	5.1	4
Finland	2,514	4.9	5
Italy	2,038	4.0	—
Total	51,336	100.0	

Sources: FLO (2005d); Krier (2005).

next decade (Ohlemeier 2005). Bananas hold a dominant position in the organic fresh produce sector. In 2002, North American certified organic banana imports totaled 48,000 tons and were rising at 23 percent per year (Dankers and Liu 2003: 33). The size of the US banana market and the success of organic labels in this market suggest that there is indeed substantial potential for Fair Trade bananas.

The Fair Trade certified banana launch[2]

While coffee defined Fair Trade certification in its first five years, bananas are defining the nature and prospects of Fair Trade for the next five years. At the time of the launch, a TransFair USA staff member observed, "Bananas are without a doubt the next big thing for Fair Trade in North America." A *New York Times* article reported that "Bananas with 'Fair Trade Certified' stickers . . . represent the new front of an international effort to help first-world consumers improve the living standards of the third-world farmers who grow much of their food" (Moskin 2004).

TransFair USA (2006a,b) documents make a strong case for certifying bananas, drawing on arguments regarding both the US market potential and the negative social and ecological attributes of conventional trade. Activists tend to emphasize the consumer education value of Fair Trade bananas. As one activist explains, "bananas can provide a useful entrée to the Fair Trade concept since they are often associated with horrible work conditions, environmental degradation, and political repression in Banana Republics." Another concurs, "bananas are key to the Fair Trade movement because they are symbols of real abuse . . . they draw attention to critical problems in the world and to the need for positive change in global power relations and social and environmental conditions."

While the potential of Fair Trade bananas is often compared to that of coffee, these commodities vary tremendously in their product characteristics and markets. The key distinguishing feature of bananas is their perishability, which necessitates their careful and timely movement from the fields to the port, across the ocean, through the port of entry, through the ripening process, onto store shelves, and into customer shopping bags. The perishability of bananas bolsters the position of large corporate distributors able to bring the fruit quickly to market and of large supermarkets able to move the fruit quickly out the door (Raynolds 2003). The introduction of Fair Trade certified bananas has thus not been able to easily avoid mainstream distribution and retail channels. A long-time ATO activist contrasts the decentralized system propelling the growth of Fair Trade coffee with the rigidities of banana distribution.

> We were able to bring in a shipment of Fair Trade coffee, store it, and roast it as needed . . . then send it out in small quantities anywhere in the United States, to coops, stores, community groups, and churches. Bananas are a different story. You have to deal in substantial quantities and it's a complicated business. You can't just ship off a box of Fair Trade bananas by UPS and have the fruit distributed on Sundays in the church basement.

Bananas also contrast sharply with coffee in that they are much less differentiated in the market. Fair Trade's major inroads in the US coffee market have been in the specialty market which is able to sustain price premiums and incorporate new quality attributes. But there is no premium banana category. US retailers typically carry only one or perhaps two (conventional and organic) types of bananas sold loose in large bins. Banana quality is assessed largely on cosmetic appearance. Price competition in bananas is fierce: while they can be one of the most profitable items in a US supermarket, they are often advertised at prices below cost to attract customers. TransFair's New Products Manager summarizes the challenges of launching bananas.

> Bananas are not something you ease into. You need to enter the market with solid volumes. You need ships arriving in the US twice a week to guarantee constant supplies of ripe bananas. Then, as they say in the produce industry "you have to sell it, or smell it." Since supermarkets do not carry multiple banana brands and varieties like in coffee, they can't market test Fair Trade fruit to see if it sells. This means you need to get commitment from the outset from retailers willing to replace their existing bananas with a Fair Trade offering.

TransFair USA got the commitment they sought from Wild Oats Markets, a natural foods supermarket chain with 108 stores across North America. In January 2004, Wild Oats became the first US retailer to offer Fair Trade certified bananas, a milestone reported in a joint press release with TransFair USA. Wild Oats replaced its entire organic banana line with dual certified organic Fair Trade bananas (though it continued to sell some nonorganic non-Fair Trade fruit). The banana launch built on Wild Oats' earlier successful conversion to organic Fair Trade certified coffee.[3] Describing the introduction of certified bananas, Wild Oats' CEO states: "Through our partnership with TransFair USA, we have extended our commitment to providing customers with Fair Trade certified product and expect to continue to grow this commitment as more products that meet our demanding standards become available" (Wild Oats and TransFair USA 2004: 2).[4]

Wild Oats' Fair Trade bananas were introduced at the same price as the fruit they replaced (US$ 0.99 per pound), because, as the Director of Corporate Communication explains, "we do not want to build profits on the backs of Fair Trade producers." According to company figures, in the first two months after the launch of Fair Trade bananas, sales grew 20 percent over their levels the prior year. Labeled banana sales were still growing at 5 percent annually a year and a half after their launch. Fair Trade bananas were Wild Oats' most popular produce item in 2004, with sales of almost 2,000 tons (4 million pounds).

Wild Oats has incorporated Fair Trade as part of its commitment to corporate responsibility. As the CEO explains, "we believe it is our responsibility to ensure the people who grow and manufacture our products are treated fairly and equitably" (Wild Oats and TransFair USA 2004). A recent Annual Report promotes this responsible image, featuring Fair Trade headlines on the front cover and text on "cultivating trust." The message, stated succinctly is: "At Wild Oats, we sell food that remembers its roots" (Wild Oats 2004).[5] Given its Fair Trade commitment, Wild Oats has been identified as "a model Fair Trade supermarket" by Oxfam America. The company has gotten positive media attention, including being compared favorably to UK supermarkets accused of price gauging in their Fair Trade banana sales (Horovitz 2004; Stecklow and White 2004).

There are two facets of the US Fair Trade certified banana launch which are likely to be remembered. One involves the commitment of a major retailer to incorporate Fair Trade into its business model and embrace this new product. The other involves the almost complete absence of the movement groups which had earlier fostered Fair Trade's launch of coffee, cocoa, and tea. The introduction of bananas was essentially configured by an informal agreement between TransFair USA and Wild Oats which granted the retailer exclusive rights to carry the first labeled fruit in exchange for a major purchasing commitment. Key allies were informed about TransFair's planned introduction of labeled bananas, but none were involved in organizing the launch. Perhaps not surprisingly, no major movement groups stepped forward to champion Fair Trade certified bananas upon their arrival. Many Fair Trade movement groups – including ATOs, religious and student groups, and development, solidarity, and consumer NGOs – were unsure about the ramifications of this launch.[6] But most sensed that it signaled a transition in Fair Trade from a movement defined by concerned consumers and groups, to a market dominated by TransFair USA's corporate collaborations.

Challenges in the Fair Trade banana chain

TransFair's introduction of Fair Trade bananas represents the move of certification into the US fresh produce sector, as it did in Europe five years earlier. TransFair has begun certifying mangos, pineapples, and grapes and has plans to launch other fresh fruits. The challenge as a natural foods grocer notes: "is to take Fair Trade out of the coffee pot and into the fruit bowl." This has not been easy: just two years after their introduction, key weaknesses have emerged in the certified banana commodity chain. While the promise of Fair Trade certification in bananas is reflected in other fresh produce areas, so too are the pitfalls.

Fair Trade bananas for the US market come from producer cooperatives and plantations, all of which are substantially smaller than the TNC plantations that supply most of the United States. Bananas were initially sourced from FLO certified producers in Ecuador who had exported to Europe for a number of years. These producers included two cooperatives (one with 160 members and 399 acres of organic bananas and the other with 350 members and 4,000 acres of conventional bananas), and one plantation (with 240 employees and 840 acres of organic bananas). The opening of the US Fair Trade market fueled the growth of these enterprises and the FLO certification of a cooperative in Peru producing organic bananas. Due to their Pacific location these enterprises are particularly well suited to supplying the US West Coast, though Ecuadorian bananas are commonly shipped around the country. Taking advantage of the growing market, five new enterprises in Colombia sought and acquired FLO certification, four of them large estates (averaging 430 acres each). These enterprises are important suppliers for the US East Coast.

The growth of the US market has stimulated a shift in the profile of FLO registered banana producer groups. Though producer cooperatives continue to outnumber plantations on the FLO banana register, an increasing share of certified bananas are coming from large-scale enterprises (FLO 2005c). The rising importance of large enterprises in bananas, and other fresh produce areas, has eroded Fair Trade's historic small farmer base and caused a reevaluation of FLO standards. In 2005 FLO (2006a: 1) did a "complete overhaul of (its) hired labor standards" focusing "much more on workers' training, management commitment, and better cooperation with local labor unions." This overhaul was motivated in part by complaints over the questionable standards of Latin American banana plantations seeking (and sometimes acquiring) certification. Most significant in this context are FLO's new standards (1) reinforcing the democratic election of a workers' committee to uphold labor rights and negotiate with management and (2) making the allocation of the Fair Trade social premium transparent.[7] FLO's changes address fears of management manipulation of worker organizations and financial misappropriations which are well-founded across Latin America.[8] They also help reinforce collaboration between Fair Trade and union movements.

Though Fair Trade is based on the idea of trading as directly as possible, in bananas there are often distinct enterprises handling exporting and importing. FLO (2006a: 9) has recently acknowledged this and has introduced direct inspections for exporters and importers to ensure that intermediaries uphold Fair Trade standards. Managing the export of bananas from Latin America, their ocean transport, and their import into the United States is complicated due to the bananas' fragility and perishability and thus the need for tight coordination and rapid movement. Given relatively small Fair Trade banana volumes, consolidating supplies so as to fill an entire refrigerated container is a challenge. Negotiating shipping space and schedules is a challenge. Even just handling the export and import fees and paperwork is a challenge. Some Latin American Fair Trade banana producer groups work with exporters who orchestrate shipping, some work with US importers who take on this task.

The US importers handling newly introduced Fair Trade certified bananas included both small progressive companies and more mainstream produce companies. TransFair USA licensed seven fresh fruit importers in 2004: four relatively small-scale importers serving regional markets specialize in organic and other socially and environmentally sensitive produce and three conventional produce importers serving national markets, including Turbana (the fifth largest US banana importer).[9] Some importers are clearly focused on the market opportunities of Fair Trade bananas, referring to them as the "new organics," produce with the growth outlook of organics in the 1990s (Kroger 2004). Yet others are motivated by broader concerns. As one importer notes: "In my job you learn ugly things about bananas... about what they do to people and the environment... that is why

I prefer to sell organic and Fair Trade fruit." Progressive companies, like Jonathan's Organics, were amongst the first TransFair licensed importers (Moskin 2004).

While large US produce importers typically ripen bananas and deliver them to retailers, many of the small Fair Trade importers ship their bananas to ripeners or wholesalers. Fair Trade bananas thus may be handled by one more entity prior to their arrival on grocery shelves. The ripeners and distributors handling Fair Trade certified bananas include businesses catering to the organic and coopera-tive sector as well as mainstream wholesalers (TransFair USA 2005b). Some of these distributors, like Co-op Partners Warehouse, pushed hard to get certified bananas as soon as they entered the United States, making them available to food cooperatives and progressive shops in their region (Anderson 2004).

A variety of smaller retailers began stocking Fair Trade certified bananas soon after they became available. In addition to being carried in Wild Oats stores, by the end of 2005, Fair Trade bananas were being sold in another 600 stores, including small natural food shops, food cooperatives, specialty grocers, and upscale regional supermarkets (TransFair USA 2005b). Since they lack the turnover to sell perishable fruits, US ATOs have not stocked bananas. According to TransFair USA staff, the early Fair Trade banana market included both highly committed progressive retailers and others looking for a profitable market niche. TransFair tried to stimulate the mainstream uptake of certified bananas by introducing this fruit to supermarket buyers and sponsoring a Fair Trade banana grower's attendance at the Produce Marketing Association 2004 trade show (Arnett 2004).

While the newly developed commodity circuits linking Latin American Fair Trade banana producers with emerging US markets appeared to work for the first year and a half, they began to unravel in the second half of 2005. Supply, ship-ping, ripening, and distribution problems together undermined the quality and quantity of Fair Trade bananas available in the United States. As the TransFair USA Produce Manager recounts,

> Getting the bananas to market has been difficult. Frankly, the logistics for West Coast bananas just fell apart. There were tremendous delays. Typically TNCs get bananas from point of export to point of entry in seven to 10 days, at most 14. But the Fair Trade bananas were taking close to 30 days. While our bananas were in transit, the corporate bananas had already hit the super-market shelf, headed out the door, and been digested.

Small suppliers and distributors could not maintain the volume of high quality Fair Trade bananas demanded by large retailers. Without steady and guaranteed fruit supplies that met their exacting standards, some retailers stopped selling certified bananas.[10] Even Wild Oats, which has made a public commitment to stocking the bananas, can not promise that they will be available in all stores all the time (or even most stores most of the time).[11] Many enterprises lost money. And for the first time, a strand of the Fair Trade market in the United States shrank. Fair Trade certified banana imports fell from 3,660 tons (8.2 million pounds) in 2004, their first year, to 3,210 tons (7.2 million pounds) in 2005.

Dedicated US retailers continue to sell Fair Trade certified bananas when they can get them, but with limited imports and limited participation by major vendors the market has stagnated.

Fair Trade/TNC bananas: symbol of success or oxymoron?

By midway through 2006 the Fair Trade certified banana market had still not revived. TransFair USA is committed to reigniting and "bringing to scale" the certified banana market. To resolve the sourcing and distribution problems and grow the market, TransFair argues, requires negotiating the Fair Trade labeling of bananas produced by one of the top three banana transnational corporations: Dole, Chiquita, or Del Monte. Fair Trade movement groups, already alienated by their exclusion from the banana launch, are upset by this corporate main-streaming strategy. While TransFair's strategy would in all likelihood propel sales, movement groups are concerned that it would also undermine Fair Trade principles. Would a Fair Trade/TNC label be a symbol of success or an oxymoron?

TransFair USA has never before had to deal with market stagnation. Two and a half years after their launch, Fair Trade banana sales are flat and the fruit is unavailable in large regions of the United States. TransFair argues that demand for these bananas has not diminished and that if consistent supplies of high quality fruit were made available, retailers that have stopped stocking the fruit (like many Wild Oats Stores[12]) would renew their purchases, and other retailers, particularly mainstream supermarkets, would commence sales. Outlining the recent problems and their strategy for reviving the banana sector, TransFair USA argues: (1) the "stalled market" is due to "logistic and quality challenges," (2) "smaller importers...do not have the transportation logistics or volumes necessary to deliver quality fruit on a consistent basis" to large retailers, (3) "most supermarkets have exclusive contracts with the Big Three banana brands (Chiquita, Dole, and Del Monte)," and (4) "it will be extremely difficult for FTC (Fair Trade Certified) bananas to break into mainstream supermarkets without the participation of one of the Big Three banana companies" (TransFair USA 2006d).

TransFair is pursuing a corporate mainstreaming strategy to maximize US banana sales based on the belief "that more volume means more farmers served" (TransFair USA 2006d). The Chief Operating Officer explains how achieving this volume requires working with large producers and being pragmatic about the market.

> The US banana market is huge. They are the top selling item in supermarkets. From a market point of view bananas offer very significant opportunities. And bananas are produced by large numbers of disadvantaged small-scale growers and plantations employing large numbers of disadvantaged workers. Bananas are a great commodity to...extend Fair Trade benefits widely. But bananas have a specific history and global sourcing pattern...three to four large banana companies dominate shipping, distribution, and supermarket

shelf space in the US. We think we have to talk to these companies if we want to bring Fair Trade certified bananas to the mainstream. TransFair must deal with this market reality; we don't think it is necessary to take on the issue of channel power.

Sidestepping issues of market concentration, TransFair USA treats all retailers and distributors as potential Fair Trade partners. As the Chief Operating Officer explains, "we believe that no company should be excluded a priori from engaging in Fair Trade, if a company fulfills the criteria and makes a commitment to expanding Fair Trade, then we want them on board." TransFair has not in the past flinched from working with large coffee companies, justifying their collaboration by asserting repeatedly that they are "certifying products not companies" (TransFair USA 2006e). A recent TransFair (2006e) document sums up their position: "We celebrate the engagement of large, mainstream businesses in Fair Trade as a sign that we are accomplishing our mission." A long-time Fair Trade activist concludes: "TransFair USA's model is to promote Fair Trade by growing the market. It is a process of reform not revolution."

Since TransFair's primary goal is to maximize certified banana sales and market shares, it should not be surprising that they are discussing labeling bananas from the corporations that dominate the US market. Nor perhaps should it be surprising that these corporations would entertain such discussions, given the potential market returns to this type of differentiated product and the public relations benefits of being associated with Fair Trade. TransFair's discussions with Chiquita initially moved quite rapidly, provoking an ATO representative to comment, "From TransFair USA's model of scaling up Fair Trade, Why not work with Chiquita?" In fact working with Chiquita makes good market sense since the company controls 25 percent of US banana sales. In addition, Chiquita argues that its corporate responsibility measures put it on a par with Fair Trade: Chiquita plantations are already certified as meeting RainForest Alliance ecological standards, many are unionized, and Chiquita has signed a labor accord with the Coordination of Latin American Banana Workers Unions (COLSIBA) and the European-based international union, IUF (Chiquita 2005). To advance discussions, TransFair signed a memo of understanding with COLSIBA in 2005 (US LEAP 2006). TransFair's negotiations with Chiquita have since slowed, but talks with Dole are now gaining momentum. Though Dole's plantations are generally not unionized this company has the advantage that it already sources organic bananas from small producers that might be able to quickly qualify for Fair Trade certification.

Fair Trade movement activists are dismayed (some outraged) by TransFair USA's corporate market strategy, arguing that it is selling out the movement and undermining decades of work in building the integrity of the Fair Trade system. The foremost concern is that Fair Trade labeling will be used as a corporate public relations tactic and that Fair Trade standards will not in fact be upheld. One activist asks bluntly: "Given their terrible history, could anyone really believe there could be a Chiquita/Fair Trade banana? Isn't this an oxymoron?" For many movement participants linking Fair Trade to Chiquita – the heir of United Fruit and a key symbol of US neocolonialism – is highly problematic. Beyond the historical distrust of this particular company is a concern that any large corporation may be able to use their power and influence to avoid meeting certification criteria. As a key Oxfam America representative argues, "the primary movement concern with TNC involvement in bananas is a concern with regulation on the ground."

Even if large corporations uphold Fair Trade standards there is a concern (expressed with varied degrees of intensity across the movement) that different levels of Fair Trade commitment should be acknowledged. For example, "Oxfam's position is that if it is clear that they are upholding the standards, then we are comfortable with any company using the Fair Trade label. That said, how can we recognize different levels of contribution?" An ATO representative extends this argument, "Our position is that all Fair Trade is good if it raises the bar on social and environmental standards, but not all Fair Trade players are equivalent and some may be more worthy of support." Those groups that are more closely aligned with the anticorporate globalization movement or the small-farmer movement express this position even more strongly. Though TransFair has a small discount for 100 percent Fair Trade firms, their volume based fees represent a significant cost and symbolic insult to small mission-based ATOs, some of whom founded the US Fair Trade movement only to now have to compete against new corporate entrants with minimal Fair Trade commitment.[13]

In the case of bananas, the concern is not just about aligning TransFair fees and other costs more closely with commitment levels. The concern is about the very survival of small mission-driven entities forced to compete with dominant corporations which benefit from substantial economies of scale in production, distribution, and sales and commonly use their market power to drive out competition. As an ATO pioneer notes, "A banana TNC could wipe out all other Fair Trade players. They could underprice their Fair Trade bananas, offsetting these losses through sales of their slave bananas. And remember they would pay licensing fees only on the Fair Trade portion."

Under-girding these particular concerns, is a more general fear among many Fair Trade activists that in striving to maximize the market TransFair USA is leaving movement groups and concerns behind. TransFair has forged ahead in launching bananas and engaging discussions with large corporate distributors with little consultation with movement groups. A long time ATO activist concludes: "The situation in Fair Trade bananas is a clear example of the market propelling the movement." In addition to concerns that movement players are being sidelined in key decisions regarding the future of Fair Trade, is the bigger concern that in the rush to capture market shares, Fair Trade will come to accept conventional market rules and thereby lose its transformative potential.

From crisis to constructive engagement

Debates over corporate mainstreaming in bananas have fomented a crisis in the US Fair Trade movement. While a commonality of interests was once assumed to exist between TransFair USA and other Fair Trade groups and allies, the banana issue reveals a strategic divide between those interested primarily in increasing certified sales and producer benefits as an end in itself, and those interested in certification as a vehicle for empowering producers, educating consumers, and fundamentally altering unequal trade relations. As an Oxfam America representative notes, "the issue of TNC certification in bananas has forced a rethinking across the movement about our key priorities, our vision of Fair Trade, and our alliances." This process has been painful, but it has also been productive in forcing a constructive engagement between Fair Trade market and movement ideas, practices, and institutions.

Over the past two years, church groups, ATOs, consumer and development NGOs, students, and others have been drawn into heated debates over the possible Fair Trade labeling of TNC bananas. Initially uncertain about the implications of Fair Trade certification in bananas, TransFair's efforts to certify Chiquita bananas galvanized significant opposition. Concerns emerged from across the US movement and were consolidated into a set of key questions and issues. To slow what appeared to be the fastlane certification of Chiquita plantations, movement concerns were presented to FLO. These concerns countered TransFair USA's presentation of corporate certification as unproblematic and reinforced FLO's review of its hired labor standards. FLO's revised criteria address movement concerns that plantation standards be strengthened and oversight improved.

Student groups have emerged as an important force in the Fair Trade banana sector as they did in earlier Fair Trade certified arenas. These groups are moving beyond campaigns to bring Fair Trade coffee to campus to campaigns to broaden the range of certified coffees as well as tea, cocoa, sugar, and bananas served regularly on campus. This effort is intended to promote an understanding that "Fair Trade isn't just a flavor it's a business model" (USFT 2005). Most university students believe that it is important for their institutional food service companies to provide Fair Trade items (Suchomel 2005). Students at Harvard have gotten their campus dining service to serve Fair Trade bananas every Friday since 2004 (Mayer 2004). Student groups at a number of other US universities are gearing up for Fair Trade banana campaigns. To enhance the understanding of banana issues, the national student association, United Students for Fair Trade (USFT), held a session on "Unions and Worker Empowerment in the Banana Industry" at their 2005 conference. USFT surveyed its affiliates to gauge reactions to TransFair's strategy of TNC certification. They found that while 63 percent of student leaders felt that "associating the Fair Trade certification label with the labels of multinational corporations (Chiquita, Nestlé, Procter & Gamble, etc.)" would improve their views of the corporation, 37 percent said this association would worsen their views of Fair Trade (USFT 2006).

The combined weight of concerns voiced by students, NGOs, and others that its strategy of corporate mainstreaming would undermine Fair Trade support and sales among the movement base has caused TransFair USA to shore up its demands in negotiating the certification of TNC bananas. TransFair's initial expectations were only that corporations meet FLO standards. Now TransFair (2006d) says that it would only reach an agreement with a major banana company if it: (1) "has a concrete plan to buy from small banana producer cooperatives," (2) "respects the right of workers to organize on its plantations and is engaging with local and/or international banana workers unions," (3) "demonstrates significant initial demand in the U.S.," and (4) "agrees to invest in marketing and promoting its Fair Trade products." Though these expectations do not address all movement issues, their specification suggests that TransFair has begun to engage movement concerns even when they counter corporate interests.

TransFair (2006f) has sought to repair the damage done to its relations with Fair Trade movement groups, publicly stating:

> TransFair USA acknowledges and values the vital role of NGOs, advocacy groups and producers in growing the FT market and movement... At times, in our efforts to extend the benefits of Fair Trade to farmers and farm workers rapidly, we have failed to adequately engage the broader Fair Trade community effectively.

This statement goes on to enumerate ways in which TransFair seeks to increase communication and collaboration with movement groups "in forming our future direction." TransFair (2006e,f) has already taken steps to address movement complaints about its lack of transparency and failure to take criticism seriously by publishing a set of responses to more than 15 "frequently asked questions" addressing thorny issues like: How TransFair protects against "greenwashing" and How TransFair feels about large-volume retailers like Wal-Mart and McDonald's carrying Fair Trade certified products. While these efforts suggest that TransFair is interested in a rapprochement with movement forces, skeptics await concrete evidence that TransFair is not simply going to "keep going it alone."

A major constructive outcome of the turmoil over bananas is the launch of an ATO Fair Trade certified alternative. Oké USA[14] bananas are being rolled out in 2006 through a joint venture between the US East Coast fresh produce ATO, Red Tomato, which is linked historically to the coffee ATO Equal Exchange, and AgroFair, a Fair Trade fruit company which is co-owned by European NGOs and ATOs and Latin American and African producers.[15] This venture builds on Red Tomato's success as a distributor of US fresh fruits and vegetables produced according to Fair Trade principles and AgroFair's success as the first and still major supplier of Fair Trade certified bananas in Europe. Starting with a regional focus in the Northeast, this ATO banana initiative seeks to supply committed Fair Trade consumers by selling to food cooperatives and university food service companies and more general consumers by selling to regional supermarkets and natural food supermarkets. Given the unease about TNC banana certification, this venture is likely to find a solid market among Fair Trade movement allies, particularly among university students and other highly committed consumers. Whether this ATO initiative can break into broader markets will depend on its ability to deliver consistent supplies of high quality bananas. While AgroFair is responsible for supply management and has a proven track record of success in this area, negotiating the US market will be a new challenge.

Conclusions

Fair Trade in the United States is without a doubt at a critical threshold. Fundamental disagreements between Fair Trade movement and market priorities, practices, and groups are emerging in the context of current debates over the future of US Fair Trade bananas. These tensions are heightened by the complexities of extending Fair Trade into the US fresh produce sector, where large-scale production dominates, perishability reinforces vertical integration, and a few corporations control supply chains and supermarket shelf space. Yet these tensions are in truth inherent to Fair Trade. These are the tensions which defined the historical split of ATOs and labeling organizations in Europe and North America, which have fueled the rift between mainstream coffee corporations and mission-based "100-percenters" in the United States, and which are now being played out in the support or rejection of a possible Fair Trade/TNC banana label. In different guises, the reoccurring divide is between (1) those that see Fair Trade as an avenue of corporate reform but basically uphold the values and institutions of the market and (2) those that see Fair Trade as an avenue for transforming these market values and institutions by promoting social justice concerns. While not discounting the challenges ahead, this chapter suggests that we may be seeing a constructive engagement between these divergent interests. How these inherent tensions are negotiated will shape the Fair Trade market and movement in the United States and beyond.

Notes

1 FLO minimum banana prices vary by country of origin and reflect local production costs. If producer enterprises export themselves, what is guaranteed is the FOB price; if they rely on FLO registered exporters, what is guaranteed is the farm-gate price. As of 2005, the guaranteed price for Colombia, Ecuador, and Costa Rica is US$ 5.50 farm-gate or 6.75 FOB for conventional bananas and US$ 7.25 farm-gate or 8.50 FOB for organic bananas. FLO price floors for other regions are higher: for example Dominican Republic prices are US$ 7.00 farm-gate or 8.50 FOB for conventional and US$ 8.50 farm-gate or 10.00 FOB for organic bananas (FLO 2006b).

2 Where not otherwise cited, information presented here was derived from a series of interviews conducted by the author between February 2005 and July 2006 with representatives of Fair Trade organizations and allied groups, supermarket and produce importer representatives, and banana union and producer group officials.

3 Wild Oats coffee is co-branded with Green Mountain Coffee Roasters (see Chapter 6).

4 This commitment is echoed in Wild Oats' 2003 Annual Report which concludes a discussion of the successful Fair Trade coffee and banana launch stating: "With more products on the horizon, expect to see an even greater commitment to Fair Trade from Wild Oats" (2004: 2).

5 For further evidence of its Fair Trade commitment, see Wild Oats' website www.wildoats.com which includes a page on Fair Trade issues, products, projects.

6 Revealing the initial sense of uncertainty about Fair Trade certified bananas, some of the movement representatives contacted in 2005 could not easily state their individual or organizational response to the banana launch.

7 Previously FLO (1) required only that management respect the right of freedom of association and collective bargaining and (2) did not require a public accounting of the allocation of the US$ 1.00 per 40 pound box social premium (FLO 2006a: 8).

8 Questions of worker organization cooptation and financial misappropriation have been raised regarding particular FLO affiliated plantations. But the President of the Latin American banana union COLSIBA argues that these problems are so widespread across the region that they must be addressed in the rules applying to all plantations.

9 Chiquita, Dole, and Del Monte control 80 percent of the US market, Noboa and Turbana control another 15 percent, with the remainder shared by small importers like those specializing in organics and regional markets (Van de Kasteele and Stichele 2005).

10 US retailers do not generally have formal contracts with small produce suppliers like they do with brand name corporate distributors. Since TransFair USA does not require that retailers establish long-term purchasing arrangements with distributors, retailers were able to simply refuse to buy the Fair Trade bananas.

11 According to the Corporate Communication Director, Wild Oats does not "have a constant, reliable supply of Fair Trade certified fruit. In the regions where we can get a high quality supply, we will always choose it for our stores… it really varies by season and by availability of the product."

12 A Wild Oats produce manager concurs, saying, "We are working with TransFair to identify a vendor who can supply us with quality Fair Trade bananas for the west coast. The problem was that the growers were too small to get to the port and through the USDA inspectors in a reasonable amount of time. The bananas took over three weeks to get from packer to ripener and the bananas ended up dehydrated… If we can work through TransFair to get one of the larger banana importers to bring them in, Fair Trade bananas would get received with other bananas we sell (nonorganic or FT) and get through the system much faster."

13 In the US coffee sector, some 100 percent, mission-based, Fair Trade firms have abandoned their TransFair USA labels over this issue.

14 This name is still being finalized.

15 For information on these groups, see Red Tomato (2006) and AgroFair (2006).

References

AgroFair. (2006) *AgroFair*, Online. Available at: www.agrofair.com (accessed July 15, 2006).

Anderson, B. (2004) "Dance that fair trade dance," *Wedge Co-op Newsletter*, February/March, Online. Available at: www.wedge.coop (accessed July 10, 2006).

Arnett, A. (2004) "Fair trade is good for farmers and products," *The Boston Globe*, Boston, MA: F1.

Banana Link. (1999) "1998 export boom in Costa Rica," *Banana Trade News Bulletin*, February: 12.

Chiquita. (2005) "Transnational banana company perspectives: Chiquita's labor and environmental programs," paper presented at the International Banana Conference, North American Preparatory Meeting, Washington, DC, February.

Cortese, A. (2003) "They care about the world (and they shop, too)," *New York Times*, July 20, Online. Available at: www.nytimes.com (accessed July 15, 2006).

Dankers, C. and Liu, P. (2003) *Environmental and Social Standards, Certification and Labelling for Cash Crops*, Rome: FAO.

EUROBAN (European Banana Action Network). (2005) "World Banana Production and Exports," paper presented at the International Banana Conference, North American Preparatory Meeting, Washington, DC, February.

FAO (Food and Agriculture Organization). (2006) "FAO statistical databases," Online. Available at: www.faostat.fao.org (accessed July 10, 2006).

FLO (Fairtrade Labelling Organizations International). (2005a) *2004/2005 FLO Annual Report*, Online. Available at: www.fairtrade.net (accessed May 17, 2006).

—— (2005b) *FLO Fresh Fruit Partners*, Online. Available at: www.fairtrade.net/ sites/products/freshfruit/partners.html (accessed October 10, 2005).

—— (2005c) *Why and How does FLO Work with Fresh Fruit Producers?*, www.fairtrade. net/sites/products/freshfruit/why.html (accessed July 27, 2005).

—— (2005d) Internal Documents.

—— (2006a) *Annual Report 2005/6 Building Trust*, FLO.

—— (2006b) *Fairtrade Standards for Bananas*, Online. Available at: www.fairtrade.net/ pdf/hl/english/Banana%20HL%20Dec%2005%2005%20EN.pdf (accessed July 27, 2006).

Forero, J. (2002) "In Ecuador's banana fields, child labor is key to profits," *The New York Times*, July 13, Online. Avaliable at: www.nytimes.com (accessed July 15, 2006).

Gereffi, G. (1994) "The organization of buyer-driven global commodity chains," in G. Gereffi and M. Korzeniewicz (eds), *Commodity Chains and Global Capitalism*, Westport, CT: Praeger.

Gereffi, G., Humphrey, J., and Sturgeon, T. (2005) "The governance of global value chains," *Review of International Political Economy*, 12: 78–104.

Global Exchange. (2006) *Fair Trade*, Online. Available at: www.globalexchange.org/ campaigns/fairtrade (accessed June 5, 2005).

Horovitz, B. (2004) "Market to sell certified fair trade bananas," *USA Today*, January 20, Online. Available at: www.usatoday.com (accessed June 10, 2005).

Kortbech-Olesen, Rudy. (2003) "The organic market," *The World of Organic Agriculture*. M. Yussefi and H. Willer (eds), Online. Available at: www.ifoam.org (accessed June 10, 2005).

Kroger, C. (2004) "Fair trade product elbows organic domain," *The Packer*, May 3, Online. Available at: www.thepacker.com (accessed June 10, 2005).

Mayer, T.A. (2004) "HUDS bases decisions on undergraduate needs," *The Crimson – Harvard University*, September 23, Online. Available at: www.thecrimson.com (accessed October 5, 2004).

Moskin, J. (2004) "Helping Third World one banana at a time," *New York Times*, May 5, Online. Available at: www.nytimes.com (accessed June 10, 2005).

Ohlemeier, D. (2005) "Organics reach for level undreamed a decade ago," *The Packer*, April 26, Online. Available at: www.thepacker.com (accessed June 10, 2005).

Oxfam America. (2006) Online. Available at: www.oxfamamerica.org (accessed August 10, 2006).

Raynolds, L.T. (2000) "Re-embedding global agriculture: the international organic and fair trade movements," *Journal of Agriculture and Human Values*, 17: 297–309.

—— (2002) "Consumer/producer links in fair trade coffee networks," *Sociologia Ruralis*, 42: 404–424.

—— (2003) "The global banana trade," in M. Moberg and S. Striffler (eds), *Banana Wars*, Durham, NC: Duke University Press.

—— (2004) "The globalization of organic agro-food networks," *World Development*, 32: 725–743.

Red Tomato. (2006) Online. Available at: www.redtomato.org (accessed August 10, 2006).

Reefer Trends. (2005) "All Windward Island bananas to be fair trade," *Reefer Trends*, Online. Available at: www.reefertrends.com (accessed June 10, 2005).

Roosevelt, M. (2004) "The coffee clash: many firms see a marketing advantage in selling politically correct beans: will Starbucks get hurt?," *Time*, March 8, Online. Available at: www.time.com (accessed March 10, 2004).

Stecklow, S. and White, E. (2004) "Some retail chains jacking up prices on fair trade products," *The Wall Street Journal*, June 8, Online. Available at: www.wallstreetjournal.com (accessed June 12, 2004).

Striffler, S. and Moberg, M. (eds) (2003) *Banana Wars*, Durham, NC: Duke University Press.

Suchomel, K. (2005) "Student knowledge and support of fair trade – an opinion poll of college students," conducted by: MPIRG. March 2005.

TransFair USA. (2005a) "Fair Trade certified produce – everyone profits when you choose Fair Trade," paper presented at the International Banana Conference, North American Preparatory Meeting, Washington DC, February 2005.

—— (2005b) *TransFair USA Licensed Partners*, Online. Available at: www.transfairusa.org/content/certification/licensees_fruit.php (accessed May 20, 2005).

—— (2006a) *Backgrounder: Fair Trade Certified Bananas*, Online. Available at: www.transfairusa.org (accessed March 20, 2006).

—— (2006b) *Fast Facts: Fair Trade Certified Bananas*, Online. Available at: www.transfairusa.org (accessed March 20, 2006).

—— (2006c) Internal documents.

—— (2006d) *Frequently Asked Questions: How Does Transfair USA Work to Grow the US Fair Trade Market with Integrity?* Online. Available at: www.transfairusa.org/content/resources (accessed March 15, 2006).

—— (2006e) *Frequently Asked Questions: How Does TransFair USA Feel about Large-Volume Retailers like WalMart and McDonald's Carrying Fair Trade Certified Products?* Online. Available at: www.transfairusa.org/content/resources (accessed March 15, 2006).

—— (2006f) *Frequently Asked Questions: How Does TransFair USA Protect Against "Greenwashing"?* Online. Available at: www.transfairusa.org/content/resources (accessed June 20, 2006).

USFT (United Students for Fair Trade). (2005) *USFT Guide to Student Organizing*, Online. Available at: www.usft.org (accessed August 10, 2005).

—— (2006) "Fair Trade certification results," Internal documents.

US LEAP (Labor Education in the Americas Project). (2005) "Bananas: the race to the bottom, paper presented at the International Banana Conference," North American Preparatory Meeting, Washington, DC, February 2005.

—— (2006) *Fair Trade and Unionized Bananas*, Online. Available at: www.usleap.org/Banana/bananatempnew.htm#fairtrade (accessed March 25, 2006).

Van de Kasteele, A. and der Stichele, M. (2005) "Update on the banana chain," paper presented at the International Banana Conference II, April 28–30, Brussels.

Wild Oats. (2004) *Annual Report 2003: Cultivating Trust*, Boulder, CO: Wild Oats, Online. Available at: www.wildoats.com (accessed February 10, 2005).

Wild Oats and TransFair USA. (2004) "Wild Oats markets offers nation's first Fair Trade certified Bananas with Transfair USA," Press Release: January 21, 2004: Wild Oats, TransFair USA, 2004.

6 Fair Trade coffee in the United States

Why companies join the movement

Ann Grodnik and Michael E. Conroy

Introduction

The consumption end of the Fair Trade movement is growing more rapidly in the United States than in any other part of the world. From the turn of the millennium in 2000, sales of Fair Trade certified coffee have grown at rates in excess of 60 percent per year. To what can we attribute the extraordinary growth? To what extent does it come from evolving internal corporate culture? Is it little more than a onetime market competition force that provides little or no benefit to late entrants into the market? Does it simply reflect advocacy pressure from Non-Governmental Organizations (NGOs) that cannot be expected to continue? Answers to these questions will make important contributions to analyses of the durability of the movement and its likelihood for continued growth.

One of the important components of this analysis relates to the changing definition of corporate social and environmental accountability in recent years. The emergence of growing demands on the part of consumers as well as shareholders, financial markets, and even the insurance industry for greater social and environmental accountability has created a climate where corporate attention to these issues is rising rapidly.

In this chapter we analyze the decisions that have brought one US company, Green Mountain Coffee Roasters, Inc. (GMCR), from reluctant and experimental embrace of one line of Fair Trade certified coffee to enthusiastic focus on dual-certified Fair Trade organic coffees as the most rapidly growing component of its total sales. In 2005 it became one of the largest vendors of certified Fair Trade coffee in the United States. Financial markets have been favorable to this growth; GMCR's share value has risen by more than 90 percent over the four years since it began to focus on expanding Fair Trade coffee sales. Yet some critics have attacked the company for not doing enough, since GMCR's business model may not allow it to become 100 percent sellers of Fair Trade coffee.

This chapter provides a case study of an individual business to complement the broader commodity, industry, and national analyses of the rest of this book. The GMCR story illustrates the interplay of shifting market expectations, internal corporate culture, and the evolving nature of corporate accountability as driving forces for the rapid expansion of Fair Trade in US markets.

The specialty coffee industry

In 1980, the world's first espresso cart went into business under the Monorail in Seattle. Starbucks had opened its first coffee shop in Seattle in 1971, but it was primarily a local retail coffee roaster until Howard Schulz became head of the company in 1982 (MagazineUSA.com 2006).

By the early 1990s, amid a bright domestic economic outlook, the specialty coffee market had caught on across America. From its roots in independent coffeehouses and family owned roasting facilities, the specialty coffee market segment today has grown into an established ecosystem of 1,200 roaster retailers, 6,800 retailers, 500 roaster wholesalers, and 150 importers (Giovannucci 2001).

Marketed mainly to middle- to high-income, educated, and cause-friendly individuals, the specialty market segment depends on product differentiation from conventional commercial-grade coffees to command a price premium for superior taste, high-quality beans, added flavors, multiple roasting processes, and freshness. Within the beverage industry, other specialty products include high-end wines, microbrewed beer, and single malt scotches.

Coffee is the world's most widely traded commodity after oil, with 5.4 million metric tons of coffee exported by 50 different countries in the 2004–2005 production year (ICO 2006a). These numbers translate to 2.23 billion cups of coffee being consumed each day (Dicum and Littinger 1999). Though the overall coffee industry is ruled by multinationals (Kraft, Procter & Gamble, Sara Lee, and Nestlé together buy half of the world's coffee beans), almost all recent growth can be attributed to the specialty coffee market. It has grown from 2 to 40 percent of the retail market by volume in the last 30 years, and now represents 17 percent of US coffee imports by volume and 35 percent by sales (SCAA 2003). The specialty market segment was valued at US$ 7.8 billion in North America in 2001 (up from US$ 1 billion in 1990) (Giovannucci 2001). Within the specialty coffee market, the fastest growth areas are certified organic and Fair Trade certified. Fair Trade certified coffee accounts for 4–5 percent of the specialty market in the United States and has been growing at a rate of 69 percent per year since 2000. Fully 85 percent of Fair Trade certified coffee sold in the United States is also certified Organic (TransFair USA 2006a).

The specialty coffee market is highly fragmented, with many companies selling coffee as a central or peripheral part of their business. The most familiar name in the industry is Starbucks Coffee Company, which had more than 7,500 cafes worldwide in 2004 and maintains a strong wholesale business as well (Starbucks 2006). GMCR has also grown to national distribution, though it maintains its strongest sales and brand loyalty in New England. Its primary competitors in specialty sales include Gevalia Kaffe (Kraft Foods), Dunkin' Donuts (a subsidiary of Allied Domecq), Peet's Coffee & Tea, Millstone (Procter & Gamble), Seattle's Best Coffee (owned by Starbucks), and New England Coffee Company. In addition, GMCR competes indirectly against all the coffee brands on the market, whether or not they are considered specialty coffee vendors. Several national coffee marketers, including Kraft, Procter & Gamble, Sara Lee, and Nestlé, distribute premium coffee lines in supermarkets alongside offerings from GMCR (GMCR 2004).

In general, competition in the specialty coffee market is becoming increasingly fierce as relatively low barriers to entry encourage new competitors to enter the market. Specialty coffee, set apart from conventional coffee only by distinctive roasting techniques, quality of beans, and brand integrity, is also easy to imitate. This becomes an issue for GMCR and other specialty roasters as they attempt to differentiate their products on the basis of quality and environmental/social responsibility.

To ensure a steady supply of a certain quality coffee, specialty coffee roasters often enter into long-term contracts with producers and importers, guaranteeing higher prices for uninterrupted delivery of high-quality beans. This process involves sending representatives to coffee-producing areas to identify suitable suppliers and build personal relationships with the farmers, cutting out the importer/distributor in the supply chain. In 2003, GMCR sourced about 40 percent of its beans from "farm-identified" estates, cooperatives, or farms (up from 34 percent in 2002). However, the timing of purchases is dictated by the availability of beans (which can vary based on annual harvests) leading to variable inventory levels (GMCR 2003a). GMCR, like other gourmet coffee vendors, uses only high-quality Arabica coffee beans, mostly grown in Central America. The lower-priced, lower-quality Robusta beans, grown mainly in Africa and Vietnam, are sold by the conventional coffee merchants. In the absence of formal tools with which to measure coffee quality, specialty roasters have traditionally depended on their personal relationships with individual producers to standardize, monitor, and evaluate growers' practices.

Owing to its dependence on environmental sustainability to sustain uninterrupted supply of quality coffee, the specialty coffee industry prides itself on an industry-wide commitment to environmental protection and social justice. Growers, importers, distributors, and roasters were generally well aware of their responsibility to environmental stewardship. Nevertheless, as consumer awareness of economic inequity and environmental degradation associated with coffee production increases, more and more pressure has been applied to the once-local specialty coffee companies that have become behemoths. "It's curious," explained the Specialty Coffee Association of America's executive director, "When it comes time to pick on an industry for not doing anything, they pick on specialty coffee, particularly Starbucks. The segment doing the most to help the farmers is specialty coffee. And the industry that continues to sit on its hands is the commercial sector" (Jedrzej 2003).

The global coffee crisis

The coffee industry is enduring a profound economic and humanitarian crisis. A decade-long recent supply glut has lowered world market prices. In 2002, world coffee prices reached their lowest level in 100 years, adjusting for inflation

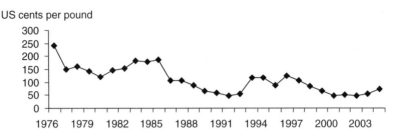

US cents per pound

Figure 6.1 ICO coffee indicator prices adjusted for trade-weighted dollar exchange rate
variation, 1976–2005.

Source: Authors' calculations on the basis of ICO 2005 prices and Federal Reserve Bank Trade-
Weighted Price Indices for Major Currencies; Federal Reserve (2006).

(see Figure 6.1). Though coffee prices rose in subsequent years, reaching
US$ 0.89 per pound in 2005 (ICO 2006b), concerns over low and highly variable
world market prices persist. As is often the case with agricultural products, only
a small portion of that price goes to the farmer who grows the beans. Lacking
market access and desperate to move their product, growers sell to middlemen
known as *coyotes* who then mark up the price and sell to importers or roasters.
At the bottom of the market, producers received around US$ 0.25 per pound from
the middleman, far below what it costs them to grow the beans. The average
US$ 3 latte thus delivered less than two cents back to the coffee farmer who grew
the beans (TransFair USA 2002).

From 1963 to 1989, coffee prices were regulated by an International Coffee
Agreement between producing countries and consuming countries under which
producing countries agreed to withhold coffee from the market, sometimes even
dumping it into rivers, in order to maintain some price stability. When the
International Coffee Agreement unraveled in 1989, production increased dramatically and the price slid. Excess supply has been fueled by a massive expansion
of government-funded coffee production in Vietnam and improved production
technology that led to increased production capacity in Brazil (see Figure 6.2).

Since it takes from three to four years for a coffee plant to produce significant
quantities of coffee, and up to seven years before the plant reaches peak produc-
tivity, it is difficult for coffee farmers to react quickly to price fluctuations. As a
result, coffee supply often increases even as market prices plummet. Further, this
leads to a collective action problem, where each farmer has an incentive to
increase production as price falls in order to reduce per unit cost and increase his
or her margins. In aggregate, this activity creates a negative feedback loop and
further depresses the world price.

Fair Trade coffee certification emerged in the United States within the context
of this global coffee crisis, seeking to counter falling producer prices, international market volatility, environmental degradation, and the vulnerability of
small-scale producers.[1]

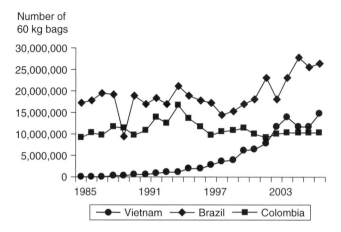

Figure 6.2 Coffee exports of Brazil, Colombia, and Vietnam, 1983–2005.
Source: Authors' graphics based on ICO (2006c).

Fair Trade certification of coffee in the United States

TranFair USA was founded in 1998 to certify coffee imported into the United States that had been fairly traded according to the criteria of the Fair Trade Labelling Organizations International (FLO). Uncertified "Fair Trade" coffee had actually been available in the United States for over a decade, supplied largely by the Massachusetts-based alternative trade organization Equal Exchange. Since Equal Exchange already followed FLO standards, it became one of TransFair USA's first licensees. Other early roasters licensed in the United States were also small socially progressive specialty coffee companies. In 2000 under strong pressure from non-governmental activist groups, Starbucks agreed to certify a small portion of its coffee according to Fair Trade criteria. The Starbucks agreement represented certified Fair Trade's breakthrough into the mainstream US specialty coffee sector and numerous other specialty coffee companies soon also began offering Fair Trade certified coffee lines.

TransFair USA tracks products from farm to market and verifies industry and farmer compliance with FLO criteria. To be licensed under FLO criteria, coffee roasters must do the following:

1   Guarantee a base price of US$ 1.26 per pound for Fair Trade nonorganic coffee and US$ 1.41 for coffee that is also certified organic.
2   Offer preharvest financing to the growers of up to 60 percent of the full contract.
3   Buy coffee only from certified family farms organized in democratically run cooperatives.
4   Maintain environmental stewardship practices as outlined by FLO regulations.

Between 1999 and 2005, TransFair certified 38 million pounds of coffee for the US market, generating US$ 74.5 million in additional revenue for coffee farmers.[2]

Roasters pay a certification fee to TransFair USA of between US 5 and 10 cents per pound on Fair Trade certified green coffee purchases, depending on the total volume they process and the proportion of their total coffee sales that is Fair Trade certified. Roasters must submit quarterly reports to TransFair USA of Fair Trade certified green coffee purchases and roasted sales. Licensed roasters are then able to market their product as Fair Trade certified, bearing a label that brands the product as fairly traded.

Though certified coffee usually commands a price premium in the market, roasters say that the guarantee of quality beans and the opportunity for product differentiation are more important factors in their decision to adopt certification (Giovannucci 2001). In reality, the price premium commanded by Fair Trade certified coffee may or may not cover the higher cost of beans. Reports by importers and roasters on the prices they pay vary widely, going as low as US$ 0.30 per pound and ranging to prices in excess of US$ 1.50, with an industry average of US$ 0.62 per pound in 2004. All told, Fair Trade certified coffee fetches slightly higher premiums than organic or shade-grown certified coffee, which is likely due to the substantial difference between the world price of coffee and the Fair Trade price floor of US$ 1.26 per pound (Giovannucci 2001). Nevertheless, roasters selling any type of certified coffee are constrained by their customers' willingness to pay for environmentally or socially superior products. Roasters cannot expect to recoup their costs for Fair Trade certification until their consumers are familiar enough with the concept to pay for it. In its retail catalog, Green Mountain Fair Trade certified coffee (nonflavored) costs US$ 7.89–8.29 per 12-ounce bag; and noncertified coffee costs US$ 7.49–8.69 per 12-ounce bag.

Eco-labeling in specialty coffee is beginning to contribute to brand identity much like price, quality, or marketing. In addition to Fair Trade and organic certification, which focus respectively on the social equity of the trade process and the production of coffee without synthetic chemicals, there are several additional eco-labels that focus on the environmental and biodiversity impacts of coffee production and do not require a floor price (e.g. Rainforest Alliance certification, Smithsonian Bird-friendly, and Utz Kapeh certification).[3] Certified organic coffee and Fair Trade coffee are the most widely recognized labels in the coffee industry (Giovannucci 2001).

Advocates of Fair Trade laud the certification mechanism as a market-based approach that creates a win–win situation for farmers, businesses, and consumers. Survey after survey proves that coffee consumers are, above all, concerned with the quality of their brew (Giovannucci 2001). TransFair USA (and certified Fair Trade coffee vendors) contend that the connection between Fair Trade certification and quality is logical: farmers who are paid more for their crops have incentive to tend them more carefully, and those farmers who sell a mix of Fair Trade certified and conventional beans will reserve the best beans for the buyers who pay the most (Jette 2004). The additional income earned by farmers is used to build schools, improve local healthcare facilities, and generally raise the standard of life in the region. The extra cash flow also allows the co-op to focus on the complexities of picking, depulping, fermenting, washing, drying, husking, and sorting with the meticulousness that the specialty market demands (Roosevelt 2004). TransFair USA asserts that the growth in Fair Trade coffee confirms that consumers are increasingly concerned about where the products that they buy come from and the social and environmental impacts of those products.

On the other side of the argument, free market advocates see the oversupply in the coffee market as an effect of economic progress and an indicator that firms should either supply a higher value product or exit the market (Lindsey 2003). They call the guaranteed price floor an inefficient subsidy, and suggest that the best answer to the coffee crisis is to stimulate demand. Wary coffee roasters worry that Fair Trade certification limits their choices as they search for the perfect crop of beans. Furthermore, since certified cooperatives can count on the US\$ 1.26 per pound price floor guaranteed by the system, some roasters argue that growers have incentive to sell their lesser quality beans as Fair Trade and sell better quality beans for the best price they can get. Even some environmentalists critique Fair Trade certification, as it does not guarantee the environmental benefits of organic or shade-grown coffee and carries less definitive standards with respect to environmental performance.

Despite these critiques, Fair Trade is gaining wide acceptance. Fair Trade coffee imports to the United States have grown at an average annual growth rate of 69 percent since 2000 as noted in Figure 6.3. Most of this growth can be attributed to mainstreaming. Coffee vendors like Dunkin' Donuts, Procter & Gamble, and Kraft

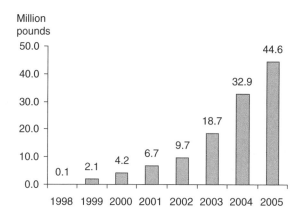

Figure 6.3 Coffee certified in the United States by TransFair USA.[a]

Source: TransFair USA (2006b).

Note

a These figures refer to green coffee imports certified by TransFair USA as meeting Fair Trade standards and receiving Fair Trade prices. They are somewhat higher than FLO figures which refer to roasted coffee sales which carry the FLO national affiliate Fair Trade label (see Chapter 2) because some US roasters blend FT coffee with other coffees and, therefore, are not entitled to use the label. But the full benefits accrue to producers from that unlabeled coffee.

all announced Fair Trade certified coffees of their own in 2004 (Jette 2004). Says Procter & Gamble spokeswoman Tonia Hyatt, "We have a goal of being a leading Fair Trade seller" (Roosevelt 2004). Dunkin' Donuts' Marketing Director Ed Valle echoes her sentiments, "This is the beginning of a movement, and we want to get in on it. We expect to serve 30 million Fair Trade *lattes* and *cappuccinos* this year" (Roosevelt 2004). Faith-based organizations, including the Catholic Relief Services and Lutheran World Relief, are working to stimulate demand for Fair Trade coffee among their congregations: with 65 million US Catholics and 48 million members of the US Lutheran and Evangelical churches, this represents a huge market (Dominguez 2003). Supermarket chains including Stop & Shop, Publix, Wegman's, and Albertson's are now offering Fair Trade coffee varieties in their aisles. Fair Trade stalwarts like coffee roaster Equal Exchange (which has always sold 100 percent Fair Trade certified, organic coffee) are thrilled by the mainstreaming of the Fair Trade ideals, but they are skeptical of the staying power of the giant retailers.

The transformation of corporate accountability

Through much of the twentieth century, corporate attention to social and environmental conditions came under the general rubric of "corporate social responsibility" or CSR. For some, such as Nobel Laureate Milton Friedman, there is "only one social responsibility of business, to use its resources and engage in activities designed to increase profits" (Friedman 1970). But for a much broader range of observers, the history of concerns about the social and environmental responsibility of businesses is almost as old as the appearance of business itself. The "corporate paternalists" of the late nineteenth and early twentieth centuries discussed their social responsibilities openly, but they tended to set the terms of the discussion as they wished, using church tithing and corporate philanthropy as the mark of their responsibility, rather than adherence to public standards for practices within their businesses.[4]

But corporate norms for responsibility are a continually changing phenomenon; and by early this century the expectations of society with respect to corporate behavior had increased dramatically. In 2005 the *Financial Times* reported that "more than half of the world's biggest companies reveal details of their environmental and social performance" (Buck 2005). The well known global accounting firm KPMG found in its study that 52 percent of the 250 largest corporations published CSR reports and that they covered a much wider range of issues in 2005 than they had covered in 2002. Socially responsible investment firms, such as Calvert Financial Services, now issue regular assessments of the social, environmental and governance performance of many companies, including the full range of activities from workplace and business practices, human rights behavior, environmental responsibility, and community relations (CSRwire 2006). And the internet has created new mechanisms for virtually instant global awareness of charges of social irresponsibility, such as human rights violations.[5]

Nineteenth-century corporate responsibility involved claims of responsibility under standards set by each company and verified only by the assertions of the company that it was following its stated practices. This is now referred to as "first-party" or self-certification of responsibility. By the end of the twentieth century, corporate disasters such as the explosion of a chemical plant in Bhopal, India, led to industry standard-setting designed to assure regulators, insurers, financiers, and consumers that industry standards were now high enough to avoid repetition of practices that led to events of this sort. But the only verification was done by company reports to an industry group, generally not released for public scrutiny, and the industry group assertions that the standards were being met. This is now referred to as "second-party" certification, where the credibility comes from the industry group, but not from any external validation. Over the past 15 years a new model of corporate responsibility has emerged, full-fledged stakeholder standard-setting and third-party independent validation. This has now become a mechanism for imposing and auditing full corporate accountability. Certified Fair Trade is one prominent model of this new form of corporate accountability.

The Green Mountain Coffee Roasters story

T.J. Whalen, Director of Brand and Market Development at GMCR, stepped outside of the Georgia World Conference Center to get a breath of the warm Atlanta spring day. He had just presented a dissection of the environmentally sustainable coffee supply chain for conference attendees at the Specialty Coffee Association of America's 16th Annual Conference. His talk focused on the prices paid to coffee growers for their product and the environmental impacts of the coffee industry. The conference, entitled "Building Our Future in Balance, Quality, Marketing and Sustainability," marked an already strong commitment on the part of the specialty coffee trade association, to the social and environmental impacts of coffee production and trade, particularly at the grower level. GMCR, as one of the most visible specialty coffee roasters and vendors of Fair Trade certified coffee in the country, was playing a leading role at the event.

Whalen, a three-year veteran of the company and an experienced brand developer with firms like Patagonia, McDonald's, and Kellogg's, knew that it hadn't always been so. GMCR had shot from selling no Fair Trade coffee to generating roughly 13 percent of its total sales from Fair Trade certified lines in little more than three years. The company was now investing heavily in educating both its wholesale and retail customers about the social and environmental impacts of coffee and using this commitment to differentiate itself from other brands. For a publicly held company that sold 80 percent of its product in supermarkets and convenience stores, this investment in social and environmental priorities made GMCR a trendsetter among firms in the coffee industry and an example of a trend that is growing rapidly in a wide array of industries in the United States. After his presentation, Whalen couldn't help but reflect on how far the company had come in so short a time.

GMCR was the brainchild of chairman, president, founder, and CEO Robert Stiller. Stiller started the company in 1981 when he purchased a single coffee café in Waitsfield, Vermont, after having enjoyed an extraordinary cup of coffee at a restaurant on a ski vacation. The coffee at the restaurant was so good that Stiller went to the café where it was roasted to learn more. He found out that the owners were looking to sell, and he promptly bought them out with US$ 100,000 of the money that he had made from selling his previous company (Grover 1991).

At the time, gourmet coffee was little known in the United States, but Stiller decided early on that he would compete on the very high end of the market. A decade later, when he was recognized as Entrepreneur of the Year by *Forbes*, he would exclaim that he could already envision the market for quality java, "When I saw how excited people got when they tasted a really good cup of coffee, I knew this would catch on" (Grover 1991). From its inception, GMCR was firmly rooted in the Vermont-based business community of socially responsible regional firms like Ben and Jerry's,[6] Cabot Cheese,[7] and Champlain Valley Chocolates. Close to home, its corporate identity grew out of both corporate philanthropy and the respectful treatment of employees. Beyond Vermont, GMCR prided itself on its long-term relationships and fair dealings with its coffee suppliers in Central and South America and Sumatra. Dependent on these farmers for the high-quality beans that set them apart from the more conventional coffee on the shelf, GMCR paid its farmers above-market prices for the best beans they could offer. The company even developed its own line of socially and environmentally friendly coffee and launched some organic varieties in the mid-1990s to illustrate this commitment. However, the measurable integration and strategic marketing of social and environmental priorities into its coffee supply chain did not take hold until 2001, when the company acquired an organic brand and was subsequently introduced to Fair Trade certification. Since then, the company has increased its offerings of Fair Trade and organic coffees to the point where 46 of its 100 coffee varieties are Fair Trade certified, while its Fair Trade sales grew by 92 percent in 2003.[8] In recent years GMCR has received numerous national awards, including #1 in the *Business Ethics Magazine's* "100 Best Corporate Citizens for 2006."

GMCR's foray into Fair Trade and organic coffee and the development of the company's larger environmental mission illustrates an increasingly common case of corporate transformation to meet changing market demands for accountability. As a publicly held company, GMCR justified its investment in environmental management and fair prices to its shareholders as an investment in quality and sustained supply. Without a certification system, however, all that GMCR could do was to publicize its responsible sourcing, which were fundamentally "first-party" claims with no independent verification or authentication. Fair Trade and organic certification provided a standardized system for quality management and long-term supply guarantees. The company went to great lengths to integrate investment and education into its overall corporate strategy, clearly aligning itself with social responsibility (despite the fact that the majority of the company's beans were still not certified Fair Trade or certified organic). Finally, GMCR used its certified coffees and environmental commitment to differentiate itself from its competitors and to partner with nationwide brands to expand the company's once-regional reach.

After his presentation at the Specialty Coffee Association of America meeting, Whalen pondered GMCR's experience with Fair Trade certification. What had the results of GMCR's strategic decision to delve into Fair Trade certified coffee been? Did the eco-labels enhance product differentiation from conventional brands? If GMCR was so committed, how could it justify selling only 13 percent Fair Trade/organic coffee? Would the company reap enough from the initiative to increase its Fair Trade offerings in the years to come or would it reach a figurative plateau? Was there a difference between the company's Fair Trade certified offerings and its other cause-related marketing?

GMCR's strategy and position in the market place

The decision by GMCR to focus heavily on Fair Trade certified and organic coffees must be understood in the context of its overall market strategy and position. Only then can we determine whether Fair Trade has been a critical or incidental component of its model. GMCR's principle activity is distribution of roasted coffee, sold wholesale in over 100 varieties to convenience stores, supermarkets, and food service outlets, as well as direct consumer operations through catalog and online sales. Coffee selections include single-origins, estates, certified organics, Fair Trade, proprietary blends, and flavored coffee that are sold under the Green Mountain, Frontier Organic Coffee, and Newman's Own Organics brands. In more recent years GMCR has also begun to custom blend and roast private-label coffees for companies such as the natural foods grocery chain, Wild Oats (see Chapter 5). GMCR has maintained strong roots in its Vermont home and continues to manage operations in Waterbury with a 90,000 square foot roasting and distribution facility. GMCR has more than 7,000 wholesale customers (GMCR 2006).

By 1985, after a few rocky years of learning the ropes, Bob Stiller had opened four Green Mountain stores in New England and was turning a profit. Through direct mail sales and word-of-mouth, the company gained momentum and added retail locations through the 1980s and early 1990s. By that time, Starbucks and other competitors were growing rapidly in the retail market. To raise money to fund retail expansion, GMCR went public in 1993, but experienced decreased earnings because expansion had outpaced sales growth (*Vermont Business Magazine* 2002).

Between 1994 and 1998, the company reorganized its sales strategies. In 1998, it expanded its certified organic coffee line, revamped its web site, and began to concentrate on its wholesale and direct mail business, providing less attention and resources to store operations. By 1999, GMCR stores had all been sold off to employees and the company was focusing wholly on its wholesale business, marked by a new partnership with the German coffee brewing machine manufacturer, Keurig, to offer one-cup brewing varieties of its coffees (Hoover's Online 2004).

In 2000, the company signed a contract with its largest customer, ExxonMobil, to supply coffee at more than 900 convenience stores and 13,000 dealer and franchise stores throughout the northeastern United States. This was considered a risky move because of the control that GMCR would give up in the decentralized brewing and sales of its coffee. However, Stiller believed that if the coffee was prepared and presented properly, then the increased exposure to quality coffee was the company's best strategy to convert new customers. "The Maxwell House coffees of the world just go into a supermarket and advertise and advertise. Everything that can be said about coffee has been said," Stiller remarked. "But at the end of the day, it boils down to what does it taste like? If we can match you with what you like and help you have that great coffee experience, well, that's where it's at. No advertising can do that" (*Vermont Business Magazine* 2002). Since 2000, GMCR's wholesale customer list has grown to include the American Skiing Company, Amtrak, ARAMARK (food services), Hannaford Bros. (grocery stores), Jet Blue Airline, Kash N' Karry (convenience store), Shaw's Supermarkets, Sodexho (food services), and Wild Oats (natural foods supermarkets).

Contracts with supermarkets and convenience stores uniquely positioned GMCR in the coffee market. On the one hand, the company sold high-quality, high-priced beans to a small local audience that appreciated the company's Vermont roots, its commitment to quality, and possibly its organic offerings. On the other hand, the company maintained kiosks at thousands of roadside convenience stores and was aggressively and opportunistically seeking new sales outlets. This seemingly schizophrenic approach to sales could be Green Mountain's strength and its weakness. While it ran the risk of disenfranchising its local customer base, it more than made up for it by accessing new distribution channels and by growing its customer base nationwide.

During the summer of 1999, TransFair USA staff approached GMCR with a case for the integration of Fair Trade coffee into its offerings. They presented the benefits and opportunities of Fair Trade to Stiller and a group of 25 GMCR employees. Though no one was familiar with what Fair Trade meant at the time, the entire team agreed that the idea was aligned with GMCR's socially responsible identity. In terms of business opportunity, the GMCR team was not convinced that Fair Trade labels would initially increase sales because consumer awareness was relatively low. However, in the long term, GMCR management envisioned increased consumer education and association of Fair Trade certification and GMCR's socially responsible image.[9] After months of deliberation, in May 2000, GMCR decided to sign on with TransFair to certify 3 percent of their coffee as Fair Trade. The deciding factor had been that Fair Trade certification offered a formal mechanism with which to standardize and monitor supplier quality and, in the long term, it could represent an opportunity to access a formerly untapped differentiating factor in the market.[10]

In mid-2001, GMCR acquired the Frontier Organic Coffee brand from Frontier Natural Products Co-op and integrated the coffee into its own organic line, bringing its tally of organic offerings from 8 to 26. A full rebranding of the company's organic varieties ensued, and GMCR turned several of its organic coffees into doubly certified Fair Trade/organic.

The company's expansion and rebranding of its organic and Fair Trade certified varieties coincided with a veritable explosion of organic purchasing and awareness in mainstream supermarkets. In April 2002, the US Department of Agriculture established national organic standards. The Lifestyles of Health and Sustainability (LOHAS) market research journal, estimated that 23 percent of the American population was making purchasing decisions based on how the products they consumed affect the world, meaning that "they have a profound sense of environmental and social responsibility." Sixty-eight percent of those consumers indicated that knowing that a company is mindful of their impact on the environment and society makes them more likely to buy that company's products and services (French and Rogers 2005). These consumers were willing to spend more money for products that allowed them to feel that they were acting in a socially and environmentally responsible fashion.

Even though GMCR devoted significant resources toward its organic and Fair Trade marketing, the company was initially thwarted by its regional limits in its early attempts to break into this market. Though GMCR had grown since its early days as a purely regional distributor, it still could not achieve the desired reach. Cate Baril, a brand and marketing manager said, "We were excited about our organic lines and we were trying to go beyond New England. But when we went to buyers for major supermarkets and tried to sell them on our organic varieties, they'd respond with 'I got one already,' meaning they already had one organic brand on the shelf and didn't need any more" (SCAA 2004).

In response to the lukewarm reception that GMCR received in mainstream supermarkets, the company initiated strategic partnerships to facilitate expansion. In 2003, GMCR partnered with Newman's Own Organics to develop a co-branded organic line of six coffees. Newman's Own is a company founded by actor Paul Newman and his family which donates all after-tax profits to charity. The coffee, sourced by GMCR, was packaged in a bag with the Newman's Own Organics label on the front and the Green Mountain Coffee Roasters label on the back. Baril notes that this was a perfect partnership because, "Newman's is a fully mainstream organic company. We wanted to get to mainstream customers who didn't yet know they wanted organic." Conversely, Peter Meehan, CEO of Newman's Own Organics, saw GMCR's coffee sourcing expertise and complementary commitment to social responsibility as the perfect entrée into the specialty coffee market (SCAA 2004).

Spurred by the positive results of the Newman's Own Organic partnership, GMCR also signed an agreement in 2003 with Hain Celestial Group (a leading brand of organic products) to sell a cross-branded line of teas. That same year, it expanded its relations with the brewing machine company Keurig, acquiring 43 percent of the company, thus allowing GMCR to sell an integrated system for quality coffee preparation in the home or office.

In 2003, GMCR did US$ 116.7 million in sales, which translates to selling 12 million pounds of coffee. Approximately 60 percent of this was to supermarkets and convenience stores (GMCR 2004). The company reported strong performance during the first quarter of fiscal 2004, with net sales up 18.4 percent from the first quarter of 2003. GMCR attributes the rise to an increase in sales of coffee and tea single-cup preparations for Keurig coffeemakers which sell at a significantly higher price per pound than other GMCR products (GMCR 2004).[11]

Despite GMCR's aggressive marketing of its Fair Trade organic coffee lines, the majority of its sales come from its noncertified products. Critics assert that GMCR is not doing enough to distribute Fair Trade or organic coffee. For example, Dean Cycon, proprietor of a 100 percent organic, Fair Trade, and kosher coffee roasting business, publicly criticized GMCR as "buying just enough fair-trade coffee to wrap themselves in the cloak of social consciousness" (Pfister 2004). In his opinion, GMCR and other coffee roasters are taking advantage of the indus-try's depressed markets to increase their profits and greenwash their business.

Fair Trade, the environment, and Green Mountain's corporate identity

Proudly headquartered in what locals call "The People's Republic of Vermont" (because of Vermont's history of liberal politics) and boasting the marketing slogan, "The Taste of a Better World," GMCR strives for a socially responsible corporate identity. It also works to couple this responsible image with high-quality coffee. According to Stiller, the company philosophy is that "coffee is a very personal type of experience. There is no 'best.' What is best is what you like, and we really help people find that and enjoy it" (*Vermont Business Magazine* 2002).

Since its business literally depends on coffee farmers' capacity to continue producing beans, GMCR frames nearly every one of its environmental initiatives as a win–win situation for the business, the environment, and the producers. Stiller describes this strategy as, "We help the farmers grow better coffee, and we help the local environment which also helps our product. We help the community…It's a very synergistic type of relationship, it's not haphazard" (*Vermont Business Magazine* 2002). This blended-value proposition is illustrated when GMCR provides startup funding for a cooperative of 100 small-scale farmers in Sumatra. They enable production at the co-op to increase six fold – with 18 percent of its Arabica beans going to GMCR (Kroll 2001).

Before GMCR had ever ventured into any formal eco-labeling or certification schemes, it offered "Stewardship Coffee," for which it used its own criteria to identify growers who were committed to GMCR environmental and social standards, focused on quality coffee, supported a healthy environment, and were respectful in their treatment of workers. Since there was no reliable industry standard for measuring both the environmental and social conditions on indi-vidual farms in the early 1990s, GMCR developed its own. The Stewardship Coffee initiative was launched in 1992, after a group of employees went on what would be the first of many company sponsored trips to coffee farms in Central America. Stewardship Coffee accounted for almost one-third of coffee purchased by GMCR until it began purchasing significant amounts of organic and Fair Trade coffee. In fact, Rick Peyser notes that "the average price that Green Mountain was paying for its coffee before it signed on with Fair Trade was higher than the Fair Trade price floor of US$ 1.26 per pound."[12]

Because the criteria for Stewardship Coffee were unique to GMCR and consumer understanding of the standards was low, GMCR's wholesale customers – particularly supermarkets – were not convinced that it would sell. In 1996, GMCR began offering organic certified coffee, which was more clearly defined and better understood by consumers.

Since its 1998 expansion of its organic coffee line, GMCR has been an active player in Fair Trade and organic coffees. In fiscal year 2002, 9 percent of the coffee sold by the company was Fair Trade certified (MacQuarrie 2003), which was a 33 percent increase from the previous year. According to Rick Peyser, Director of Public Relations, the company intends to increase that portion to 25–30 percent by 2008. Eighty-five percent of the company's Fair Trade coffees are also certified organic. In 2003, GMCR claimed to have the largest offering of double-certified Fair Trade and organic coffees in the market (12 percent of their total sales, up by 57 percent from 2002) (GMCR 2003b). GMCR's sales may soon surpass those of Equal Exchange, the United States' first 100 percent Fair Trade coffee company, which currently is the country's largest supplier of certified Fair Trade coffee.

Fair Trade and organic certification has allowed GMCR to increase and reposition its value proposition and boost wholesale and consumer sales, particularly in segments where consumer awareness is high. For example in April 2004, the company piloted its Fair Trade organic coffee in 17 Bruegger's Bagels stores nationwide. Breugger's was relaunching its brand in its 125 stores and identified their store-branded "Bruegger's" coffee as a weak component of their selling proposition. While Bruegger's had never considered Fair Trade (the purchasing team had never heard of it), Green Mountain convinced them to test out a fully branded Green Mountain Fair Trade organic coffee program, complete with an in-store education program and Bruegger's-specific cups and packaging.[13]

Unlike other coffee roasters (and unlike Starbucks in particular), GMCR has avoided negative press and public pressure from social development groups. This is mostly a result of the company's willingness to partner with activists and NGOs to educate consumers and drive demand for certified coffee. Despite GMCR's national growth plans, its wholesale and online sales and distribution channels allow it to operate with a relatively small ecological footprint, avoiding the issues associated with building new coffee shops around the globe.

GMCR has not avoided, however, criticism from both NGOs and competitors about the fact that it is not yet focused on buying *all* of its coffee on Fair Trade terms. The boom in sales – and, therefore, in benefits to farmers – has come as mainstream companies like GMCR have introduced lines of Fair Trade products alongside their ordinary commercial grade (often less-expensive) products. The competition between the "100-percenter companies," totally dedicated to selling Fair Trade products as the basis for their company success, and the mainstream corporations selling much larger amounts of Fair Trade products, though smaller percentages of their total sales, has become acute. Some of the small companies began seeking a competitive edge by publicly criticizing their larger competitors whose commitment to Fair Trade, they argued, was suspect. This was, apparently, a violation of their TransFair USA licensing agreements, which barred attacks upon other licensees. When warned of that violation, a small number of the 100-percenters cancelled their links to TransFair USA and set out to become independently identified as "Fair Trade" without TransFair USA certification.[14] These companies claim that their products are at least as worthy as those that carry the TransFair USA label. Some of these companies use a Fair Trade Federation membership symbol as evidence of certification, even though the Fair Trade Federation does not verify compliance with its code of conduct for members.

Dean's Beans provides a good example of the "Fair Trade Plus" approaches of a small number of companies in the United States.[15] Dean's Beans advertises that it adheres to the FLO minimum prices, that is, US$ 1.41 per pound for the certified organic coffees it sells. It suggests that it purchases only from organizations that are on the FLO registry or who have become members of the International Fair Trade Association (IFAT). The company then publishes the list of cooperatives from which it purchases, provides documentation on the extra six cents per pound social premium it pays, and has its transactions with producers audited independently by Quality Assurance International to verify the validity of its claims.

The Dean's Beans website contains a passionate and personal critique of the practices of its competitors who don't commit fully to selling only Fair Trade products. Although these 100-percenters appear to represent a very small proportion of total Fair Trade sales in the United States, they represent the leading edge of the push for higher levels of commitment.

The importance of Fair Trade certification to GMCR success[16]

GMCR is a successful company of moderate size that has embraced social and environmental product differentiation as central to its business strategy. That commitment has rewarded the company in recent years, more than doubling its total sales between 2002 and 2005 (see Figure 6.4). Rick Peyser describes the company's commitment to sustainability in human terms, "Fair Trade puts the farmer's face on the cup of coffee. Our customers want the human link" (Roosevelt 2004). While GMCR is not the only company to put the farmer's face on their cup of coffee, nor is it the most vigilant in terms of Fair Trade, it is nevertheless a company that has gone to great lengths to integrate its commitment to the environment and equitable trade into its overall corporate strategy.

Environmental and social product differentiation usually involves a company offering products that provide greater environmental and/or social benefits (or smaller costs) than its competitors' products. These tweaks to the product or the production process raise the firm's costs, but they also enable it to command a price premium in the marketplace or to capture additional market share, leaving it at least as well off as before. In order for the differentiation to be successful, the quality of the product must be, at a minimum, equivalent to its competitors. This is exactly the case in Fair Trade certification, where GMCR increases its costs by buying its coffee at fair prices, maintaining the quality of the beans, and then

Dollars per share

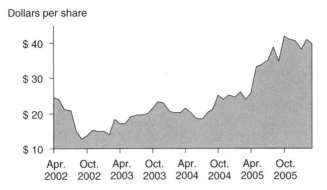

Figure 6.4 GMCR share value 48 months through March 2006.

Source: Authors' graphic, based on Yahoo! Finance (2006).

investing in education about the process. These investments allow GMCR to differentiate the product – and the company – from competitors.

In addition to engaging its suppliers and partners in the Fair Trade supply chain, GMCR has actively educated its customers and the general public about the global coffee crisis. This strategy plays a dual role. First, it creates a connection for consumers between the growers and the final coffee product. This objective has been lauded by NGO's working for market penetration by more Fair Trade certified coffee and is also a boon for sellers of certified coffees. In effect, GMCR's consumer education campaigns create a "club good" for the entire industry. Second, it positions Green Mountain as a socially responsible and proactive company leading the way in environmental and social justice issues.

For environmental or social product differentiation to succeed, the first require-ment is that consumers are willing to pay for the public goods provided. GMCR maintains a customer base comprised of people who are loyal to the GMCR brand (and willing to pay for it) and people who have never heard of GMCR but found it at their local supermarket and have continued to buy. Once their brand loyalty has been established, GMCR's customers may be willing to pay more for its Fair Trade and organic coffee for altruistic reasons. The company's marketing tells the story of coffee "from tree to cup," creating a compelling story for contributing to the support of local communities and biodiversity hotspots. Willingness to pay can also grow from a desire to convey a commitment to social and environmental responsibility to friends and acquaintances. However, as opposed to the coffee transaction in a coffee shop, GMCR's product is most commonly consumed at home, so customers do not get the added benefit of being able to show off their socially and environmentally responsible purchases in public.

The criticism of GMCR for "not doing enough" is a common result when a company attempts to horizontally differentiate their products based on environ-mental and social criteria. By offering different versions of coffee (Fair Trade certified and noncertified, organic and nonorganic), GMCR is vulnerable to perceptions of insincerity in their environmental and social commitments. If the company sold exclusively to a wealthy, educated customers willing to pay for public goods, then it could steadily increase its offering of certified coffees without risk. However, as GMCR's largest wholesale customers are gas stations and supermarkets where the willingness to pay a premium for certified coffee is presumed to be low, the risk of alienating a segment of the market is noteworthy.

The company's integrated communication of its commitment to Fair Trade and organic certification, its philanthropic giving, its investment in coffee-growing communities, its Vermont roots, and its folksy, familial tone creates an unusually strong bond with customers. This relationship bundles together the company's concerns about living wage, environmental protection, and product quality and all these factors ultimately contribute to the Green Mountain brand. Other companies can copy this convergence only to the extent that they too have invested in a similar culture and similar relationships with customers. Whether this combination of commitment, responsibility, and action can be replicated remains to be seen. Others seem sure to try.

Conclusion

The rapid growth of Fair Trade in the United States has been fueled in large measure by the adoption of Fair Trade certified products by coffee roasters and retailers who use these products to distinguish their brands in the market. While some of these coffee roasters and retailers sell Fair Trade coffee due to external pressure from activist groups, others like Green Mountain Coffee Roasters have turned increasingly to Fair Trade certification as a way to communicate their corporate commitment to socially and environmentally responsible products and to position themselves in the highly differentiated specialty coffee industry. Given GMCR's success we can expect this company and others following a similar strategy to comprise an increasingly large share of the US Fair Trade certified coffee market. While this growth raises questions from 100 percent Fair Trade companies, it suggests that Fair Trade certification is solidifying its position as a mechanism for engaging demands of corporate accountability within large mainstream corporations.

Notes

1 For a discussion of these issues from the perspective of coffee producers see for example, Bacon (2005).
2 These figures are calculated by the authors from TransFair USA 2006b: 6.
3 See Raynolds et al. (forthcoming) for a comparative analysis of these certifications.
4 Much of this section is drawn from Michael E. Conroy, Branded! How the "Certification Revolution" Is Transforming Global Corporations (2007).
5 See, for example, www.businesshumanrights.org, where weekly updates list these charges, along with corporate responses to them.
6 Ben and Jerry's Ice Cream Company, now part of Unilever, has had an extraordinary record of social and environmental responsibility (see www.benjerry.com/our_company/about_us/social_mission/social_audits/2004/sea_2004.pdf).

7 Cabot Cheese is a 100-year old brand associated with one of the oldest and most successful US farmer cooperatives producing high quality cheeses and other dairy products.
8 Interview with Rick Peyser, VP of Public Relations, Green Mountain Coffee Roasters, April 28, 2004.
9 Interview with Rick Peyser, VP of Public Relations, Green Mountain Coffee Roasters, April 28, 2004.
10 Interview with Rick Peyser, VP of Public Relations, Green Mountain Coffee Roasters, April 28, 2004.
11 K-Cup coffee sales accounted for 19 percent of GMCRs fiscal 2002 sales revenue. "Green Mountain Coffee Reports FY04 Q1 Results," Business Wire, February 19, 2004.
12 Interview with Rick Peyser, VP of Public Relations, Green Mountain Coffee Roasters, April 28, 2004.
13 Cate Baril, email communication, May 2004.
14 The group included Dean's Beans, Café Campesino, Larry's Beans, and several others.
15 See, for example, www.deansbeans.com/fair_trade_roadmap.html?id=Nhue3W2f
16 This section includes several interpretations of principles from Forest Reinhardt, *Down To Earth: Applying Business Principles to Environmental Management.* Harvard Business School Press: Cambridge, MA.

References

Bacon, C. (2005) "Confronting the coffee crisis: can fair trade, organic, and specialty coffees reduce small-scale farmer vulnerability in northern Nicaragua?," *World Development*, 33: 497–511.

Ben and Jerry's. (2004) *Social and Environmental Assessment 2004: One Scoop at a Time*, Online. Available at: www.benjerry.com/our_company/about_us/social_mission/social_audits/2004/sea_2004.pdf (accessed July 12, 2006).

Buck, T. (2005) "More companies reveal social policies," *Financial Times*, July 12, 2004: 8.

Business Wire. (2004) "Green Mountain Coffee Reports FY04 Q1 results," *Business Wire*, February 19, Online. Available at: www.businesswire.com (accessed July 12, 2006).

Conroy, M.E. (2007) *Branded! How the "Certification Revolution" Is Transforming Global Corporations*, Vancouver and London: New Society Publishers.

CSRwire: The Corporate Social Responsibility Newswire Service, Online. Available at: www.csrwire.com (accessed June 10, 2006).

Dicum, G. and Luttinger, N. (1999) *The Coffee Book: Anatomy of an Industry from Crop to the Last Drop*, New York: The New Press.

Dominguez, A. (2003) "Coffee program expands to more churches," CRS: Fair Trade, October 16, 2003.

Federal Reserve. (2006) Online. Available at: www.federalreserve.gov/pubs/bulletin/2005/winter05_index.pdf (accessed May 2, 2006).

French, S. and Rogers, G. (2005) "LOHAS Market Research Review: Marketplace Opportunities Abound," *LOHAS Journal*, Online. Available at: www.lohas.com/journal/trends.html (accessed August 13, 2006).

Friedman, M. (1970) "The social responsibility of business is to increase its profits," *The New York Times Magazine*, September 13: 31–33.

Giovannucci, D. (2001) "Sustainable Coffee Survey of the North American Specialty Coffee Industry," Philadelphia: Summit Foundation, Online. Available at: www.cec.org/files/PDF/ECONOMY/CoffeeSurvey_EN.pdf (accessed July 10, 2006).

GMCR (Green Mountain Coffee Roasters). (2002) *Annual report.*

—— (2003a) SEC filings, form 10-Q, August 2003.

—— (2003b) *Annual report.*

—— (2004) SEC filings, form 10-Q, March 2004.

—— (2006) *Company Profile*, Online. Available at: www.gmcr.com/investor_services/scripts/company_profile.asp (accessed June 20, 2006).

Grover, M.B. (1991) "Hippie redux," *Forbes*, December 9, Online. Available at: www.forbes.com (accessed April 23, 2004).

Hoover's Online. (2004) Online. Available at: www.hoovers.com/green-mountain-coffee/–ID__45721–/free-co-factsheet.xhtml (accessed March 21, 2004).

ICO (International Coffee Organization). (2006a) *Exports by Exporting Countries to all Destinations, June 2006*, Online. Available at: www.ico.org/prices/m1.htm (accessed August 13, 2006).

—— (2006b) *ICO Indicator Prices Monthly and Annual Averages 2004 to 2006*, Online. Available at: www.ico.org/coffee_prices.asp (accessed July 18, 2006).

—— (2006c) *Historical Statistics*, Online. Available at: www.ico.org/historical.asp (accessed May 15, 2006).

Jedrzej, G.F. (2003) *Transnational Corporations and Human Rights*, New York: Macmillian.

Jette, J. (2004) "Fair trade expanding beyond the specialty coffee aisle: gaining ground," *The Patriot Ledger*, January 24, 2004.

Kroll, L. (2001) "Java man," *Forbes*, October 29, Online. Available at: www.forbes.com (accessed April 23, 2004).

Lindsey, B. (2003) "Why 'fair trade' isn't fair: should coffee drinkers be coffee activists, too?," *Consumers' Research*, June 2003: 22–26.

MacQuarrie, B. (2003) "Bitter feelings over coffee bean prices," *The Boston Globe*, November 18: A6.

MagazineUSA.com (2006) *Starbucks History*, Online. Available at: www.magazineusa.com/us/info/show.aspx?unit=originals&doc=33 (accessed July 10, 2006).

Pfister, B. (2004) "Some coffee drinkers pay a premium for social conscience," *San Antonio Express-News*, January 10: 01C.

Raynolds, L.T., Murray, D., and Heller, A. (forthcoming) "Regulating sustainability in the coffee sector: a comparative analysis of environmental and social certification and labeling initiatives," *Agriculture and Human Values*, 24.

Roosevelt, M. (2004) "The coffee clash," *Time Bonus Section: Inside Business/Trade*, April 2004.

SCAA (Specialty Coffee Association of America). (2003) *Annual report.*

—— (2004) 16th Annual Conference Proceedings, April 23, 2004.

Starbucks. (2006) *Starbucks Timeline and History*, Online. Available at: www.starbucks.com/aboutus/timeline.asp (accessed April 23, 2004).

TransFair USA. (2002) *Annual report.*

—— (2006a) *Coffee Facts*, Online. Available at: www.transfairusa.org/pdfs/fastfacts_coffee.pdf (accessed June 22, 2006).

—— (2006b), *Fair Trade Almanac 2005*, Online. Available at: http://www.transfairusa.org/pdfs/2005FTAlmanac3.17.06.pdf (accessed August 13, 2006).

Vermont Business Magazine. (2002) "Q&A: Robert Stiller and Green Mountain Coffee Roasters," *Vermont Business Magazine*, January 1, 2002.

Yahoo! Finance. (2006) Online. Available at: http://finance.yahoo.com/q/hp?s=GMCR (accessed April 2, 2006).

7 Mainstreaming Fair Trade in global production networks

Own brand fruit and chocolate in UK supermarkets

Stephanie Barrientos and Sally Smith

Into the mainstream – supermarket own brand Fair Trade

Since 2000 Fair Trade has grown rapidly in Europe. Much of this growth is a result of supermarket retailing, which has expanded Fair Trade to consumer groups traditionally thought to have less affinity with its underlying principles. Of particular note is the introduction of supermarket "own brand" Fair Trade goods which carry the name of the supermarket alongside the "Fairtrade" certification logo of Fairtrade Labelling Organizations International (FLO). Supermarket own brand Fair Trade has potential for further expanding the consumer base and bringing Fair Trade fully into the mainstream. But it may also have a marked effect on the dynamics of Fair Trade production networks, given the recent changes in global agrofood systems described by Raynolds and Wilkinson in Chapter 3. These include growth and concentration in the supermarket sector and the concurrent emergence of "buyer-led" production networks in which supermarkets play a dominant role and require suppliers to meet an expanding range of standards for food "qualities," including social and environmental attributes (Dolan and Humphrey 2004; Gereffi 1994; Ponte and Gibbon 2005). This allows supermarkets to capture market share and maximize returns without getting involved in low-value activities directly or developing close relationships with suppliers, but can put tremendous commercial pressure on suppliers within their networks (Barrientos and Kritzinger 2004; Gereffi et al. 2005; Vorley 2004).

Supermarket own brand Fair Trade has brought it further into the ambit of the more conventional agrofood system and potentially enhanced the power that supermarket buyers can exert within Fair Trade networks. This is compounded by an anomaly in the FLO system that allows supermarkets to use the FLO mark on their own brand products without having to become a licensee, due to the fact they outsource packing and labeling. Since supermarkets are therefore not necessarily bound by Fair Trade rules and regulations, their suppliers are potentially being exposed to the types of practices and pressures that exist in conventional production networks.

In this chapter, we explore whether Fair Trade integration into supermarket own brand ranges provides a route for advancing greater social justice within the commercial mainstream, or whether it is instead leading to the co-opting of Fair Trade by the same agrofood system it was set up to oppose. We do so through a case study of Fair Trade in UK supermarkets, illustrated by two products marketed under own brand labels: cocoa from Ghana (processed into chocolate) and fruit from South Africa.[1] The cocoa is sourced from a cooperative of small-scale producers and its production network reflects a relational Fair Trade model that has been incorporated by the Co-operative Group supermarket chain ("the Co-op"). The fruit is being sourced from larger-scale commercial farms and passes through more conventional networks to be retailed by various UK super-markets. We examine in the following section the broad dynamics of own brand Fair Trade, and then the production networks of these two products, concluding with an assessment of the implications for the future of Fair Trade.

Fair Trade in the United Kingdom and the challenges of integration into supermarket own brand production networks

Growth of Fair Trade in the United Kingdom

The Fair Trade sector in the United Kingdom saw some growth from its inception in the 1960s through charity-based outlets, but by the end of the 1980s the Alternative Trading Organizations (ATOs) and Non-Governmental Organizations (NGOs) recognized that to expand sales they would need to follow the example of Max Havelaar in the Netherlands and develop a "certified Fair Trade" label. The Fairtrade Foundation was set up as the UK's National Initiative in 1992, tasked with marketing the Fair Trade mark and licensing firms to use it.

The first certified Fair Trade products became available in 1994 and by 2006 there were over 1,500 labeled retail and catering products available in the United Kingdom (Fairtrade Foundation 2006a). Sales grew from £16.7 million (US$ 27.7 million) in 1998 to £195 million (US$ 355 million) in 2005 (see Table 7.1),

Table 7.1 Growth in retail value[a] of labeled Fair Trade sales in the UK (US$ million)

Year	Coffee	Tea	Cocoa products	Honey products	Bananas	Other[b]	Total retail sales
2005	119.8	30.2	39.9	6.4	86.8	71.9	354.9
2004	90.2	23.6	30.2	6.2	56.0	50.0	256.2
2003	55.9	15.5	17.8	9.9	39.6	11.7	150.4
2002	34.7	10.8	10.6	7.4	26.0	5.3	94.5
2001	26.8	8.5	8.6	4.6	21.0	3.2	72.7
2000	23.6	7.8	5.5	1.4	11.9	n/a	50.0
1999	24.3	7.3	3.7	0.2	n/a	n/a	35.3
1998	22.7	3.3	1.7	n/a	n/a	n/a	27.7

Source: Fairtrade Foundation (2006b).

Notes
a Assumes margin of 40 percent for retailers (30 percent on bananas).
b Fresh fruit, sugar, fruit juice, nuts and snacks, preserves and spreads, rice, roses, sports balls, wine and beer.

with the United Kingdom surpassing all other European countries (Fairtrade Foundation 2006b). Although only a small percentage of total UK food sales – 0.17 percent of the £144 billion (US$ 235 billion) is spent on food and drink in 2003 (Tallontire and Vorely 2005) – this represents a significant achievement in a relatively short space of time. Cocoa is the third most successful product by value, reaching nearly £22 million (US$ 40 million) in 2006. Fresh fruit has not yet reached a sufficiently high level of sales to be listed as a separate category, due to the relatively short period it has been available, but demand is reportedly dynamic in the United Kingdom, which has acted as a pioneer market, and is growing elsewhere (FLO 2006).

Fair Trade in UK supermarkets

Food retailing in the United Kingdom has become increasingly concentrated in the supermarket sector, with the leading four supermarkets (Tesco, Asda, Sainsburys, and Morrisons) capturing nearly three-quarters of total grocery sales (Taylor Nelson Sofres 2005). In order to significantly expand sales of food products, Fair Trade needed to penetrate this market and the Fairtrade label enabled them to do so. In 1994, Sainsbury's became the first British supermarket to sell a Fair Trade labeled product, with other supermarkets quickly following suit, stocking branded Fair Trade products from "mission oriented" companies like Cafédirect and Traidcraft (Fairtrade Foundation 2006a). By the end of 2002 all the major supermarkets sold at least one labeled product and were seeing impressive growth in Fair Trade sales – a 112 percent increase from 2002 to 2003 for the Co-op, 70 percent for Tesco and 24 percent for Waitrose (Freshinfo 2003).

In reality it was only when the Co-op threw its weight behind the Fair Trade movement in the late 1990s that supermarket sales really started to take off. The Co-op is a relatively small supermarket in the United Kingdom accounting for approximately 5 percent of grocery sales (Taylor Nelson Sofres 2005). It is one of the largest consumer cooperative organizations in the world and is owned and controlled by its membership, comprised of other Cooperative societies and individuals who shop in its stores.[2] It realized in the early 1990s that it had to develop a strategy which differentiated it within the UK market and in 1994 undertook a survey of 30,000 consumers to identify their key concerns. The results led to a decision to spearhead Fair Trade within the UK market. In 2000 the Co-op achieved two supermarket firsts: it began selling Fair Trade certified bananas, the first fresh fruit product and soon to be a top Fair Trade line; it launched the first supermarket own brand Fair Trade certified product, a milk chocolate bar. It has since taken the unprecedented step of converting *all* of its own brand chocolate and coffee lines to certified Fair Trade, rather than just running separate Fair Trade products alongside conventional lines. In 2004 the Co-op achieved Fair Trade sales of £24 million (US$ 44 million) (Co-operative Group 2005), which equates to 17 percent of the UK's total certified Fair Trade sales that year. Although the Co-op is a long-term supporter of Fair Trade, it now vies with the UK's leading supermarket, Tesco, for the number one spot in terms of actual sales due to its much smaller share of the grocery market (around 5 percent compared to Tesco's 30 percent). Tesco's 2005 Corporate Responsibility Review claims that one in three certified Fair Trade products bought in UK supermarkets come from their stores (Tesco 2006). These figures clearly demonstrate the importance of the supermarket sector to Fair Trade sales in the United Kingdom.

The uptake of Fair Trade by UK supermarkets relates to the fact that they are engaged in a fierce battle for market share, and closely monitor both competitor and consumer behavior for signs of possible market advantage. Consumers are increasingly aware of Fair Trade, with one in every two adults in the United Kingdom now recognizing the FLO logo (Fairtrade Foundation 2005). Many are engaged in a process of changing social beliefs and accepted norms around the fairness of trade, influenced not only by Fair Trade but also by wider campaigns and social movements, such as the Trade Justice Movement. Supermarkets aim to cater to all consumer needs with a "one stop shopping" format, and consumer interest therefore necessitates the inclusion of Fair Trade products in their range. Although customers might buy only one or two Fair Trade items, supermarkets monitor their purchases through loyalty card schemes and do not want to risk losing their patronage. Most supermarkets see Fair Trade as a niche, high value "feel good" line which sits alongside organic and eco-friendly labels to complement their value and premium ranges. As well as appealing to a consumer group that supermarkets are keen to capture ("ABs" in market research terms, that is, professionals and other skilled people), Fair Trade also has public relations spinoffs.

The commercial reasons for stocking Fair Trade were summarized by the Fair Trade Product Manager at Tesco, who named three sound business factors behind the company's decision to increase their Fair Trade range: customer demand, commercial opportunity, and brand value (Nicholls and Opal 2005). This makes it clear that supporting marginalized producers and workers is important only in the extent to which it adds value to the Tesco brand. A battle for brand dominance has become a defining feature of food systems across the globe (Grievink 2003), and supermarkets work hard to protect and promote their brands. However, this generalized picture disguises some important differences between supermarkets. There are "champions" within certain supermarkets with a high degree of sympathy and commitment to the objectives of Fair Trade, who drive forward the Fair Trade agenda both within the company and in the wider environment. There are also supermarket brands that are more closely identified with corporate social responsibility in general, who could be said to be acting with "enlightened self-interest" (Humphreys 2000). Most notable of these is the Co-op which may be expected to empathize with the values of Fair Trade. Another UK supermarket perceived to have more affinity with corporate social responsibility is Waitrose, part of the John Lewis Partnership which gives all staff a share in the company. Though not quite "mission oriented" retailers, these companies both cite ethical reasons for increasing their commitment to Fair Trade.

But even the Co-op sees Fair Trade as strategically important for retaining their market share in an increasingly competitive environment, as expressed by one of its corporate social responsibility managers: "Fair Trade is part of the responsible retailing brand that we are trying to develop as a business strategy." The customer-led rather than producer-led approach to Fair Trade that super-markets have adopted has driven them to go out in search of sources of Fair Trade rather than wait for Fair Trade products to be offered to them as has traditionally been the case. This has a significant impact on the dynamics between actors in Fair Trade production.

The rise of supermarket own brand Fair Trade

The Co-op was the first UK supermarket to introduce an own brand Fair Trade certified product, but all others have since also done so. By 2005 there were at least 130 separate supermarket own brand Fair Trade products, accounting for nearly a quarter of all labeled goods retailed in the United Kingdom (see Table 7.2). The top three supermarkets in terms of number of products stocked were the Co-op, Tesco, and Waitrose, in that order.

The upward trajectory of supermarket own brand Fair Trade is perhaps strongest in the United Kingdom, but is mirrored in other European countries. A recent survey of Fair Trade sales in 25 European countries found that 56,700 of the 78,900 "points of sale" were supermarkets (Krier 2005). The United Kingdom is certainly not unique in experiencing increasing concentration of food retailing in the hands of a few supermarkets – there are 12 other European countries in which the combined market share of the top three food retailers is over 50 percent (Grievink 2003). An increase in supermarket retailing is also taking place in many

Table 7.2 Number and type of Fair Trade certified products stocked by UK supermarkets (March 2005)

Supermarket	Fair Trade product categories [a]		Fair Trade product lines [b]	
	Number of categories stocked	% categories with own brand lines	Number of product lines stocked	% product lines that are own brand
Asda	6	50	38	16
Co-op	16	94	123	54
Morrisons	4	75	23	17
Safeway	6	17	29	10
Sainbury's	14	9	68	15
Somerfield	6	50	27	15
Tesco	16	4	107	22
Waitrose	11	9	73	16

Source: Fairtrade Foundation data (2005b).

Notes
a The Fairtrade foundation lists 22 categories of Fair Trade certified products (e.g. coffee, tea, fresh fruit and vegetables, etc.).
b Within each category there are a number of different product lines (e.g. coffee product lines include roast and ground, organic dark roast, instant freeze dried, etc.). Each type of fresh fruit was counted as a separate line.

other parts of the world, in part due to the global vision of leading supermarket chains in the North which now have stores in a growing number of countries and see various emerging markets (especially China) as key to future growth (Grievink 2003; Reardon et al. 2003; Vorley 2004). These combined trends indicate that events in the United Kingdom may be an important signpost for Fair Trade elsewhere.

The expansion of supermarket own brand Fair Trade points to an important anomaly in the FLO licensing system. Licensing is under the National Initiatives and in the United Kingdom only companies that actually put the FLO label on Fair Trade products are required by the Fairtrade Foundation to register as licensees. UK supermarkets outsource the job of labeling to packers or importers rather than do it themselves. This means that even though a Fair Trade product may carry the name of a UK supermarket next to the FLO logo, that supermarket does not necessarily have any direct connection or obligation to the Fairtrade Foundation, FLO, or any other Fair Trade organization.[3]

The increase in supermarket own brand Fair Trade reflects both the success of Fair Trade and the challenges it faces. On the one hand, it is an indication of the potential for Fair Trade to expand further within the mainstream, particularly given that supermarkets' share of retail markets is growing and an increasing amount of their sales are under their own brand labels. But this also represents challenges, as tensions between the commercial trajectory of supermarket sourcing and the social principles of Fair Trade come more sharply into focus.

Challenges of supermarket own brand Fair Trade

Growth and concentration in the supermarket sector has given supermarkets enormous power over producers and agents within their supply chains (Vorley 2004). This reflects a general shift from market based agrofood systems toward "buyer-led" global commodity chains, or production networks, in which lead firms exercise control over what is produced, how, when and at what price (Gereffi 1994; Ponte and Gibbon 2005). As detailed in Chapter 3, this trend is accompanied by a tendency to go beyond a simple price orientation to the tangible and intangible "qualities" of food, including the conditions under which it is produced and processed. Buyers increasingly govern these qualities using "standards" which codify complex information into generic criteria (Gereffi et al. 2005).

The global networks through which supermarkets source are not homogeneous and different forms of coordination may be used according to the type of product, its origin and availability. Gereffi and colleagues characterized five different types of coordination on a continuum from vertically integrated "hierarchical" chains through "modular," "relational," and "captive" coordination to arms length, "market" systems (Gereffi et al. 2005). The same supermarket may use market coordination for some suppliers or products, and much closer relational coordination for other suppliers or products. There are also differences between supermarkets based on corporate ethos. However, many of the large UK supermarkets exhibit a trend toward modular governance, whereby a relatively small number of first tier suppliers ("category managers") are given responsibility for ensuring year round supply of products according to strictly defined terms and standards, without any long-term commitment (Gereffi et al. 2005).

Fair Trade production networks have traditionally relied on relational forms of coordination, with transactions undertaken through regular direct contact and sustained by notions of solidarity and trust (Raynolds and Wilkinson Chapter 3; Smith and Barrientos 2005). They have involved civic actors in social movements and development NGOs who question the injustices of the global trading system and seek to develop an alternative by linking disadvantaged producers with sympathetic consumers in the North on more equitable terms. From the perspective of these Fair Trade actors, labeling provides a vehicle for accessing mainstream retail and food service outlets and thereby expanding the consumer base. In contrast, for supermarkets the FLO mark establishes the social credentials of the Fair Trade products on their shelves, having evolved through a process of negotiation among civic actors and achieved legitimacy in the eyes of consumers (Raynolds and Wilkinson Chapter 3; Renard 2002). Their interest in the underlying values embodied in the mark is likely to be secondary to their interest in what the mark can offer in terms of providing assurances to their customers. In the case of Fair Trade brands, such as Cafédirect or Traidcraft, this may not be problematic (although as Raynolds and Wilkinson point out in Chapter 3, dealing with supermarkets may put considerable pressure on Fair Trade companies to conform to the industrial/market conventions). However, for supermarket own brand Fair Trade goods there are likely to be inherent tensions between the underlying social values of Fair Trade and the commercial principles and practices which characterize supermarket production networks.

In particular, supermarket own brand Fair Trade potentially challenges the traditional Fair Trade model by introducing new types of coordination into Fair Trade production networks. It might not change the relational ties of Fair Trade organizations with producers, but it could affect the overall dynamic of networks and ATOs could be reduced to the role of category managers in modular value chains. Unless the ATO or producer retains some unique quality, supermarkets will be able to switch between Fair Trade suppliers on the same basis that they switch between all suppliers, that is, very often based on price. The fact that supermarkets are not required to be licensed gives them freedom to pursue a largely commercially oriented agenda.

On the other hand, the extension of supermarket own brand retailing into Fair Trade could challenge their conventional buying practices. Since supermarket retailing of Fair Trade goods rests on the social legitimacy that the FLO logo provides, they risk devaluing the Fair Trade "brand" if their commercial practices contravene the social principles underlying Fair Trade. They also risk public condemnation if they are exposed for exploiting Fair Trade for their own benefit. They may therefore have a vested interest in abiding by Fair Trade rules, even if they are not technically required to do so. In this scenario it could certainly be argued that Fair Trade is expanding its influence within the conventional agrofood system through supermarket own brand Fair Trade ranges, and thereby moving closer to its goal of changing the way all trade is practiced.

Chocolate and fruit – the dynamics of two supermarket own brand Fair Trade production networks

Our aim is to explore these issues through two UK supermarket own brand Fair Trade products, looking at the network dynamics and outcomes in each case. The first case represents a more traditional Fair Trade network in which cocoa is sourced from a small-scale producer cooperative in Ghana and processed into chocolate for retail by the Co-op. Relational forms of coordination predominate in this network. The second example is of fresh fruit sourced from farms in South Africa (categorized as "plantations" in the Fair Trade certification system) and sold under the own brand label of various supermarkets.[4] In this production network modular forms of supermarket governance tend to be used. Through these case studies we consider whether integration into supermarket own brand retailing is leading to the co-opting of Fair Trade by the conventional agrofood system or instead helping Fair Trade challenge and influence the principles, and practices of that system.

Cocoa from Ghana – a "relational" Fair Trade production network

Fair Trade chocolate made with cocoa from the Kuapa Kokoo cooperative in Ghana has long been a part of the ATO Fair Trade range. Kuapa Kokoo was established following partial deregulation of state controlled cocoa marketing in 1992–1993 when a visionary member of the State Marketing Board enlisted the support of a UK ATO and a Dutch NGO to form a cooperative of cocoa producers in two regions around Kumasi. With an initial membership of 2,000 farmers, Kuapa Kokoo rapidly increased in size to over 40,000 producers organized into 890 village societies covering all Ghana's cocoa growing regions. By 2002/2003 it exported 38,700 metric tons of high quality cocoa and had gained international recognition for both its commercial and social activities (Doherty and Meehan 2005; Tiffen et al. 2004).

The conventional international cocoa value chain is arms length, market based and fairly complex in comparison to many other products. Cocoa passes through a long trading network involving intermediaries, exporters, commodity exchanges, processors, and manufacturers (Bedford et al. 2001). In 1998 Kuapa Kokoo established an independent marketing arm in the United Kingdom by setting up The Day Chocolate Company in association with NGO partners.[5] This provided direct access to its main market, with Day selling Fair Trade labeled chocolate under the Divine and Dubble brand names. Kuapa owns 33 percent of the equity of Day, has two members on the Board, and received a 66 percent share in its profits as well as a social investment levy that is passed to the Kuapa Kokoo Farmers Trust (Mayoux 2001, n.d.). In comparison to conventional cocoa production networks, Kuapa/Day has a tighter supply chain with much greater transparency and direct relations between the key actors, reflecting a set of relational ties that have been established over a period of time based on regular face to face contact and interaction. These facilitate the coordination of a complex set of trading relationships, positioning Kuapa/Day as an established Fair Trade supplier within European markets. Support from NGOs and other actors has also provided Kuapa social legitimacy and a wider social terrain within its main export market.

Fair Trade guarantees a minimum price for cocoa of US$ 1,600 per metric ton and a social premium of US$ 150 per metric ton, as well as stable supply relations.[6] Fair Trade has always been a fairly small percentage of Kuapa Kokoo's total output (approximately 3 percent in 2002/2003), but the social premium and minimum price still contributed approximately US$ 1 million to Kuapa Kokoo's income between 1993 and 2001 (Tiffen et al. 2004). The rest of Kuapa's exports are into the conventional cocoa market, much of it purchased by large-scale chocolate manufacturers and multinationals.[7] However, the international network developed through engaging in Fair Trade has expanded its trading contacts and its exposure to external markets (Doherty and Meehan 2005; Ronchi 2002). The benefits derived are thus not solely from Fair Trade sales, but from the support and capacity building Fair Trade has provided for general commercial expansion.

The conversion of the Co-op's entire own brand line of milk chocolate bars to certified Fair Trade in 2002 marked a significant step in the mainstreaming of Fair Trade by supermarkets. For the first time, Fair Trade goods were not being sold as a high price niche product under a separate Fair Trade label, but within a supermarket's conventional own brand range and in competition with conventional brand name bars (such as Cadbury's and Nestlé). The Co-op's move into Fair Trade chocolate was galvanized in 2001, following extensive media coverage of child labor, forced labor, and severe exploitation of migrant workers in the production of cocoa in West Africa, particularly the Ivory Coast. It emerged that much of the chocolate sold in the North was likely to be made from cocoa from this area (Co-operative Group 2002; Save the Children Fund 2003). Given the complexity of the chocolate value chain, the Co-op could not guarantee that its chocolate did not come from illicit sources. In response, it decided to move to sole sourcing of certified Fair Trade cocoa for its own brand chocolate range. Initially it sought to work with large chocolate manufacturers to achieve this, but ultimately chose to work with the Day Chocolate Company and Kuapa Kokoo.[8] This had three advantages: first, Kuapa operated on the basis of cooperative principles providing synergy with the Co-op's own principles; second, Kuapa and Day provided direct linkages and transparency for the sourcing of the certified Fair Trade cocoa; third, Ghana is the source of some of the highest quality cocoa in the world, producing chocolate with a strong appeal to consumer tastes.

The Co-op developed strong relational ties with Day and actively supports Kuapa's social programs and commercial development. For example, it has promotional information on Kuapa's activities on its website and in its publications, and provides ongoing support to its community program. But despite having shared values, the Co-op still operates within a competitive supermarket environment. Negotiation of the commercial relationship between Day and the Co-op was subject to the requirements of operating within the tough commercial environment of the UK supermarket sector. While the Fair Trade strategy within the Co-op was led by those engaged in corporate social responsibility, the practical commercial details had to be agreed between Day and the buying staff responsible for the whole chocolate range. The latter's primary incentives are ensuring brand development, margins and delivery to customers.[9]

One of the first priorities was ensuring consistent, year round supply – running out of all Co-op chocolate on store shelves would be a commercial disaster. The Co-op developed a relationship with the German processor that had traditionally worked with Day, who committed to being able to handle the larger quantities required by the Co-op. Pricing was a potentially sensitive issue. The chocolate bars sold under the Co-op name had to be able to compete alongside conventional bars on its shelves. A potentially disadvantageous price differential was overcome by selling a slightly smaller bar at a more competitive price. The Co-op sold its snack size 45 gram Fair Trade milk chocolate bar at 39 pence (72 cents) against larger conventional bars of the same type which retailed at 41 pence (75 cents).[10] Although the Co-op committed to a long-term commercial relationship with Day, the supplier agreement signed was similar to that of any commercial supplier. The commitments made by the Co-op in terms of its engagement in the principles of Fair Trade for an entire own brand range were therefore tempered by the hard commercial reality they operated in.

The success of Co-op's strategy depended on the reaction of consumers. The figures quickly assured skeptics (including conventional chocolate companies that had distanced themselves from the Co-op's wholesale entry into Fair Trade), that expanding Fair Trade own brand was a potential "win–win" scenario. The Co-op Fair Trade chocolate was 15 to 20 percent more expensive, but its sales of chocolate increased by approximately 21 percent in 2003, despite an overall 1.1 percent decline in chocolate sales in the United Kingdom over the same period (Co-operative Group 2002; Doherty and Meehan 2005). The high quality of the cocoa supplied by Kuapa was deemed an important factor in this, as well as the allegiance of Co-op consumers.

The Co-op's order resulted in a 30 percent increase in Kuapa's Fair Trade sales, and contributed to an increase in Day's chocolate sales from £103,500 (US$ 181,125) in 1990 to £5.5 million (US$ 10.1 million) in 2004. This gives an indication of the potential impact of supermarket own brand Fair Trade. However, it is a specific case, where a producer cooperative is linked to a supermarket with cooperative roots through relational forms of coordination, based on shared principles – a scenario that could not necessarily be replicated elsewhere. In the next section, we explore a different model of supermarket own brand Fair Trade in which the commitment and relationships formed between supermarkets and producers are more tenuous.

Fresh fruit from South Africa – Fair Trade in a conventional own brand production network

Building on the success of Fair Trade bananas, other types of fresh fruit (mangos and pineapples) first went on sale in UK supermarkets in 2002. In 2003, a key new source of certified Fair Trade fruit became available from a "Black Economic Empowerment" initiative in South Africa, the Thandi project.[11] Thandi aims to support the empowerment of historically disadvantaged groups through giving them "equity share ownership" in farms producing fruit and wine for international markets. The fruit is marketed by Capespan, South Africa's largest fruit exporter, under the brand name Thandi. The Capespan Foundation, a charitable arm of the Capespan Group of Companies, provides a program of support for participating farms and has negotiated cost reductions with other actors in the South African end of the supply chain, including suppliers of packaging and transport. However, upon approaching supermarkets with the Thandi concept Capespan found that many (especially in the United Kingdom) were not interested in taking on another "ethical" brand, instead suggesting that FLO certification would be a more appropriate vehicle for marketing Thandi products.[12] Thandi farms sought accreditation from FLO and in 2003 their first Fair Trade certified apples and oranges entered UK supermarkets.

Fair Trade certification increased the marketability of Thandi fruit, but it also opened up the possibility for non-Thandi fruit to enter the market, FLO soon found itself overwhelmed by applications from South African farms seeking accreditation. What followed was a critical point in the history of Fair Trade, as described by Kruger and du Toit in Chapter 12, when producers themselves decided that FLO plantation criteria should be locally interpreted to require that workers have at least a 25 percent legally protected interest in the business. Most supermarkets are rationalizing their supply base in order to reduce transaction costs and have little interest in taking on new suppliers unless they can offer something different. If their customers show an interest in Fair Trade products they will respond to this by seeking Fair Trade sources, but it is more convenient and less costly for them if these come from their current supply base. The Fair Trade system does not prevent any company or individual from registering as a trader or licensee so long as they commit to abide by the Fair Trade trading standards and pay the appropriate fees. As a result, fruit importers and exporters are registering as Fair Trade traders in the belief that offering a Fair Trade line could give them an advantage over competitors in securing supermarket programs. Until the requirement for worker ownership was introduced, the same was true of South African producers, with FLO reportedly receiving around 350 applications from farms seeking accreditation by early 2004. This is hardly surprising given that, according to a key figure in the South African fruit industry, there are approximately 100,000 fruit farmers in the Southern hemisphere all trying to get into five supermarkets in the United Kingdom. In such a situation producers will jump at any opportunity to differentiate themselves from the pack. These commercial motivations to get involved in Fair Trade are a new development for

Fair Trade networks, which have traditionally been populated by actors motivated by sympathy for the plight of small producers. They have the potential to dramatically change how and by whom the majority of Fair Trade products are taken to market, and also which producers are selected as sources of Fair Trade.

By the 2004/2005 season South African Fair Trade certified fruit was being sourced from both Thandi and non-Thandi farms, principally by the Co-op, Tesco, and Waitrose. Much of it was traded by Capespan but not all was sold directly to supermarkets, as some supermarket buyers only wanted to work through their established category managers. At least one UK supermarket worked with the South African exporter that already supplied it to develop direct sources of Fair Trade. With a growing number of exporters and importers now involved, the South African Fair Trade value chain developed more of a network structure, and the close connections with the Thandi initiative began to diminish. In this sense the production network took on a more conventional structure, particularly at the UK end.

The similarities between conventional and Fair Trade production networks become more apparent when we look at the way supermarkets govern them. Most UK supermarkets exhibit a trend toward modular governance in which they pass the responsibility for supply chain management, product development, and consumer research to a small number of category managers, but reduce risk by avoiding relational ties with those suppliers (Gereffi et al. 2005). Although they may supply a particular supermarket for many years, category managers are given no long-term contracts or guarantees and therefore compete fiercely with their rivals to secure as many supermarket listings as possible. As for all their own brand products, supermarkets want to be assured that Fair Trade fruit meets their exacting standards for food safety in order to protect them from the risk of litigation. They also demand high and consistent quality, and reject any fruit that does not meet the grade, in order to reduce wastage costs. Meeting these standards is simply a condition of supply and while supermarkets dictate the standards, it is up to the category managers and others in the production network to ensure that they are met. This raises questions about the kind of producers that are able to participate in supermarket own brand Fair Trade, and who provides the support necessary to enable producers to reach the required standards.

Even more challenging for Fair Trade are the terms on which fresh fruit is purchased. According to the FLO trading standards for fresh fruit, long-term relationships should be established between buyers/importers and producers through the use of quarterly or seasonal sourcing plans, contracts outlining volumes and prices, and shipment orders specifying the Fair Trade volume per shipment. Fifty percent of the payment for the shipped fruit should be paid upon delivery, with the remainder paid after reception of documents. However, in the case of Fair Trade fruit sourced from South Africa, it has proven extremely difficult for traders to meet these criteria because of the "just in time" distribution systems used by supermarkets. While UK supermarkets do give suppliers seasonal programs outlining the volumes they anticipate purchasing of each type of fruit, often they do not stick to them as they base their purchases on day-to-day sales and current trends in consumption. This is no different for Fair Trade lines. For example, in one case a Fair Trade producer was expecting to sell to five UK supermarkets based on programs that had been secured during a preseason marketing trip. The fruit was packed and shipped according to the volumes outlined in the programs, which involved additional costs to keep the Fair Trade fruit segregated from conventional fruit. Upon arrival in the United Kingdom, only two of the five supermarkets honored their programs and purchased the fruit, leaving the trader with no choice but to off load the rest on conventional markets. Furthermore, one supermarket did not take the Fair Trade fruit at the time that they said they would, instead waiting four weeks before taking a lower than expected quantity. In the meantime the quality of the fruit diminished which resulted in a "fine" for poor quality, reducing the overall price received per fruit shipped.

Similar problems have been reported by other producers, including super-markets switching from one importer, and therefore producer, to another after fruit has been shipped. Since Fair Trade fruit has to be packed separately to ensure traceability through the system, it then has to be repacked in order to sell it to other markets, thereby incurring costs. Not only this, producers budget and plan based on expected sales to the Fair Trade market. FLO even asks producers to draw up detailed plans for spending the social premium they anticipate earning from Fair Trade sales, including consulting with workers and local communities about how they want the money to be spent. These processes raise expectations among the intended beneficiaries of Fair Trade (equity share producers, workers, and community members) which, if the sales do not end up being realized, can create skepticism and disillusionment among them. This can do lasting damage to the process of empowerment that Fair Trade is supposed to support.

Some Fair Trade producers in South Africa are now questioning whether it is worth participating in Fair Trade if supermarkets are willing to commit to taking the volumes that they program. While Fair Trade does guarantee them a minimum price, and has in some cases fetched more than double the market price, there are considerable extra costs involved in terms of logistics and administration. With the consolidation of supermarkets in most Northern markets, being listed by a supermarket becomes the primary aim for producers exporting to the North. Price is used as the main mechanism for achieving that in the fresh fruit sector. Because it's perishable, price reductions and promotions are used to respond dynamically to market conditions and product quality. Some producers therefore feel that the Fair Trade minimum price is actually counterproductive, limiting the extent to which Fair Trade can move beyond a high value niche to a genuinely mainstream item. With the added costs of certification and product segregation, the benefits of participating in Fair Trade may therefore be minimal. Some producers are even starting to see Fair Trade as just another certification that they need to acquire in order to supply UK supermarkets.

It should be emphasized that this does not mean South African workers do not benefit from Fair Trade, but if the trading standards are not adhered to, the processes by which those benefits come about will become more random and less sustainable, and may be lost altogether if the owners of farms remove their support or supermarkets switch their supply source. This raises questions about the long-term development gains from Fair Trade in fresh fruit.

Insights from chocolate and fruit for the future of Fair Trade

The examples of chocolate and fruit illustrate how the mainstreaming of Fair Trade in supermarket own brand ranges has played out within two different products. In both cases the final product carries the same FLO logo, but there is a clear contrast in the processes through which it arrives on supermarket shelves and the outcomes for those that Fair Trade seeks to support. In this section, we identify key features of the two production networks and explore how these may provide some insights for the future development of Fair Trade.

One feature important for determining outcomes is the type of product and its market position. Cocoa is a nonperishable product that can be stored for fairly lengthy periods until a suitable market is found. Once processed into chocolate, it is sold under separate Fair Trade brands as well as under supermarket private labels. This gives it an independent route into the market and the potential for sustaining at least a proportion of Fair Trade sales even if an individual supermarket drops it as an own brand line. The level of commitment of 100 percent Fair Trade companies like Day Chocolate is unquestionable, especially given producer co-ownership, and some might argue that the most risk-free and successful way to mainstream is through Fair Trade brands such as Divine. However, this opportunity does not exist with fruit in the United Kingdom. Fruit is highly perishable and needs to move quickly from field to plate. There are few retail options outside the supermarket sector and most supermarkets are not interested in branded fruit. This leaves other actors in the network little room for negotiation, and in a fierce competition with each other for market access. Although Fair Trade certification can act as a means for product differentiation and help in getting access to supermarket shelves, once the number of FLO traders and producers goes beyond a minimal level this competitive advantage is lost, given there are now so few supermarket chains to sell to.

The type of coordination employed by supermarkets is another key feature affecting outcomes. In the chocolate case relational forms of coordination predominate at all levels, with strong ties between the Co-op, Day Chocolate Company, and Kuapa Kokoo. In committing to an ongoing trading relationship based on dialog and proactive support, the Co-op is contributing to the continued evolution and success of Kuapa as a business and as a social organization. While it requires Kuapa and others in the production network to meet the same high standards as any other own brand supplier, it works closely with them to identify problems and find solutions. This has helped to resolve tensions between the commercial principles underlying supermarket retailing and the social objectives of Fair Trade. In contrast, the production networks for own brand Fair Trade fruit from South Africa involve more conventional forms of governance by UK supermarkets. Supermarkets generally treat Fair Trade fruit just as they would any other line, and employ all the same processes for pushing cost and risk onto other actors in the network. Although traders and producers may exhibit relational forms of coordination (such as between Capespan and Thandi producers), it can be very difficult for them to operate according to Fair Trade principles if supermarkets are not. For example, there is an explicit tension between the commercial practice of "just in time" ordering systems and the Fair Trade principles of advance purchasing and long-term supply relations. As supermarkets are unwilling to commit upfront to taking a certain volume of Fair Trade fruit, traders and producers have to bear the costs when fruit is shipped as Fair Trade but sold as conventional. A critical factor is that supermarkets are not required to become licensees, and therefore are not themselves bound by FLO trading standards. But exacerbating the problem is their use of modular governance, in which their requirements are codified into standards and first-tier suppliers are responsible for ensuring those standards are met. In this situation they can distance themselves from any tensions between commercial imperatives and Fair Trade principles.

A third point of difference between the two production networks is their structure and the degree to which they involve civic actors focused on the interests of producers. In the case of chocolate the network is fairly tight, having just one cocoa supplier (Kuapa Kokoo) and a single marketing company which is part owned by producers. The supermarket involved is cooperatively owned and its customer base has expressed concern about producers in developing countries. NGOs have been involved in the network from the start and play a central role in strategic decisions. This contrasts with the production network for fruit which is almost entirely populated by commercial actors and, as more farms and traders are certified/registered by FLO, is increasingly loose. This illustrates a subtle shift that has taken place in Fair Trade from being driven exclusively by those focused on development objectives and social justice, to include those that see it as a commercial opportunity. Ironically this shift is facilitated by the same vehicle that the Fair Trade movement has used so successfully to bring Fair Trade into the mainstream – the FLO standards. When the standards were introduced, there was almost an assumption that those who registered to use them would intrinsically support and uphold the Fair Trade principles of social justice that they enshrined. In the early days monitoring against the standards was fairly ad hoc, with trust playing an important role in ensuring the Fair Trade brand was not abused. As Fair Trade grew and more actors entered the system, the Fair Trade movement realized that a more formal monitoring system was needed and FLO processes were tightened. This was important to ensure the continued credibility of the Fair Trade mark, but increased reliance on standardization and certification has reduced the need for close relations between network actors.

While fruit may be a particularly problematic Fair Trade product, there is mounting anecdotal evidence (across both own brand and branded product sectors) of supermarkets switching between Fair Trade suppliers on the basis of price, asking suppliers for price reductions in return for continued listing, and pushing for sources of Fair Trade from among suppliers, many of which are large farms or plantations. There are also reports of Fair Trade traders undercutting established

Fair Trade suppliers, or cutting them out of the chain, in a bid for supermarket listings. While the Fair Trade standards may not be breached in any of these cases, it contrasts with the definition of Fair Trade as a "trading partnership based on dialogue, transparency and respect" and reduces possibilities for stable relationships with producers. Fair Trade producers may be guaranteed a minimum price and social premium for any sales they do achieve on the Fair Trade market, but the long-term perspective important for achieving sustainable development objectives may be absent. Creating and sustaining solidarity rather than competition among actors in Fair Trade networks is also more challenging, thereby reducing opportunities for using their collective power to bring about social change.

The dynamics described earlier suggest that it may be increasingly difficult for traders with a social mission (especially ATOs) and producers with low capacity to participate in Fair Trade if supermarket own brand Fair Trade continues on its current trajectory. ATOs' commercial objectives are framed within the broader social goals of Fair Trade. They typically invest considerable resources in building up Fair Trade producers' capacity to trade and may give preference to producer organizations that face particular challenges, such as those that are geographically or socially isolated (e.g. indigenous groups). While this may incur extra costs, this is seen as part and parcel of achieving their goals. In contrast, conventional trading companies operate principally from the standpoint of commercial objectives. Although they may also have social goals, due to the interests of individuals within the company or a broader recognition of their responsibility to society, they are usually incorporated into an existing commercial framework. Therefore they are less likely to choose to work with producers that require substantial support or are more costly to trade with. FLO standards contain nothing that requires registered traders or licensees to support or favor weaker producer groups. The fact that producers need to meet FLO standards, including paying for certification, could actually favor stronger producers, including plantations over small-scale producers. Not only may this disadvantage more marginalized producers, it has the potential to squeeze ATOs that support them out of the Fair Trade market, as they may be unable to compete with the lower costs of conventional traders working with strong producer groups or plantations.

Parallels can be drawn between the situation of ATOs and that of supermarkets like the Co-op that are going the extra mile to embrace Fair Trade. Both are operating in competitive commercial environments, where levels of commitment to Fair Trade (including resources that are channeled to it) do not necessarily give you an advantage in the market, because of the way the Fair Trade labeling system operates. Both may be pushed out by those that are able to take advantage of economies of scale to reduce their costs. This risk has been magnified by the recent decision of FLO Cert to work toward ISO 65 (an international standard for bodies operating product certification services). Aimed at ensuring consistency and equivalency in FLO's accreditation systems, this move is controversial because ISO 65 principles of nondiscrimination mean that FLO cannot distinguish between one producer and another, or one trader and another. This potentially opens the gate for any conventional company to enter Fair Trade, regardless of their background and motivations.

Despite some of these tensions, there are reasons for cautious optimism arising out of the experience with own brand Fair Trade fruit. There is evidence of closer relationships being developed between commercial actors, with some traders talking about going the extra mile to make Fair Trade work and "being in this together" with Fair Trade producers. Clearly there are solid commercial reasons for this, as well as local drivers in the South African context of government targets for Black Economic Empowerment, but the result is that this may create the kinds of long-term relationships necessary for development outcomes to be achieved. Furthermore, there is a growing network of Fair Trade producers and support organizations (as described in Chapter 12) which will hopefully serve to strengthen solidarity in production networks and create space for joint, mutually beneficial action. This may offset, or at least mitigate, potential negative impacts arising from competition for market access, as well as provide some degree of counterbalance to the dominant power of supermarkets.

In both chocolate and fruit, Fair Trade has also introduced new links between the spheres of production and market through FLO and in the UK the Fairtrade Foundation. Direct contact between supermarket buyers and Fair Trade producers is rare. Some supermarkets actively resist relationships being developed between supermarket buyers and producers by rotating staff frequently between product sectors, which makes it difficult to take a process approach in line with the development objectives of Fair Trade producers. To date the Fairtrade Foundation's focus with supermarkets has been on growing the market, particularly through new product development, but in the process relationships are being formed. The Fairtrade Foundation has even created a new Account Manager position within its ranks, with the specific objective of maintaining relationships with supermarkets. This presents opportunities for raising awareness of the challenges faced by producers and the critical role of stable supply relationships for achieving development objectives. Since it is difficult for producers or traders to raise complaints directly with their clients, for risk of losing business, this could be an important role of Fair Trade in the future.

Finally, it should also be emphasized that the Fair Trade movement still retains some control over how the market develops. For example, FLO limits the number of producers that are certified so that registered producers can be guaranteed a market, although the difficulty lies in predicting just how big the market is, and so far the estimations seem to have been somewhat wide of the mark. The Fairtrade Foundation tries to ensure that supermarket own brand lines will grow the market rather than just shift Fair Trade purchases from one segment (branded Fair Trade) to another (own brand). It also requires supermarkets to grow their branded Fair Trade range prior to licensing own brand lines. There is considerable consumer loyalty to Fair Trade brands and so it is possible that growth in own brands will be limited to areas where there aren't Fair Trade brand alternatives, such as fruit.

Concluding remarks

The question this chapter set out to address was whether the integration of Fair Trade into supermarket own brand ranges is leading to cooptation by the same agrofood system it was set up to oppose, or whether instead it has provided a route for advancing social justice within the commercial mainstream. The answer, perhaps predictably, is that this is a complex issue with no single outcome. Drawing on analysis of two global production networks, we found that mainstreaming using the FLO standards may change the dynamics of Fair Trade at all levels from retailer to trader and producer. Supermarkets have contributed to the rapid growth of Fair Trade in the United Kingdom, and in some cases are playing an important role in supporting producers in developing countries, but they are also driving a shift from producer- to consumer-led Fair Trade. Supermarkets are not themselves required under current FLO rules to be licensed and there may be inherent tensions between their trading practices and the social principles of Fair Trade. As they expand their Fair Trade sourcing for commercial motives there is a risk that competition may drive out traders with the most affinity to Fair Trade principles, and that producers able to meet their exacting standards have a comparative advantage over the more disadvantaged producers Fair Trade originally set out to support. However, supermarket own brand Fair Trade may also facilitate new relational ties in conventional production networks and allow civic actors to influence dominant commercial actors in the global food system. It remains to be seen which of these dynamics has most impact in the coming years as Fair Trade continues to be mainstreamed.

Notes

1 The case study is based on research undertaken by the authors during 2004 and 2005, involving in-depth interviews with retailers, traders, producers, Fair Trade organizations, and other key informants in the UK, Germany, Ghana, and South Africa. The research was funded by the Leverhulme Foundation and the Ford Foundation. The views presented in this chapter are those of the authors alone.
2 The Co-op's aims are: "to deliver a quality service to customers and to contribute to the well-being and enrichment of society through good operating practices and by reinvesting our profits in our business and in the communities we serve" (Co-operative Group 2005).
3 At the time of writing it was up to the discretion of individual National Initiatives whether they allowed retailers to include the Fair Trade logo on their labels without registering as a licensee, with the Fairtrade Foundation in the United Kingdom permitting this while some other National Initiatives apparently do not.
4 We classify fresh fruit as own brand when it is sold in packaging with a label showing the supermarket's name.
5 Partners in Day Chocolate include Kuapa Kokoo, Twin, Body Shop, Christian Aid, and Comic Relief. Support was also received from the UK Department for International Development (Doherty and Meehan 2005).
6 In 2004 the world market price for cocoa was US$ 1,500 per metric ton, having recorded a 27-year low in November 2000 of US$ 714 per metric ton (Doherty and Meehan 2005).

7 Cocoa is also used as an ingredient in cosmetics and Kuapa has long sold cocoa to the Body Shop, which has been an important supporter through its Community Trade program, but not as certified Fair Trade.

8 The chocolate sector is dominated by four large multinationals (Nestlé, Cadbury and Mars/Masterfoods alone had a combined market share of 80 percent by value in 2002), and most chocolate production takes place under their control in developed countries (Doherty and Meehan 2005).

9 In recent years the key performance indicators for buying staff have included responsibility for ensuring buying practices conform with the Co-op's "responsible retailing" commitments.

10 This was not possible in the case of own brand coffee, which came later, because of the difficulty of varying the quantity contained in a standard jar. For coffee the Co-op had to absorb the price differential to ensure its Fair Trade own brand range was competitive with conventional brands.

11 The Thandi project is described in more detail in Chapter 12.

12 This is in line with the general trend in UK supermarkets to rationalize their product lines.

References

Barrientos, S. and Kritzinger, A. (2004) "Squaring the circle: global production and the informalization of work in South African fruit exports," *Journal of International Development*, 16: 81–92.

Bedford, A., Blowfield, M., Burnett, D., and Greenhalgh, P. (2001) *Value Chains: Lessons from the Kenya Tea and Indonesia Cocoa Sectors*, London: Resource Centre for Social Dimensions of Business Practice.

Co-operative Group. (2002) *Chocolate: A Campaign for Fairtrade Chocolate and an End to Exploitation*, Manchester: Co-operative Group.

—— (2005) *Why We Support Fair Trade*, Manchester: Co-operative Group, Online. Available at: www.co-opfairtrade.co.uk/pages/why2.asp (accessed June 16, 2006).

Doherty, B. and Meehan, J. (2005) *Competing on Social Resources: The Case of Day Chocolate Company in the UK Confectionary Sector*, Liverpool: John Moores University.

Dolan, C. and Humphrey, J. (2004) "Changing governance patterns in the trade in fresh vegetables between Africa and the United Kingdom," *Environment and Planning*, 36: 491–509.

Fairtrade Foundation. (2005) *Awareness of the Fairtrade Mark Rockets to 50%*, London: Fairtrade Foundation, Online. Available at: www.fairtrade.org.uk/pr270505.htm (accessed June 16, 2006).

—— (2006a) *Chronology of Fairtrade in the UK*, London: Fairtrade Foundation, Online. Available at: www.fairtrade.org.uk/about_chronology.htm (accessed June 16, 2006).

—— (2006b) *Sales of Fairtrade Products in the UK*, London: Fairtrade Foundation, Online. Available at: www.fairtrade.org.uk/about_sales.htm (accessed June 16, 2006).

FLO (Fairtrade Labelling Organizations International). (2006) *FLO Fresh Fruit Markets: Offer and Demand*, Online. Available at: www.fairtrade.net/sites/products/freshfruit/markets.html (accessed June 16, 2006).

Freshinfo. (2003) *Freshinfo News Bulletin*, July 7, 2003, Online. Available under subscription only.

Gereffi, G. (1994) "Capitalism, development and global commodity chains," in L. Sklair (ed.) *Capitalism and Development*, London: Routledge.

Gereffi, G., Humphrey, J., and Sturgeon, T. (2005) "The governance of global value chains," *Review of International Political Economy*, 12: 78–104.

Grievink, J. (2003) *The Changing Face of the Global Food Industry*, paper presented at OECD Conference on Changing Dimensions of the Food Economy, The Hague, February 2003.

Humphreys, L. (2000) *Which Way to Market? Exploring Opportunities for Marginalized Producers in Developing Countries to Supply Mainstream Commercial Companies in the UK*, London: Traidcraft Policy Unit.

Krier, J.M. (2005) *Fair Trade in Europe 2005: Facts and Figures on Fair Trade in 25 European Countries*, Brussels: Fair Trade Advocacy Office.

Mayoux, L. (2001) *Impact Assessment of Fair Trade and Ethical Enterprise Development*, Online. Available at: www.enterprise-impact.org.uk (accessed November 12, 2005).

—— (n.d.) *Case Study: Kuapa Kokoo, Ghana*, London: TWIN.

Nicholls, A. and Opal, C. (2005) *Fair Trade: Market-Driven Ethical Consumption*, London: Sage.

Ponte, S. and Gibbon, P. (2005) "Quality, standards, conventions and the governance of global value chains," *Economy and Society*, 34: 1–31.

Reardon, T., Timmer, C.P., Barrett, C.B., and Berdegue, J. (2003) "The rise of supermarkets in Africa, Asia, and Latin America," *American Journal of Agricultural Economics*, 85: 1140–1146.

Renard, M.C. (2002) "Fair trade: quality, market and conventions," *Journal of Rural Studies*, 19: 87–96.

Ronchi, L. (2002) *Monitoring Impact of Fairtrade Initiatives: A Case Study of Kuapa Kokoo and the Day Chocolate Company*, London: TWIN.

Save the Children Fund. (2003) *Children (Still) in the Chocolate Trade, the Buying, Selling and Toiling of West African Child Workers in the Multi-Billion Dollar Industry*, Canada, Save the Children Fund.

Smith, S. and Barrientos, S. (2005) "Fair trade and ethical trade: are there moves towards convergence?," *Sustainable Development*, 13: 190–198.

Tallontire, A. and Vorley, B. (2005) *Achieving Fairness in Trading Between Supermarkets and Their Agrifood Supply Chains*, London: UK Food Group, Online. Available at: www.agribusinesscenter.org/docs/Marketplace_6.pdf (accessed June 16, 2006).

Taylor Nelson Sofres. (2005) *Market Share of the Leading Supermarkets in the UK, TNS Superpanel 3rd Quarter 2005*, UK: Taylor Nelson Sofres, Online. Available at: superpanel.tns-global.com/ (accessed November 12, 2005).

Tesco. (2006) *Tesco Corporate Responsibility Review 2005*, UK: Tesco Plc., Online. Available at: www.tesco.com/csr/p/p2.html (accessed June 16, 2006).

Tiffen, P., MacDonald, J., Maamah, H., and Osei-Opare, F. (2004) "From tree-minders to global players: cocoa farmers in Ghana," in M. Carr (ed.) *Chains of Fortune: Linking Women Producers and Workers with Global Markets*, London: Commonwealth Secretariat.

Vorley, B. (2004) *Food Inc. Corporate Concentration from Farm to Consumer*, London: UK Food Group.

Part III

Fair Trade in the Global South

8 Southern social movements and Fair Trade

John Wilkinson and Gilberto Mascarenhas

Introduction

The Fair Trade movement has grown rapidly in the past ten years. Yet despite its success, the movement faces fundamental challenges if it is to become a real alternative for sustainable development in the South. The challenges arise from the demands of Southern actors regarding the movement's adaptation to specific national contexts and the goals of sustainable local development (Cotera and Ortiz 2004). Key Southern demands revolve around the development of Southern Fair Trade markets, greater participation in Northern markets, and adaptations of Fairtrade Labelling Organizations International (FLO) policies in the multilateral trade context (Asia Fair Trade 2005; Declaración 2005). Whether these demands lead to a reshaping of Fair Trade and strengthening of its global legitimacy or to a fragmentation of the movement and greater divisions between Northern and Southern conceptions of Fair Trade is as yet unclear (Elsen 2005; Wills 2005).

In this chapter, we outline the principal characteristics of the Fair Trade movement in the Southern context, the role of Southern actors in building networks and alternative markets, and Southern priorities for the movement. Subsequent chapters in this section provide more detailed analyses of particular products and regions, focusing on case studies from Mexico, Brazil, Peru/Bolivia, and South Africa. The Mexico and South Africa chapters (Chapters 9 and 12) complement each other in exploring the principal tensions in the Fair Trade movement around the certification of plantations. South Africa, a major growth pole for Fair Trade, has recast the issue of plantation registration in the context of this country's Black Economic Empowerment (BEE) policies and in ongoing negotiations over FLO's plantation policies. Mexican small farmer cooperatives are confronting the dilemmas of shifting Fair Trade market trends as new labels compete with FLO and the registration of new mainstream actors appears to threaten the gains of these traditional suppliers. Chapter 10 focuses on Brazil, highlighting the emerging tensions within Fair Trade between the global movement and domestic strategies, particularly in the development of national Fair Trade labels in large middle-income developing countries. Chapter 11 explores the implications of Fair Trade's expansion into new products, in this case the transformation of an Andean basic foodstuff, quinoa, into a highly valued health food for Northern markets.

To structure our understanding of the Southern movement, we first analyze the activities of the key Fair Trade labeling organizations (FLO affiliates) and Alternative Trade Organizations (ATOs) (International Fair Trade Association (IFAT) affiliates), across producer regions and the role of regional actors in promoting convergences within the global South. We then identify a set of emerging issues central to developing a Southern Fair Trade agenda. We conclude with a brief discussion of the challenges and opportunities a Southern agenda opens up for the global movement. Our discussion relies heavily on analyses of the Latin American experience since this has been central to the consolidation of Fair Trade and to chapters which comprise this section. Where possible we draw on considerations from Africa and Asia.

Fair Trade in the South

The role of Northern actors

The IFAT and FLOs have been key actors in the development of North/South Fair Trade. As outlined in Chapter 2, FLO and IFAT represent two distinct branches of the Fair Trade movement. IFAT and its members have had the longest presence in Southern countries, mainly supporting handicraft activities (IFAT 2005a). Labeling initiatives have over the past 15 years incorporated a range of products and regions under the aegis of FLO. Despite their convergent interests and movement ties in the North, there has been little coordination between the two organizations in developing common strategies in the Global South.

We sketch first the activities of FLO across the Global South. The 433 producer organizations registered with FLO supply 126,000 tons of labeled commodities, worth US$ 1.4 billion (FLO 2006). As noted in Chapter 2, Latin America is home to the majority of FLO registered groups and generates the vast majority of labeled products (77 percent of total value; 76 percent of the volume). Africa is the next most important producer region, with 20 percent of FLO certified groups generating 19 percent of the value and 22 percent of the volume of labeled products. Asia has 17 percent of FLO registered producer organizations, accounting for 2 percent of the value and 3 percent of the value of Fair Trade labeled products (see Tables 2.6 and 2.7).

The centrality of Latin America in certified Fair Trade production is due to the historical importance of coffee and more recently bananas, orange juice, and other items. Quinoa, a traditional grain of the Andean peasantry, has recently been certified by FLO as will be discussed in Chapter 11. In Africa, cocoa and tea have been the major FLO certified products, but as demonstrated in Chapter 12 the rapid growth of Fair Trade in this region is based in large measure on the introduction of certified fruits, juices, and wine, particularly in South Africa. In Asia certified Fair Trade production revolves around the early FLO commodity tea.

FLO is expanding the number of certified organizations, commodity areas, and sales. Over the past five years, FLO has developed standards for new products in line with the evolution of both Northern demand and Southern pressure.

Certification is now available for 18 different products. FLO's growth is clearly evident in Latin America with certified volumes increasing from 83 to 110 million tons between 2003 and 2004 (Sacca and Penchévere 2005). The number of Latin American organizations certified by FLO rose from 185 in 2000 to 399 in 2005 (FLO 2005b). There are currently 22 certified Fair Trade products exported from Latin America and although the majority of groups produce coffee or bananas, 49 producer groups export new items like wine, fresh fruits, and nuts. Mexico maintains its regional dominance, with 16 percent of producer organizations, followed by Colombia and Peru (see Chapter 2).

Rising sales in mainstream markets has altered the character of importers and sourcing arrangements. The number of FLO affiliated commodity traders has increased even faster than the number of producer organizations, with many new traders oriented toward the conventional retail sector. Southern producers are finding themselves more dependent on the demands of Northern supermarkets, where standardized quality and adjustments to perceived consumer expectations are the rule. These changes are leading to the rise of two new expectations in the sourcing of Fair Trade certified products.

First Fair Trade products are increasingly expected to receive dual Fair Trade/ organic certification. In cocoa, the percent of FLO certified goods also certified organic rose from 78 to 96 percent between 2001 and 2002 (FLO 2005c). About half of Fair Trade bananas are also now organic (see Chapter 5). In coffee, organic certification is even more prevalent. In Mexico, almost all Fair Trade certified coffee for domestic and international markets is now organic (see Chapter 9). The growth of dual certified coffee is also clear in Brazil, Peru, and other Latin American countries. The expansion of dual certification has been fueled by the dictates of Fair Trade buyers, the decline in chemical input use during the recent economic crisis, and the influence of organic and agroecological movements. FLO predicts that the greatest future demand for Fair Trade will be for items also certified as organic (FLO 2005c).

The second major change in the sourcing arrangements of Fair Trade certified items is the increasing prioritization of product quality and scale of supply. This emphasis has fueled the certification of plantations and the preferential selection of more market-oriented small farmer organizations (Ferreira 2003; Tallontire 2001). These changes are evident for example in items like orange juice that demand large continuous supplies and selective quality standards. As Chapter 10 demonstrates, in this commodity importer demands have limited the partici-pation of some producers and favored commercially oriented small farmers and plantations in Brazil able to provide the required product homogeneity and special blends.

Reviewing the activities of IFAT across the Global South, we find that this organization remains more closely linked to Fair Trade's traditional beneficiaries than FLO. As outlined in Chapter 2, IFAT works with organizations of artisans and small producers of handicraft and food items primarily in Asia. In 2000, Asian groups represented 55 percent of IFAT producer membership and 66 percent of its sales (Vizcarra 2002). As IFAT membership increases, African participation appears to be rising the most rapidly, balancing out Asia's historical dominance. The number of Latin American producer affiliates is declining somewhat. In 2004, 47 percent of IFAT's 167 producer organizations were located in Asia, 32 percent in Africa, and 20 percent in Latin America (IFAT 2005b).

IFAT reflects the agendas of producers and aligned movements in the Global South. There are clear complementarities between IFAT and Southern movements focused on the solidarity economy, family farming, counterglobalization, ethical and solidarity consumption, and agroecology. To become more attuned to these diverse movements, IFAT has recently founded a set of regional and national forums, including the African Fair Trade Forum (discussed in Chapter 12), the Kenya Federation for Alternative Trade, and the Latin American and Caribbean Coordination of Fair Trade Small Producers (CLAC) based in Ecuador (Kocken 2003; Willis 2005).

IFAT's biannual conferences have stimulated exchanges on the future directions of the Fair Trade movement from a Southern perspective. IFAT continues to uphold most of the original Fair Trade principles, but expanding markets for Southern products through its traditional outlets represents a serious challenge. Since food markets have grown more quickly in recent years than handicrafts, IFAT producer organizations are seeking to move into the food sector (Elsen 2005).

While maintaining its focus on disadvantaged Southern producers, IFAT has modified its market activities along some of the lines already pursued by FLO, adopting a higher degree of professionalism in production and retailing, improvements in product quality, and other measures to fuel market growth. IFAT has worked to build capacity and empower small producers to cope with increasing competition in Northern markets and has also sought to create new markets in countries such as Brazil, Russia, China, and India through domestic and South/South Fair Trade (Wills 2005).

Southern convergent initiatives

The Northern Fair Trade movement has become more flexible in response to new constituent and market demands. The key challenge is perceived to be the need to broaden producers' market access while preserving the movement's principles of solidarity and social values. A further challenge, and opportunity, involves the possibilities of joining forces with new types of Southern actors (such as social movements, alternative networks, governments, and enterprises), to bolster Southern Fair Trade markets. To the extent that Fair Trade is seen as a vehicle of sustainable development, its representatives tend to become increasingly associated with other Southern actors (Bisaillon et al. 2005). Given the specific characteristics of Southern markets – limited producer power, low consumer income, and the lack of traditional Fair Trade initiatives – governments, social movements, and enterprises are all central to the building of alternative production/consumption networks.

A number of initiatives across the Global South forge relationships between producers and consumers, exhibiting a "close kinship to what is conventionally understood as Fair Trade" (Jaffee et al. 2004: 170). In some cases different traditions have made collaboration difficult. For example in India, there has often been strong opposition to international movements, yet this is changing and the potential for interaction between Fair Trade and Indian movements is rising. In South Africa, national movements for empowering black farm workers are negotiating the social criteria for FLO certification of plantations (see Chapter 12). In Latin America, strong ties are emerging between national Fair Trade proposals and the solidarity economy movement, paralleling the convergence between IFAT and the Northern solidarity economy movement, particularly in France and Canada.

Collaboration between these different social movements and initiatives, despite their varied interests, organizations, and objectives, offers important opportunities for the consolidation of strategic alliances (Hassanein 2003: 82). There are considerable potential synergies between these movements and Fair Trade, facilitating the collaborative construction of Southern initiatives for fairer markets and sustainable development (Low and Davenport 2005; Medina 2004; Ortiz 2002; Relacc 2002). The main social movements emerging in the South with the potential to both influence and benefit from Fair Trade are those engaged in: the solidarity economy, community trade, family farming, agroecology and organic agriculture, and ethical and responsible consumption (see Table 8.1).

The solidarity economy movement emphasizes market participation, the development of solidarity-based production networks, and involvement in national and global policy initiatives supporting disadvantaged producers, workers, and consumers, particularly in the informal sector. Organizations and initiatives linked to this movement are involved in networks throughout Latin America (Encuentro 2005a). Internationally, the movement is promoted by the RIPESS (Intercontinental Network for the Promotion of the Social and Solidary Economy) which brings together solidarity economy groups focused on poverty alleviation in the North and South.

As previously noted there is significant overlap between organic and Fair Trade certification and there is also important overlap between the two movements. Organic production for domestic and international markets is flourishing across the Global South (Fonseca 2005). Domestic and regional organic certification systems (such as Certimex in Mexico, and Ecovida in Brazil) have been established to limit certification costs and increase local participation. The potential synergies between organic and Fair Trade initiatives are being explored in other regions of the Global South.

There are new synergistic opportunities for Fair Trade related to the growth of ethical trade and corporate social responsibility in the Global South (see for example the supermarket initiatives in Brazil in Chapter 10). Corporate social responsibility is, as Bisaillon et al. (2005) point out, central to the ethical trade movement due to their shared social and environmental objectives. Fair Trade and ethical trade share numerous common objectives and increasingly "producers are

Table 8.1 Southern social movements and initiatives and their potential linkages with the Fair Trade movement

Social movement initiatives and public policies	Main convergencies with Fair Trade
Solidarity economy	Popular cooperatives (networks of production and consumption), democratic participation, inclusion of disadvantaged people (small producers, artisans, and consumers), alternative micro-finances, social, money, gender, and child issues
Family farming	Empowering of small farmers, policies of food safety and sovereignty, local markets, social appeal, low use of chemicals, social justification for Community Supported Agriculture (CSA)
Organic agriculture	Environmentally driven production, health foods, and certification
Agroecology	Social and environmental concerns with production, direct linkages between producers and consumers, local markets, CSA initiatives, and alternative systems of certification
Community trade	CSA, farm markets, and alternative outlets
Religious initiatives	Capacity building, group organization, alternative market systems, human rights, and land reform
Responsible consumption	Ethical, solidarity, sustainable and responsible consumption, consumer awareness, inclusion of disadvantaged consumers
Ethical trade	Improving working conditions, limitation of child work, and labor rights
SMEs	Capacity building, market driveness, local development, and job creation
CSR	Alternative procurement programs, and market access
Other movements	Gandhian movement (India), Co-operatives, Work Unions, and Landless
State	Market regulation, support policies for disadvantaged people, multilateral negotiations

Source: Authors' research 2005/2006.

now applying simultaneously both ethical and Fair Trade standards" (Smith and Barrientos 2005: 195). As these initiatives expand across the South we would expect to see mounting convergences with Fair Trade.

The need for rethinking the role of the State has been taken up by several social movements in the South, focusing particularly on the need for government support for the sustainable development of small-scale operations whether in farming or other activities (Declaración 2005; Encuentro 2005c; Ortiz 2002). In addition, there is increasing pressure from social movements for greater participation of the State, either in the context of promoting policies supporting small-scale production in domestic markets or in the articulation of South/South market cooperation (Bisaillon et al. 2005; Roca 2004).

A Southern agenda

Initiatives in the Global South have shaped demands for the adaptation of the Fair Trade movement to Southern needs. The Southern agenda is built around four interrelated domains: (1) the need for greater participation in Northern markets by existing and new small producer organizations; (2) the need for changes and adaptations in FLO policies and the development of national Fair Trade systems; (3) the need for local and regional Fair Trade aimed at supporting disadvantaged producers and workers and developing fairer markets which do not exclude low income consumers; and (4) the need for changes in the multilateral arena, acknowledging the economic and social asymmetries between the North and the South. While these issues are of concern across the Global South, specific engagements in reshaping Fair Trade assume greater or less weight given the diversity among countries and regions.

Greater participation in Northern markets

Southern producers face restrictions on the demand for their Fair Trade products in Northern markets. Despite movement efforts in recent years to increase the number of consumers and access mainstream distribution channels, Northern markets can not absorb the full supply or potential range of Southern Fair Trade products.

In practice, only a small group of Southern producers have access to Fair Trade markets. This creates an image of exclusiveness that counters Fair Trade's goal of incorporating disadvantaged producers. Even among producer organizations integrated into Fair Trade networks, only a small percentage of producer output can be absorbed. While Fair Trade seeks to promote Southern partners' access to domestic markets and avoid dependence on Northern Fair Trade, the costs of adapting to Fair Trade conditions may prove an obstacle to competitive access to domestic markets as well.

The potential range of Fair Trade products is also restricted. Many basic Southern products have not been incorporated into Fair Trade due to their limited acceptance in Northern diets and lack of FLO certification standards. In recent years there has been a considerable diversification of Fair Trade products and new health demands in Northern markets are opening up opportunities for some traditional products, repositioned as functional foods. The case of quinoa, a traditional Andean grain now valued for its healthful properties, will be analyzed in Chapter 11.

Questions regarding greater producer participation in the value chain and in value-added activities remain largely unresolved. Integration into high-value activities remains central in empowering Southern producers. Successful experiences, such as the case of Cafédirect and Day chocolate, demonstrate that producer organizations can be integrated further down Fair Trade value chains (Doherty and Tranchell 2005). Rather than maintaining colonial-based practices of simply exporting raw material, producers must be able to increase their technical and marketing knowledge and strengthen their position in alternative and conventional markets if Fair Trade movement goals are to be advanced.

Changes and adaptations in FLO policies

FLO's political, operational, and strategic decisions are increasingly being questioned by Southern producers. As discussed in Chapter 9, there is a growing demand for greater participation and deliberative responsibility in FLO's leading bodies. Producer organizations propose that the president of the FLO Board of Directors be elected from the external members, rather than being selected from among national initiative representatives, as is currently the case. They further propose that national initiative representation on the Board be reduced to match that of producer organizations. Demands for greater producer representation have emerged in response to unilateral decisions by FLO regarding issues such as the selection of regional representatives, the establishment of certification fees, and the possible reduction in FLO's coffee floor price (see Chapter 9).

Discontent among Latin American small farmer organizations has been fueled by the extension of FLO certification to an increasing range of plantation products, including tropical fruits already cultivated by small producer cooperatives and the strong pressure to integrate plantations into coffee. Small farmer groups argue that Fair Trade plantation production could restrict their already limited exports, since larger more capital intensive producers can produce at lower cost. It is argued that if FLO keeps its policies favoring small producers, plantation workers will persist, but that if these policies are eliminated small producers could disappear entirely. This issue has provoked heated discussions among Latin American producer organizations linked to FLO (Bisaillon et al. 2005). Mexican organizations and the Latin American and Caribbean Coordination of Fair Trade Small Producers (CLAC) have challenged plantation certification and are threatening the unity of the Fair Trade movement by exploring openings for an alternative small farmer certification. Small scale producer groups in Latin America appear largely sympathetic to this position (Comercio Justo 2004; Declaración 2005; Medina 2004; Norberto 2004).

While opposition to Fair Trade plantation production is strongly expressed in Latin America, this is not necessarily a universal Southern position. In South Africa, for example, the inclusion of plantations under Fair Trade represents a move to empower black rural workers and advance land reform (see Chapter 12). The vulnerability of rural workers in Southern countries is well demonstrated and a number of non-governmental organizations (NGOs) focus explicitly on bolstering the position of these groups (Allen et al. 2003). This vulnerability renders more complex the plantation vs. small farmer debate.

In addition to the plantation debate, FLO's style of intervention and the recent imposition of certification fees have stoked anti-FLO feelings among producer groups. These groups argue for the adaptation of certification systems to Southern contexts, greater transparency along the Fair Trade value chain, greater emphasis on sustainable development, and support for the creation of Southern markets.

In Latin America and Asia, there are specific proposals for cutting certification costs, adopting alternative participatory methods of assessment, and promoting joint Fair Trade and organic certification. FLO's requirements are considered to exclude the most disadvantaged producers, given the prohibitive costs of certification, exacting product quality standards, and need for infrastructure and skilled personnel to deal with export markets (Jaffee et al. 2004). If FLO continues to prioritize market demands, it will distance itself from its target producer base (Bisaillon et al. 2005).

Producer organizations complain further that there is a lack of transparency along the Fair Trade value chain and limited information available on Northern demand and markets. In this context, the low share of Fair Trade certified exports as a percentage of the total production of certified producer organizations is a source of concern. When the huge numbers of small producers who could potentially be certified by FLO (if certification costs were lower) or participate in the integrated Fair Trade chains are taken into account, the position against plantation certification becomes readily intelligible.

Development of South/South Fair Trade markets and national systems

Southern initiatives to create national Fair Trade systems are discussed in light of specific production and consumption characteristics. Mexico has led the way in Latin America and is currently being followed by Brazil, Peru, and Ecuador. South Africa and India are involved in similar discussions. Proposed national systems prioritize the enlargement of the Fair Trade product range to include basic foodstuffs and value-added products, such as beans, corn, milk, and manioc, currently not certified within FLO (Comercio Justo Mexico 2004; Cotera and Ortiz 2004; Ferreira 2003).

Supplying these products requires the creation of a national label to differentiate them from conventional items as well as structures for monitoring and managing production and marketing. As explored in Chapter 10, there is considerable debate regarding the most appropriate (third party or participatory) certification for domestic markets (Cotera 2003; Declaración 2005). The development of Southern markets faces the additional challenges of increasing consumer awareness, defining market strategies, developing market channels and involving key private and public actors.

Several alternative market initiatives already exist in the South, but they remain tied to local, solidarity, or health concerns. There is to date virtually no research on attitudes to Fair Trade products in the Global South. It is argued that Northern consumers base their purchasing decisions largely on price, quality, value, and brand familiarity, rather than charity concerns. In Mexico, *Comercio Justo* upholds this outlook, basing its strategy on better product and services and justifying higher prices which translate into increased farm prices (Comercio Justo Mexico 2004). In Brazil, the Altereco is seeking to launch Fair Trade supermarket sales based on better product characteristics and prices only slightly higher than conventional products, with higher producer prices generated by tighter logistics and lower margins along the value chain (Altereco 2005).

Latin American alternative market discussions highlight the need to play down the notion of a fair price in favor of fair negotiations, the elimination or reduction of intermediaries, and greater market access (Medina 2004; Mittiga 2004b). It is argued that price in local and domestic markets should not become a mechanism for the exclusion of low-income consumers (Jaffee et al. 2004). In Latin America as well as Africa and Asia, domestic market initiatives must grapple with the rising power of large-scale retailers. In countries where Fair Trade is closely linked to the solidarity economy movement, there is considerable resistance to working with mainstream distribution channels. Southern movements increasingly prioritize local and regional markets, with the aim of breaking the pattern of enclave growth in favor of development.

Another key actor in the development of alternative markets in Southern countries is the State. Public policies are seen to be essential to deal with deficiencies in technical assistance, credit, and capacity building for small producers. On the consumer side, the exclusion of a large part of the population from basic consumption has deepened the social divide in these countries, creating pressure for income redistribution policies. Such policies could take the form of preferential purchases of Fair Trade products, which would, simultaneously, contribute to creating an alternative market for small producers and incorporate low-income consumers to the benefits of consuming good quality products with positive socio-environmental characteristics.

Main Southern demands in multilateral context

Demands for "Fair Trade" have become common in key international forums over recent years. In some cases these demands involve general issues of trade justice – such as opposing regional trade agreements which are seen as disadvantaging poor producers – voiced by a range of progressive groups. Yet increasingly we are seeing key Fair Trade movement organizations and their allies taking to heart the advocacy goals of the movement and formulating a Fair Trade political platform.

This advocacy was clearly evident at the 2004 United Nations Commission on Trade and Development (UNCTAD) meeting in Brazil, where a large number of Fair Trade groups presented "The Fair Trade Declaration."[1] This document calls for (1) strengthening the role of UNCTAD in promoting sustainable development through trade; (2) promoting South-South technological cooperation; (3) enhancing civil society participation in multilateral negotiations; (4) developing policies to support small farmers; (5) officially recognizing Fair Trade as a tool for development and fairness in trade; (6) establishing programs supporting Fair Trade activities in Southern countries; and (7) promoting UN and governmental Fair Trade purchases (Fair Trade Declaration 2004). Importantly this document merges broad global social justice goals (items 1–4) with more specific goals to enhance Fair Trade recognition, programs, and markets (items 5–7).

Key Fair Trade demands were reiterated at the 2005, Meeting on Solidarity Economy and Fair Trade in Latin America, held in Bolivia. Participants came from 12 Latin American countries and included representatives of major regional social movement groups. A "Declaration of Cochabamba" was agreed on calling for (1) the promotion of Fair Trade and the solidarity economy, including strengthening Latin American coordination; (2) the implementation of participatory certification systems and the unification of monitoring criteria; (3) the establishment of alliances with other social movements to promote public policies favoring Fair Trade and the Solidarity Economy; and (4) the opposition to FLO plantation certification (Declaración 2005). The meeting forges important links between Fair Trade and related groups throughout the region.

Though groups from the South have played the most important role in advancing international calls for Fair Trade, the FINE group (FLO, IFAT, NEWS, and EFTA) prepared a position paper for the 2005 Sixth Ministerial Conference in Hong Kong. This document, "Fair Trade Rules," incorporates many Southern demands including (1) greater sovereignty for states in regulating their economies; (2) domestic policies to develop agriculture and strengthen internal markets in the South; (3) protection for Small and Medium Enterprises (SMEs) in developing countries; (4) defense of food security and sovereignty; (5) an end to trade-distorting subsidies and dumping; and (6) prioritizing the needs of small and marginalized producers in negotiations.

In spite of the tensions between FLO-affiliated Southern producer groups and the Northern movement, these initiatives point to important convergences that can foster the emergence of a global Fair Trade movement. To a great extent North/South tensions are reproduced within the North between advocates of mainstreaming and those more identified with alternative trading networks. These tensions have been accentuated by FLO's registration of transnational corporations such as Nestle and Sara Lee (see CTM Altromercato 2006). FLO and IFAT, in their turn, have adopted different strategies. Nevertheless, there are indications of increasing convergence as IFAT moves more into foodstuffs, strengthens its presence in Latin America and pays greater attention to the professionalization of trading practices.[2] While the gravity of the conflicts should not be underestimated there are grounds for seeing these as a condition for the emergence of a global Fair Trade movement in which the Southern actors are no longer reduced to the role of beneficiaries but assume the status of autonomous partners.

Conclusions

Two complementary trends can be detected in the Southern axis of the global Fair Trade movement generating critical tensions that will be explored in subsequent chapters. First Southern beneficiaries have become organized members of the Fair Trade movement with their own positions on procedural and substantive questions. This is evident across continents and corresponds to both specific features in each region and to the identification of common "Southern" interests. In Latin America, the small farmer basis of the movement informs the programmatic challenges to the inclusion of plantations and transnational corporations, while in South Africa the key question is to redefine Fair Trade policy on plantations in line with local realities. In Asia, on the other hand, the inclusion of small and medium enterprises is central to their conception of Fair Trade. All regions converge on the need to develop Fair Trade in domestic markets and to promote horizontal South/South Fair Trade relations.

Second, to the extent that the orientation to domestic market becomes central, Fair Trade in the South situates itself firmly as a development strategy and enters into dialogue with other movements having similar goals. In addition, Fair Trade looks to the State as a natural partner (in times of democracy), given its shared interest in offsetting market exclusion. The Fair Trade movement in the South must therefore simultaneously define itself in relation to the public sector and to alternative development strategies.

Notes

1 Some 133 organizations participated in the parallel Fair Trade Forum at the São Paulo UNCTAD meeting in 2004.
2 FLO for its part, with the certification of cotton, has moved into the nonfood sector.

References

Allen, P., FitzSimmons, M., Goodman, M., and Warner, K. (2003) "Shifting plates in the agrifood landscape: the tectonics of alternative agrifood initiatives in California," *Journal of Rural Studies*, 19: 61–75.
Altereco. (2005) "Étude Altereco Brasil: Vers un Commerce Équitable Sud-Sud," Paris: Altereco.
Asia Fair Trade Forum. (2005) "A consumer campaign to develop domestic markets for fair trade: a recommendation," IFAT Conference, Quito, May 2005.
Bisaillon, V., Gendron, C., and Turcotte, M.F. (2005) "Fair trade and the solidarity economy: the challenges ahead," Montreal: Alliance21/UQAM.
Comercio Justo Mexico. (2004) "Comercio Justo: el poder de un mercado diferente," *Informe de actividades 1999–2004*, Oaxaca: Comercio Justo.
Cotera, A. (2003) "O comercio justo a partir da perspectiva dos países do Sul," *França, C.L. Comércio Ético e Solidário no Brasil*, São Paulo: FES.
Cotera, A. and Ortiz, H. (2004) "El comercio justo: documento resumen de enfoques y propuestas," *Comercio Justo, Consumo Etico. Marco conceptual y experiencias en curso*, Lima: CEP/COR/GRESP.
CTM Altermercato. (2006) *Lettera Aperta Sull Inclusione Delle Grandi Compagnie Transnazionali nel Settore del Fair Trade*, Online. Available at: www.altromercato.it (accessed October 18, 2005).
Declaración de Cochabamba. (2005) *Encuentro Empreendedor de Economía Solidaria y Comercio Justo en America Latina*, Cochabamba, Bolívia.
Doherty, B. and Tranchell, S. (2005) "New thinking in international trade? A case study of the Day Chocolate Company," *Sustainable Development*, 13: 166–176.
Elsen, J. (2005) "Are we moving towards a variety of fair trade concepts?," IFAT Conference, Quito, May 2005.
Encuentro Emprendedor de Economia Solidaria y Comercio Justo en America Latina. (2005) *Otro comercio es posible*, Cochabamba, September 2005.
Fair Trade Declaration. (2004) UNCTAD XI, São Paulo, Brazil.

Ferreira, V. (2003) "O sistema de certificação internacional de comércio justo: a experiência da FLO," in C.L. França (ed), *Comércio Ético e Solidário no Brasil*, São Paulo: FES.

FLO (Fair Trade Labelling Organizations International). (2005a) "Overview of FLO activities," Biofach Conference, Rio de Janeiro.

—— (2005b) *About FLO*, Online. Available at: http://www.fairtrade.net/ (accessed November 4, 2005).

—— (2005c) "Tendencia de mercado productos de Comercio Justo," Presentation, Rio de Janeiro.

—— (2006) *FLO 2005/2006 Annual Report: Building Trust*, Online. Available at: www.fairtrade.net (accessed July 10, 2006).

Fonseca, M.F.A.C. (2005) "A Institucionalização do Mercado de Orgânicos no Mundo e no Brasil: uma Interpretação," unpublished doctoral thesis, CPDA/UFRRJ, Rio de Janeiro.

Hassanein, N. (2003) "Practicing food democracy: a pragmatic politics of transformation," *Journal of Rural Studies*, 19: 77–86.

IFAT (International Fair Trade Association). (2005a) *IFAT*, Online. Available at: www.ifat.org.br. (accessed October 13, 2005).

—— (2005b) "Overview of IFAT's actuation," Biofach Conference, Rio de Janeiro, November 17, 2005.

Jaffee, D., Kloppenburg, J.R., and Monroy, M.B. (2004) "Bringing the 'moral charge' home? Fair trade within the North and within the South," *Rural Sociology*, 69: 169–196.

Kocken, M. (2003) *Fifty Years of Fair Trade: A Brief History of the Fair Trade Movement*, London: IFAT.

Low, W. and Davenport, E. (2005) "Postcards from the edge: maintaining the 'alternative' character of fair trade," *Sustainable Development*, 13: 143–153.

Medina, P.F. (2004) "Comercio justo y consumo etico: el comercio justo hacia una economía al servicio de las personas," *Foro Nacional de Comercio Justo y Consumo Etico*, Lima, Peru.

Mittiga, S. (2004) "El comercio justo hacia una economía al servicio de las personas: documento de trabajo sobre certificación. Documento base de taller 2," *Foro Nacional de Comercio Justo y Consumo Etico*, Lima, Peru.

Norberto, E., Leroy, A., Perez, A., Galon, B., Parravicini, M., and Foubert, S. (2004) "Comércio justo: uma oportunidade de negócio à espera de um arranjo institucional," *Bahia Análise & Dados*, 4: 603–614.

Ortíz, H. (2002) "El comercio justo y su potencial transformador," Boletín n.2. Perú: Gresp.

Relacc. (2002) "Gobiernos locales y desarrollo rural en los Andes: casos y experiencias," Conferencia electrónica, Online. Available at: www.condesan.org/e-foros/Gobiernos_locales/gobloc3_2.htm (accessed December 15, 2006).

Roca, H.O. (2004) "El comercio justo hacia una economia al servicio de las personas: taller las politicas publicas y el comercio justo, Documento del taller 3," *Foro Nacional de Comercio Justo y Consumo Etico*, Lima, Peru.

Sacca, J. and Penchévere, S. (2005) "Opportunités du marché Brésilien pour Altereco: Vers un Commerce Equitable Sud-Sud," Paris: Altereco.

Smith, S. and Barrientos, S. (2005) "Fair trade and ethical trade: are there moves towards convergence?," *Sustainable Development*, 13: 190–198.

Tallontire, A. (2001) "Challenges facing Fair Trade: which way now?," DSA Conference, Manchester: NRI, September 10, 2001.

Vizcarra, K.G. (2002) "El comercio justo: una alternativa para la agroindustria rural de América Latina," Santiago, Chile: FAO.

Wills, C. (2005) "Renewing our vision," IFAT Conference, Quito, May, 2005.

9 Fair Trade coffee in Mexico

At the center of the debates

Marie-Christine Renard and
Victor Pérez-Grovas[1]

Introduction

Coffee has been the core commodity of the Fair Trade movement from its inception, with Mexico the leading supplier throughout the movement's development. Mexican small producer organizations pioneered the Fair Labeling concept and one of the founders of the movement lives in Mexico, further establishing its historical importance to the Fair Trade movement. While a relatively small number of small-scale coffee producers in Mexico are members of Fair Trade cooperatives,[2] their importance far exceeds their numbers because of their organizational capacity. The coordination among Mexican Fair Trade cooperatives has extended to cooperatives in other countries in the region. Together these cooperatives form a unified front, defending the interests of small-scale producers in the face of changes that are taking place in the regulation and certification systems of Fair Trade.

In this chapter we describe how Fair Trade contributed to strengthening small producer coffee organizations in a period of crisis, and how these organizations are attempting to move beyond a market niche strategy to pursue a more ambitious development goal. This goal will not be achieved without confronting a number of problems. Current concerns include competitive pressures from transnational exporting firms, the continued precariousness of small-scale producer livelihoods, and the lack of knowledge of Fair Trade that leads some producers to sell their coffee to "coyotes" (local intermediaries), weakening their own organization. Other challenges are coming from within the Fair Trade movement through the rise of complex regulation and certification organizations, as producer organizations see themselves increasingly in a struggle to keep Fair Trade from abandoning its founding objective of supporting small-scale producers.

The case of Fair Trade coffee in Mexico demonstrates the impact on Southern producers of Fair Trade's integration with conventional markets in the Global North. While this integration brings the benefit of increased demand and sales of Fair Trade coffee, it also brings a number of negative effects. The overriding priority of increasing sales volume means the market has gone beyond a means for development to an end in itself. The need to respond to market exigencies, increasing market concentration and the normalization of Fairtrade Labelling

Organizations International (FLO) as a regulatory body have created new imperatives for producers which represent barriers to market participation and new tensions between Northern initiatives and Southern producer organizations.

An escalating tension is developing between two visions: one is the vision of Southern producers, where Fair Trade is an inseparable part of a broader development strategy (see Chapter 8). In this vision, Fair Trade is a North/South partnership based on solidarity, equality, and transparency (Bisaillon et al. 2005; Yepez and Mormont 2006). The other vision is based on the dynamics of Fair Trade in the North and the pressures to increase sales volume which is driving integration with the conventional market, new economic standards such as quality controls; new actors such as large distributors and transnational corporations seeking to establish their "ethical" image. This is contributing to the breakdown of the consensus upon which Fair Trade was established in the Alternative Trade and Fair Labeling initiatives, and threatens the dilution of the broader concept of ethical trade. Trade becomes an end in itself, part of the development of the market (Trade, not Aid) a vision of the market as synonymous with development (Aid to Trade) (Yepez and Mormont 2006).

To begin, we will describe the gains coffee producer cooperatives have made through Fair Trade along with some of the problems they have encountered. We will then explore how these advances frame a broader development and organizational strategy, both economic and political, which goes beyond the borders of Mexico. Then we will explore how the dynamics of mainstreaming affect Fair Trade organizations and how they have defended their own vision through the debates over plantation certification, participation of transnational corporations, and the governance structures of FLO and the Fair Trade movement.

Coffee producer organizations in Fair Trade

With a few exceptions, international coffee prices have faced a continuous decline since the process of market liberalization began after the collapse of the International Coffee Agreements in 1989. Prices reached their lowest level in 2002, at US$ 0.41 per pound for Mexican prime washed coffee (premium grade quoted on the New York Exchange). Production costs were estimated at US$ 0.90–1.00 per pound. Further aggravating the impact of declining prices, transnational exporting firms deduct a quality penalty from the price (up to US$ 0.24 per pound in 1999–2000), arguing that Mexican coffee does not meet international standards. These firms at times have manipulated the market price by sending inferior quality coffee samples to importers for cupping (Pérez-Grovas et al. 2002: 50).

In contrast, Fair Trade certified cooperatives have received a guaranteed minimum price of US$ 1.26 per pound for conventional coffee and US$ 1.41 per pound for organic coffee, thus avoiding the fluctuations in market prices, covering production costs, and providing a profit. This price includes a "social premium" of US$ 0.05 per pound for local development projects. The price premium has made the difference between the disappearance of these cooperatives and their survival during periods of low prices, even if they are unable to sell 100 percent of their crop in the Fair Trade market. On average, Mexican Fair Trade certified cooperatives sell only 20 percent of their production in this market niche. The necessity of responding to market demands, including volume and quality, as well as administrative and logistical expectations, favor the more well-established and organized cooperatives. These producers sell the majority of their coffee at Fair Trade prices based on the ability of their advisors and their long-standing contacts with roasters and alternative trade organizations (ATOs) (Taylor et al. 2005). As we will see, Fair Trade Certified cooperatives have turned to increasing collaboration to overcome unequal access to the Fair Trade market.

Not only have these cooperatives survived, they have consolidated their membership during this period of crisis. Their members' loyalty to the cooperatives has been strengthened in part through the payment of higher prices than those offered by local intermediaries. In addition, individual producers receive indirect benefits from belonging to cooperatives that are on the FLO Fair Trade registry.

Cooperatives have been able to translate Fair Trade earnings into investment in capital funds or financial reserves (Renard 1999a: 281). These funds are especially important in times of high prices in the local markets when the Fair Trade price differential is reduced and the temptation to sell to local intermediaries increases. Some organizations have created community credit funds with low interest rates for their members, or they have purchased land for production projects. The social premium has been invested in public goods and programs including transport vehicles, new processing facilities, the construction of warehouses, production projects, health centers, latrines, schools and educational centers, community stores, and the promotion of organic agriculture (Aranda and Morales 2002; Murray et al. 2003; Pérez-Grovas and Cervantes 2002; VanderHoff 2002).

Another important benefit for the cooperatives is prefinancing: Fair Trade standards require roasters to provide the producers with credit that is repaid after the harvest. This credit is provided to the cooperatives so they can pay their members for the coffee upon delivery. In a time when banks offer limited credit to small-scale coffee producers at high rates of interest, this prefinancing is welcomed even though it is not sufficient to allow the producers to pay their harvest laborers. In order to prevent their members from selling their coffee to other buyers, cooperatives find themselves obliged to seek financial resources in other places. Some succeed in spite of the credit restrictions, thanks to the reputation that they have gained from repaying previous loans on time, whether it was through private or public financial organizations, or in the framework of governmental support programs for the coffee sector.[3]

Professionalism in business activities and on time payments are part of the organizational skills required to satisfy the conditions for admission to the FLO Fair Trade registry and to achieve Fair Trade certification, as are improvements in other administrative processes. Another benefit has been training in the production of high-quality coffee through improved cultivation and processing procedures to meet market demands for high-quality coffee. Many of the cooperatives have staff agronomists that advise and assist the producers. Being organized also allows the cooperatives access to resources for public infrastructure projects, such as drying patios and de-pulpers. For example, the program Alliance for the Land (Alianza para el Campo), which resulted from policies for which these same organizations have lobbied, provides funds for such projects. There are other advantages to participating in Fair Trade: the cooperatives establish long-term business relationships with roasters and importers and acquire the knowledge and the abilities to participate in the market in a self-assured manner (Renard 1999a: 274).

We do not claim here that Fair Trade is a panacea that will solve all the problems of small-scale producers. On the contrary, much still needs to be done before these producers can achieve truly satisfactory living standards. One serious limitation is the size of landholdings among the small-scale producers, as the division of arable land has reached its limits (Renard 1999a: 311). For many families, the out-migration of at least one child is already an integral part of their survival strategies; during the coffee harvest, it is common to see the fields full of older people, women, and children. Nonetheless, it is true that Fair Trade strengthens the cooperatives and raises the confidence and self-esteem of individual members that have managed to be successful in the midst of both a generalized crisis and the multiple failures and corruption in national social organizations (Murray et al. 2003: 8).

Vulnerability in periods of high prices

The long-term relationships between Fair Trade cooperatives and Northern roasters depend on the ability of the cooperatives to meet their contract terms. Central to these terms is the timely delivery of coffee at agreed upon standards of quality and quantity. The cooperatives, in turn, depend on the delivery of coffee from their members. They face competition from the local intermediaries employed by the transnational export firms that have controlled the market since 1989. The strength of these firms comes from their access to capital that allows them to pay for coffee as soon as it is delivered, an important priority for poor, small-scale producers in a country where credit is scarce and costly. When the international market prices are low, as has been the case in most of the period since 1989, the price premium offered by the cooperatives that have access to the Fair Trade market makes them very attractive. Producers do not hesitate to deliver their coffee to them: coffee is abundant, the competition from other local buyers is scarce, sufficient coffee is easy to collect and store. The situation changes radically when the market prices are high and the difference between what Fair Trade and the local intermediaries offer is reduced. In these periods producers get many offers for their coffee, with the "coyotes" competing for the producers' business.

In the context of the post-1989 market, the transnational export firms have adopted a strategy of protecting themselves from market instabilities through forward contracts. They have committed to supplying large quantities of coffee without actually having sufficient physical stocks, and therefore need to compete in order to fulfill their contracts. They sell futures at high prices, and therefore have high-enough margins to offer higher prices to the producers. They enter coffee producing communities and offer the same prices as the cooperatives. While the export firms sell their coffee before actually buying it, the Fair Trade cooperatives buy it first and sell it later. The cooperatives cannot assume the risk of selling coffee that has yet to be harvested. The immediate needs of the coffee growers often lead them to direct part of their harvest to those buyers who can pay them up front. Although the members keep the majority of their coffee harvest for the cooperative, this practice, repeated by many of the producers, can make it difficult for the cooperatives to fulfill their commercial obligations and puts them at risk of default (Renard 1999a: 275–276).

Supply problems can be particularly severe if the members are unaware, due to their lack of knowledge of Fair Trade, of the consequences of not selling their coffee to the cooperative. Since much of Fair Trade activities are carried out at the cooperative level, many members are unaware of what happens to their coffee. In contrast, cooperative members are actively aware of organic coffee production because it involves labor carried out by the producers themselves (e.g. the use of organic fertilizer, the construction of terraces, and the implementation of mixed cropping systems). Cooperative managers negotiate Fair Trade contracts with market participants. The delegates to the member assembly in each cooperative possess some knowledge about the marketing arrangements, especially in organizations that offer training courses, but the producers have no knowledge of these arrangements. At most, they know that their coffee travels to Europe and the United States (Pérez-Grovas and Cervantes 2002: 14; Renard 1999a: 300–302). Cooperatives frequently do not have the time to take up this task of educating their members, or fear doing so because of the risk of misunderstandings. For example, not all of the US$ 1.21 per pound FLO minimum price (US$ 1.36 for organic coffee) reaches individual producers since cooperatives do not sell all their coffee in Fair Trade markets and typically average total (Fair Trade and conventional market) earnings in producer payments. Though the additional US$ 0.05 per pound social premium is often viewed as part of the minimum price, this is used at the cooperative level and does not elevate producer prices. Finally, the cooperatives have processing, transportation, and administration costs that are discounted, before an average price for sale of the total harvest is paid to the members. The cooperatives also have to use some of the earnings for reinvestment. Sometimes it is difficult to explain to the members that they will not be paid the full guaranteed minimum price without arousing suspicions of mismanagement. This helps explain why the producers' lack of understanding and precarious economic position leads them to divert part of their coffee to other buyers, placing the whole Fair Trade system in jeopardy.

The cooperatives experienced this problem in the 1994 harvest when the prices jumped due to speculation in the market. This occurred again in the 2004–2005 harvest, when there was a scarcity of coffee in Mexico and Central America. The trading companies began visiting members of the cooperatives, knowing that high-quality coffee was produced there. The largest trading company in Mexico, Agroindustrias de México, S.A. (AMSA), organized a coffee quality competition in each coffee producing state, awarding winners with public recognition and diplomas. The organizations naïve enough to participate in the competition discovered after the fact that it had been a market research endeavor searching for producing zones, organizations, and communities with the highest quality coffee.

The competition from local intermediaries poses a challenge for the cooperatives, especially if the relationship between the cooperatives and their members is more instrumental than holistic. In general, cooperatives are made up of a strong core of members who are completely loyal, a second group that is more or less loyal, and a large number of opportunistic members. Some cooperatives resort to sanctions to maintain loyalty, such as prohibiting members who fail to deliver a predetermined percentage of their harvest to the cooperative from selling to the cooperative for a period. Even with these measures, in 1994–1995 the Union of Indigenous Communities of the Isthmus Region (Unión de Comunidades Indígenas de la Región del Istmo or UCIRI) from Oaxaca collected 15 percent less coffee than in previous years and the State Coordinator for Coffee Producers of Oaxaca (Coordinadora Estatal de Productores de Café de Oaxaca or CEPCO) bought only 50 percent of its previous volume (Renard 1999a: 277).

High coffee prices lead to financial pressures on the cooperatives because they have to pay their members before exporting the coffee and finalizing their contracts. Even though the final price will be higher than that offered by the intermediaries, this causes a liquidity problem for the cooperatives. In the 2004–2005 harvest, the Majomut cooperative in the highlands of Chiapas had to reach into its reserve funds to supplement the prices paid to the producers so as not to pay less than what the "coyotes" were offering, even though there were only a few days in which high prices were offered. Cooperatives that lack funds due to low coffee volumes lose members, clients, and contracts in these years of high prices.

A changing vision: from niche market to development

Economic logic assumes that cooperatives compete among themselves for access to the market, and that competition favors the larger and well established over the newer entrants. But contrary to traditional logic, the Fair Trade coffee producer organizations moved from competition to solidarity. UCIRI, the first organization that sold coffee in the Fair Trade market, opened the door for many other organizations in Oaxaca and Chiapas. Through its marketing activities, it exported coffee from other more recently organized cooperatives until they were able to market on their own (Renard 1999a: 274). With a few exceptions, most cooperatives assisted in the extension of Fair Trade to other cooperatives. They understood that collaboration and mutual aid were more profitable than competition for a market niche. The network of solidarity that resulted from the cooperation in Mexico has extended to the coffee growing organizations in Central and South America.

There is a dynamic link between Fair Trade cooperatives and the cooperative movement more generally in Mexico and throughout the region. Cooperatives respond to requests for assistance in times of need: they assist each other in the training of coffee cuppers, they exchange techniques, and they advise each other on the issues of commercialization, marketing, and organic cultivation. The "independent"[4] organizations of Mexican coffee producers have formed an umbrella organization, the National Coordinator of Coffee Producing Organizations (Coordinadora Nacional de Organizaciones Cafetaleras, or CNOC), to represent the interests of its member organizations before government agencies. It also strives for increased regulation of the market at both the national and international levels. CNOC is made up of 70,000 coffee growers, 15 percent of the national total. There are also officially recognized second-level organizations of coffee producers of various states of Mexico, like the State Coordinator of Coffee Producers of Oaxaca (CEPCO) and the Coordinator for Small Coffee Producers of Chiapas (Coordinadora de Pequeños Productores de Café de Chiapas or Coopcafé). The cooperatives that participate in Fair Trade are quite experienced and they provide a strong dynamism for the second-level organizations. In addition, this network has managed to influence public policies in recent years, as some coffee sector programs have taken up their proposals. There are strong links between Fair Trade cooperatives and the cooperative movement in coffee in other countries: the president of the National Coffee Council of Peru came from the Center of Coffee Grower Cooperatives of Concepción (COCLA); Café Nica, a network of Nicaraguan cooperatives, is very influential in the coffee sector; in Costa Rica, the Fair Trade cooperatives have their own assistant secretary of Agriculture; and in Honduras, the president of the Honduran Coffee Institute comes from a cooperative background.

Development passes through stages of self-management, the creation of cooperative-owned companies and the autonomy of regulatory institutions. The Mexican coffee grower organizations have advanced on several fronts. They have a national certifier, Certimex, a Mexican company founded at the insistence of independent coffee grower organizations. Prior to the founding of Certimex all Mexican organic coffee was certified by international certification organizations such as Naturland. The goal of Certimex, whose work is guaranteed by these international organizations, is to provide less expensive certification services, saving the cooperatives unnecessary expenses. Certimex has now expanded to Fair Trade coffee certification. It has also obtained ISO 65 accreditation, something that FLO is still seeking.

There is now a national initiative called Comercio Justo México, which was formed in 2001 to create a domestic Fair Trade market in Mexico. Producer organizations realized that creating a domestic market was essential to their long-term survival, which until then had relied on expanding and diversifying export markets for growth. Under Comercio Justo México, coffee is sold with its own label. Other labeled products such as honey are about to be introduced into the market. In its first years, the initiative languished due to insufficient Fair Trade consumer demand. Given the economic plight of most Méxicans, Fair Trade was not a central public concern. The fact that Fair Trade products are sold in small specialty or organic produce stores has further curtailed sales. The domestic market does not support prices that cover certification costs. The poor quality of the coffee sold in the domestic market further compounds Comercio Justo México's problems. Cooperatives export their highest quality coffee because European or North American consumers pay a premium for specialty coffee. In Mexico, the concept of Fair Trade has also been criticized as being elitist. As a result, Comercio Justo México has to offer coffees of different quality levels with varying prices, stigmatizing some coffees as inferior.

Together with Comercio Justo México, Certimex is developing a self-evaluation manual for cooperatives based on Fair Trade standards, indicators, parameters, and supporting documents that inspectors use to evaluate cooperatives.[5] FLO still lacks a measurement instrument of this type. Instead, its inspectors write a general report which leaves room for personal interpretation and a certain level of arbitrariness. The Certimex and Comercio Justo México self-evaluation manual should aid producers who, until now, have been unaware of what the inspectors are looking for.

This will also help these same producers give substance to the notion of "Fair Trade" quality. Quality, in a broad sense, is constructed by incorporating social values such as equality of exchange, which is one of the ways in which economic value is determined (Renard 1999a,b, 2003). The assignment of value requires a standardization process, or the development of criteria and certification procedures to guarantee that these criteria are met. This entire process requires a regulatory organization that establishes these standards and criteria (Renard 2005). In this sense, the work of Comercio Justo México and Certimex, is a form of quality management. This work is carried out in conjunction with producer organizations seeking clarification of the rules determining access to the market, a clarity that FLO has not always provided. Further, Comercio Justo México and Certimex are working to harmonize the criteria that are shared between different certification agencies.

Comercio Justo México is a "national initiative" of Fair Trade, much like Max Havelaar Holland or TransFair USA. The most important difference is that it is located in a producing country, giving it a different perspective than those situated in the North. It is not a member with the full rights of FLO, but rather an invited guest while soliciting membership. Comercio Justo México's application involves a set of particular requests. First, Comercio Justo México wants to keep its own system of standards for the national market. Comercio Justo México argues that the increasingly complex Fair Trade regulatory system needs to be tailored to the distinct needs of each country. In contrast, FLO believes that all the functions and decisions regarding standards should remain universal and centralized. Second, Comercio Justo México wants to continue to be certified by Certimex at reduced cost. And finally, Comercio Justo México wants 95–99 percent of its certified products to come from small-scale producers and not from plantations. This point will be addressed further below.

Some of the Mexican Fair Trade cooperatives have created joint social corporations, including a business directed at the national market, Agromercados, and an export company, Mexican Commercializer of Agroecological Products

(Comercializadora Mexicana de Productos Agroecológicos or COMPRAS). Agromercados is a public corporation created to combine the efforts and resources of the cooperatives in the promotion and distribution of Fair Trade products. Ultimately, the goal is to place Fair Trade products in the major supermarkets of Mexico. The corporation was formed in 1999, with the current shareholder structure in place since 2000. Coffee was designated as the product to open the market and studies were carried out to define the target market segment and best product type. In 2002, Agromercados launched the Café Fértil coffee line which was targeted to university students because of their greater buying power, their attraction to the Fair Trade concept, and their appreciation of specialty coffee. Agromercados had a good initial performance and was able to obtain credit for operating capital to purchase roasting, grinding, and packaging infrastructure, and to carry out market studies and advertising campaigns. Beginning in 2004, sales fell due to poor management and the enterprise began to have liquidity problems. But by late 2005 it was in a state of financial recovery and was preparing for a large-scale promotional campaign. Agromercados is considering launching new products, including a chain of tortilla factories using non-GMO white corn directly from Mexican farm organizations.

The idea for COMPRAS was born in 2000 during the negotiation process for Fair Trade coffee contracts. Three cooperatives from Chiapas (Majomut, San Fernando, and MásCafé) were separately negotiating with their principal buyer on volume, delivery date, and coffee quality conditions. Based on this experience, the cooperatives decided to initiate a contract together with two buyers for the 2001–2002 harvest. This resulted in an increased contracted volume and a larger distribution of their coffee. The cooperatives also decided to experiment with using a single transaction for the different parts of the export process: insurance contracts, custody, transportation to the port, customs, and shipping. For that harvest, they saved up to 50 percent in the costs of these different services. By the following harvest (2002/2003), the decision was made to create the export company, COMPRAS, adding the organization Ecological Farmers of the Sierra Madre of Chiapas (Campesinos Ecológicos de la Sierra Madre de Chiapas or CESMACH) as a partner. The business was based on an equal stock distribution: 25 percent for each organization. A Board of Directors was created, with each organization having one vote. The producer groups agreed to export all their volume through the new corporation and to support all the groups with which the four organizations were working, benefiting 22 cooperatives. The management team was comprised of people from each organization in different positions: sales, shipping, administration, and quality control. The costs were distributed according to the export volume for each organization.

In the first harvest cycle COMPRAS sold 31,000 bags (60 kilograms each). By the following harvest (2003/2004) the volume grew to 39,000 bags, 67 percent of which was organic, and close to 90 percent sold in Fair Trade markets. In the 2004/2005 harvest, the volume fell by 5,000 bags, far less than the 35 percent decline in overall Mexican coffee production that year. It is estimated that COMPRAS now exports 8 percent of all Fair Trade certified coffee in the world (COMPRAS 2005). This initiative faces some resistance from FLO and FLO-Cert since the principles of Fair Trade require that each cooperative remain economically independent, a rule seen by initiative participants as inhibiting the coordination between cooperatives and preventing the creation of joint social businesses.

The coordination between producer organizations does not remain at an economic level, but also covers the political arena, including discussions of decision-making processes and how power is exerted in FLO. This discussion is carried out within a new organization, the Latin American and Caribbean Coordination of Fair Trade Small Producers (CLAC). This organization originated from the unification of two previous Latin American groups, the Union of Coffee Producers (la Unión de Productores de Café or UPROCAFÉ), with close ties to the Max Havelaar initiatives, and the Solidarity Front (Frente Solidario), connected with the TransFair groups and the Catholic Church. CLAC is composed of approximately 300 small producer organizations of 100,000 families in 16 countries, producing a variety of products including coffee, bananas, other fresh fruits, juices, honey, and cacao.[6] A unifying element for CLAC has been the need to present an organized voice to FLO.

FLO against small producers? Fair Trade at issue

These organizational developments raise a question: Why do the producers feel the need to defend themselves from an initiative created to give them an advantageous position in the market? At its inception, the model for Fair Labeling grew out of a request by the small-scale producers and defined these producers as the primary beneficiaries. Fair Trade was devised to support them, not only to access the markets, but also to pursue broader development. Fair Labeling was organized around basic principles defining a mode of operation in a niche market: minimum guaranteed prices, direct, and long-term business arrangements, and prefinancing (Renard 1999a,b). Developing this initiative was not easy, as it required its founders to resist the pressures of corporations that dominated the coffee market and opposed its launch (Roozen and VanderHoff 2002).

As Fair Trade certification has expanded to more countries and products, and has included plantation production, small producer organizations have lost their central place in the FLO system. The position of small producer groups has shifted further with FLO's increasingly bureaucratic administration of the producer registry, of the organizational decision-making process, of standard-setting, and of marketing (Renard 2005). Centralization and professionalization within FLO has reduced regional producer meetings to a consulting status. It has also led to a reshuffling of personnel in national initiatives in consumer countries, resulting in the loss of personal contacts. While Fair Trade founders came from backgrounds in social activism in solidarity with the "Third World," some current members of the national initiatives come from very different business-related backgrounds. FLO decisions are now directed more toward commercial considerations ("what the market demands") than political considerations. This is due in part to the desire to make Fair Trade grow as much as possible and in part to the interest that some of the dominant corporations in the agrofood sector are showing in Fair Trade products (Renard 2005).

The recent creation of FLO-Cert, the certification body of FLO, has involved an increasing role of certification professionals far removed from FLO's former activist mentality. Consequently, the inspection process for the cooperatives has changed. On the one hand, there are more standards to meet. On the other hand, the parameters used to confirm that the standards are being met are more complex. The certification process has become quite complicated for producer organizations. It has also become a financial burden, as the cooperatives must now pay for the certification that was previously covered by the Fair Trade label license-holders. For some organizations the certification process has become a barrier to entry to the Fair Trade market rather than a guarantee of market access.[7]

All these factors have led to disagreements, many very heated, between the small-scale coffee producer organizations and FLO. As the literature on the process of quality assessment and certification in the agrofood sector has made clear, regulatory organizations for quality products have among their duties the management of market access through standard-setting, the distribution of the differentiatial premium by coordinating the network actors, and the protection of the label (Renard 2005; Sanz and Macias 2005; Sylvander 1995; Watts and Goodman 1997). These responsibilities doubtlessly represent a source of power and, by definition, are an object of negotiation. In the case of Fair Trade, they tend to concentrate power in the regulatory body. With stricter application of standards, this leads to increasing control of Southern activities (Yépez and Mormont 2006).

Conflicts over the use of power

Producers complain about the lack of transparency in FLO's structure and its decision-making processes, their own lack of representation, and the absence of communication channels between producers and FLO (Murray et al. 2003: 21; Pérez-Grovas and Cervantes 2002; VanderHoff 2002). Power has concentrated in the national initiatives (Max Havelaar, TransFair, Fairtrade Foundation and others). When FLO was formed in 1997, only the national initiatives were members and the Board of Directors was made up of representatives of six national initiatives with one producer representative who had only observer status. In 1999, two producer representatives were added, one from Latin America and the other from Africa. In 2001, the FLO Board grew to four producer representatives (two from Latin America, one from Africa and one from Asia) selected in regional meetings and two buyer representatives (one from industry and one from an ATO). As a result of continued producer pressure, the number of national initiative representatives was reduced to five in 2005,[8] and two "external" members representing consumers were added.

The maneuvering for posts on the FLO Board demonstrates the controversial nature of Fair Trade policies. Despite recent changes the national initiatives currently have the majority of FLO votes, challenging Fair Trade's original procedures when consensus was more the norm among participants. Producer organizations seek to return to this original sense of partnership: "FLO cannot have a promising future while the opinion of one of its fundamental parts, the producers, does not have enough influence in its decision-making structure. Nor can it face a promising future while FLO's vision is not shared and supported by all its actors" (CLAC 2004c).

One example of the contentious nature of FLO policies involves the payment of certification costs. Producer organizations did not question the fact that they would have to cover some of the costs of certification, recognizing that certification by an independent third-party strengthens the credibility of the label. A consensus was reached over a system of payments at the FLO Forum in September 2003. But two months later the Operational Board of FLO approved a different system in a meeting at which the producers were not present. This decision generated disagreement. The members of the national initiatives decided upon a tariff based on volume (0.45 percent of the FOB value of the product), which the producers argued punished larger organizations for the benefit of those that sell less. CLAC decided in April 2004 that none of its organizations would pay FLO-Cert (CLAC 2004b). In response, the national initiatives threatened to remove them from the registry, with the producer organizations responding that they would deal directly with their buyers without FLO. Since some cooperatives already sell their coffee directly to Carrefour France, bypassing Max Havelaar France, the threat was taken seriously (Renard 2003, 2005). At CLAC's Regional Meeting in August 2004, a compromise was reached in which a percentage-based payment system would continue for two years, at which time the actual cost for inspections and certification would be charged. Discussions continue over the inspection fee, the costs of double certification in the case of organic coffee, and the frequency and scope of monitoring (CLAC 2004b).

Another point of disagreement has been the recurring discussions of lowering the minimum guaranteed coffee price. Currently, Fair Trade is faced with an imbalance between relatively slow growing demand and the potentially large supply of coffee from certified or potentially certified cooperatives. Fair Trade is also pressured by the competition of labeling initiatives with weak or less demanding criteria, such as coffee certified by Utz Kapeh. Utz Kapeh coffee costs much less than Fair Trade coffee because it does not apply the basic Fair Trade principles, including paying a minimum guaranteed price, prefinancing, a social premium, and long-term contracts. The introduction of other certified coffees creates confusion among consumers (Renard 2005). In light of this, some argue for lowering the minimum price as a means of increasing the consumption of Fair Trade coffee. The cooperatives, supported by small and medium-sized roasters in the United States and Europe oppose this proposal, arguing that a lower price would damage the message to the consumer regarding Fair Trade (CLAC 2004a). Nonetheless, the proposal to evaluate coffee prices continues to resurface with the FLO Board of Directors.

The controversy surrounding plantations

When Fair Trade certification was first offered to plantations, it was agreed that it would be only for those products not grown by small producers, such as tea. But increasingly plantations are being certified that produce goods also produced by small producers, like bananas (see Chapter 5). This is occurring over the opposition of the small producer organizations. The quantity of plantation products has grown rapidly, primarily in Asia and Africa. This growth is the result of demand from supermarkets and corporations seeking to market Fair Trade products in the same way that they have previously embraced organic products. Plantations are better able to maintain quality controls which cooperatives, made up of hundreds of small producers, find more difficult. If supplies are not available, supermarkets are prepared to bypass Fair Trade certification and instead establish arrangements with other initiatives (such as Utz Kapeh), or with already consolidated ATOs (e.g. Carrefour and Oxfam in Belgium), or even to launch their own initiatives (Renard 2005). This, in turn, brings further pressure on FLO to certify new items produced under systems other than small-scale producer cooperatives.

Strong pressure existed to open Fair Trade to coffee plantation production, even while the majority of the cooperatives were not able to sell all of their products in this market. The plantation discussion began when the Italian company Illy Coffee, whose blends contain Brazilian plantation coffee, made plantation certification a condition of their participation in Fair Trade, arguing it could not change the sourcing of the blends it had taken years to develop. The proposal was accompanied by assurances that the plantations would not compete with the small coffee producers. Small producers argued that to allow plantations to be certified exerts greater pressure on prices, thereby eliminating small producers from the Fair Trade market and endangering their very existence. It was resisting the market pressures that historically forced small-scale producers from the market, they argued, that led to the creation of Fair Trade in the first place. In 2004, taking a position branded by some as "protectionist," but supported by ATOs such as Equal Exchange, the small producers succeeded in establishing four products: coffee, cacao, cotton, and honey, as exclusively sourced from small producer organizations.

A second argument in favor of certifying plantations is that the problems faced by plantation workers are worse than those faced by small producers. The small producer organizations acknowledged the difficult situation of the workers, but countered that they do not consider the FLO system as best suited to lead this struggle (CLAC 2004c). They argued that the primary beneficiaries of Fair Trade certification would be the plantation owners, not the workers, and only if the plantations were converted into worker-owned collectives could real worker benefits be assured. They went on to argue that the cooperatives are pursuing a fundamentally different development model to the one implied by plantation certification. Small producers are the owners of their organization and their production processes, and consequently FLO's small producer certification system stresses democratic self-management. In contrast, FLO's plantation certification only requires the creation of a "joint body" of workers and owners to implement certain labor policies. These standards do not go further than those established already in local legislation or international agreements. In addition, the structure and level of costs of plantations are different from those of small producer organizations. The minimum price guarantee, which is one of the most important pillars of Fair Trade, would be undermined if different cost calculations were introduced. Finally, they argued Fair Trade Labeling was built around the small producers. Consumers still identify the FLO label as a label of small producers.

The debate over transnational companies

The debate over plantations is linked to the admission of transnational corporations as licensed users of the Fair Trade label. For the national initiatives, the participation of transnational corporations is a means of increasing the size of the Fair Trade market and to increase revenue through the licensing fee that firms pay to use the Fair Trade label. This increase in sales would benefit Fair Trade producers as well. Some national initiatives are signing agreements with transnational corporations to sell products with the Fair Trade label. Corporations, such as Starbucks and Nestlé, have chosen to participate in Fair Trade often in response to Non-Governmental Organization (NGO) campaigns against them.

In the coffee sector, the concerns over corporate engagement abound. Starbucks offers one Fair Trade coffee blend representing only a tiny share of its total sales. Starbucks has agreements with small producer cooperatives in the buffer zone of the Triunfo Biosphere Reserve of Chiapas, Mexico for both its Shade-Grown and Fair Trade blends of coffee. In addition to Fair Trade standards, Starbucks also has an internal system of best practices, but these are not very well understood by producers. Starbucks uses Conservation International, which is financed by the United States Agency for International Development and large corporations including Starbucks itself,[9] as its certifying organization. Conservation International evaluates producers to determine if they meet the quality standards demanded by Starbucks, in the process controlling the productive process and the organization of the cooperatives (Gonzalez and Nigh 2005). All Starbucks producers in the region are required to sell their coffee through the trading company AMSA, part of the transnational group Omnicafé Atlantic Coffee. Some argue that this violates one of the basic criteria of Fair Trade: direct purchasing from producers and their cooperatives. Further, the use of this trading company means that complete traceability of the coffee is not possible and that the entire Fair Trade price will not reach the cooperatives. Some cooperatives severed ties with Starbucks to free themselves from this intermediary relationship. The growers that continue now provide coffee that is Shade-Grown but not Fair Trade certified.

In 2002, Oxfam International organized a large campaign blaming Nestlé for the collapse of coffee prices in world markets. Because of this campaign,

Nestlé initiated conversations with the Fairtrade Foundation (FtF) in the United Kingdom. Nestlé offered to buy 3,000 bags of Fair Trade coffee a year – barely 0.02 percent of the company's purchases – and to increase that amount depending on sales. In addition, it proposed creating new cooperatives in El Salvador and Ethiopia rather than buying the coffee from cooperatives already in the FLO producer registry.[10] In October 2005, Nestlé launched Nescafé Partner's Blend with FtF certification. This entry into the Fair Trade market has been criticized by some because Nestlé has been the target of numerous boycotts, although others argue that this is a step in the right direction for a large transnational corporation.

In the United Kingdom, 60 percent of the Fair Trade coffee market belongs to Cafédirect, the brand name of a company founded in 1991 by four NGOs.[11] Currently, Cafédirect is the sixth largest coffee brand in the United Kingdom, representing 7.27 percent of the national market for roasted and ground coffee and 4.35 percent of the instant coffee market.[12] According to the FtF, Cafédirect and Nescafé Partner's Blend will not compete directly since they target different consumer sectors. Others argue that consumers who already bought Nestlé instant coffee may buy the new Fair Trade blend, which represents an advance for Fair Trade.[13]

But the tension between Nestlé and Cafédirect remains. It holds a special significance for Mexican Fair Trade producers, since Twin Trading-Cafédirect is known for treating coffee cooperatives as equal partners via a relationship that goes beyond commercial interactions and supports the social organization and development processes in a more direct link between producers and consumers. Cafédirect pays the cooperatives a 10 percent social premium above the contracted coffee price. In addition, it pays a gourmet premium of US$ 2 per pound and a US$ 0.05 premium above the Fair Trade price for organic coffee. In short, while the guaranteed minimum price for Fair Trade organic coffee is US$ 1.41 per pound, Twin Trading-Cafédirect pays US$ 1.61. Cafédirect also reinvests part of its company earnings, 8 percent last year, in workshops and social and business development programs. This relationship contrasts with the tension that characterizes the relationship between the Fair Trade certified cooperatives and FLO. In 2004, Cafédirect became a public company, retaining a 45 percent share while offering 10 percent ownership to its suppliers through a trusteeship located in London. As a result of their shares in Cafedirect, the producers have two seats (one for Africa and one for Latin America) on the Administrative Council. Many of the Mexican cooperatives in Chiapas and Veracruz dedicated the gourmet premiums earned over two years to the purchase of shares. They plan to reinvest further earnings in the purchase of more stock.

For the producers, Cafédirect represents the "gold standard" for "trade, not aid" in its dedication to an equal partnership without paternalism, the sharing of projects and ownership of companies between the North and the South. Producers fear that Cafédirect will be weakened by the introduction of Nescafé Partner's Blend. On the other hand, many recognize that if Nestlé had not obtained FLO certification, it might have sought certification from UtzKapeh or Rainforest Alliance, further weakening producer interests.

Meanwhile, in Mexico, the coffee growers suffer from Nestlé's conventional policies, exerting its economic power to oppose any attempt to regulate the domestic coffee market or to raise the quality and price of the coffee that is consumed in the country.[14]

Conclusions

Coffee continues to be the most important Fair Trade product and its supply still comes largely from Mexico. Because it was created a year before the collapse of the International Coffee Accords and the crisis that still continues in the coffee sector, Fair Trade has been a key factor in the continued successful existence of a number of coffee producing organizations. Fair Trade coffee grower cooperatives have managed to strengthen themselves and to create collective social enterprises that allow them to fulfill their goal of autonomous development. They also have created a Mexican Fair Trade organization and a national certifying organization with international accreditation and recognition. Above all, the cooperatives have built a relationship of solidarity and mutual support among themselves and with other Fair Trade cooperatives in Latin America.

These achievements face new challenges arising, paradoxically, from the success of the Fair Trade model itself. This success is attracting the dominant players in the global market: the transnational agrofood corporations. These corporations are seeking to improve their public image and increase their earnings in a profitable segment of the agrofood market. All of this is being pursued without modifying their general economic strategy, the very same strategy which Fair Trade was created to counter. The national initiatives and FLO have increasingly adopted a market-oriented approach to Fair Trade, to the detriment of the small producers. This has happened for a number of reasons: the importance of the new actors' demands, the prospect of rapidly increasing sales of "fair" products, and the pressure created by the exponential growth of new, weaker certification labels. Coffee producers perceive the evolution of the structure of FLO and its policies as a shift from an initiative that helped its member cooperatives, to a foreign and sometimes hostile system that acts not in its members' interests but with its own bureaucratic logic.

Small producer organizations have continued to resist what they see as the fundamental challenges to the future of Fair Trade, namely the entrance of plantations into the FLO registry, and the participation of transnational corporations. These developments threaten to displace the cooperatives from the Fair Trade market, while calling into question what is "fair." While the coffee producers are evolving from a vision of niche market to one of development, FLO is evolving from a strategy of support for the disadvantaged small producers to mainstreaming. Doing so in the name of greater sales, Fair Trade is in danger of losing its original vision: to create a different market (Raynolds 2002; Renard 1999a,b). In the process, Fair Trade is becoming a movement with divisions at its very heart that may yet undermine consumer confidence and cost the movement its legitimacy.

Notes

1 The authors are grateful to Jerónimo Pruijn, Executive Director of Comercio Justo México A.C., for his collaboration. This chapter was translated by the Center for Fair and Alternative Trade Studies (CFATS) Staff.
2 In Mexico there are 38 coffee cooperatives registered with the FLO, which together sold 1,740,753 kilograms of coffee in the Fair Trade market in the past year. These cooperatives are located in the states of Chiapas, Oaxaca, Veracruz, Puebla, and Guerrero and are made up of around 34,500 members, out of approximately 483,000 total coffee producers in the country. Data from FLO and the Support for Commercialization Services, ASERCA (September 2005), respectively. The number of members in the cooperatives is approximate because some organizations refer to active members and others to registered but not necessarily active members.
3 For example, the credit that was available through the Solidaridad program and FONAES, the National Foundation for Social Businesses, in the 1990s.
4 As opposed to the official State-organized cooperatives that are integrated into the State party apparatus.
5 For example, Fair Trade cooperatives must be democratically governed. How does one evaluate this norm? The indicator would be the occurrence of member assemblies and the parameter the number of acceptable assemblies. The supporting documentation would be an assembly accord or an interview with a producer (Information from Comercio Justo México).
6 CLAC launched the small producer symbol in 2006.
7 Meanwhile, no one verifies how democratic the industrial roasters or the supermarkets are where Fair Trade coffee is sold.
8 CLAC proposed that the national initiatives have four representatives, like the producers. Presently, the five national initiatives are TransFair USA (25 percent of the volume of Fair Trade), Max Havelaar France, Max Havelaar Denmark, Max Havelaar Belgium, and the UK's Fairtrade Foundation. The industrial representatives are Green Mountain USA and Oxfam WW Belgium. One producer representative comes from Mexico (coffee), another from Brazil (orange juice), another from Tanzania (coffee), and a tea plantations representative comes from Sri Lanka.
9 Funders of Conservation International include Citigroup, Exxon Mobil, ICBG, and McDonalds (Choudry 2003).
10 Interviews with CLAC representatives, March 2006. See also www.oxfam.org.uk/ generationwhy/blog/2006/03 (accessed May 3, 2006).
11 Twin Trading, Oxfam, Tradecraft, and Equal Exchange.
12 Information from CaféDirect administrator.
13 Presentation by Harriet Lamb, FtF, at the 2° International Meeting on Solidarity Tourism and Fair Trade. Chiapas, Mexico, March 2006.
14 Nestlé buys 30 percent of all Mexican coffee and its instant coffees make up 70 percent of national consumption (Mexican Coffee Council).

References

APPC (Asociación de Países Productores de Café). (2001) "Resolution for the improvement of the quality of coffee in the world," *Revista Cafés de México*, May 20.
Aranda, J. and Morales, C. (2002) "Poverty alleviation through participation in fair trade coffee networks: the case of CEPCO, Oaxaca, México," Report prepared for Fair Trade Research Group, Colorado State University, Online. Available at: www.colostate.edu/ Depts/Sociology/FairTradeResearchGroup (accessed June 12, 2006).
Bisaillon, V., Gendron, C., and Turcotte, M.-F. (2005) *Commerce Équitable et Économie Solidaire: Les Défis pour L'avenir. Synthèse des Activités du Chantier Commerce*

Equitable,   Online.   Available   at: http://fairtrade.socioeco.org/fr/documents. php#list_docs_id_doc_7412 (accessed June 4, 2006).

Choudry, A. (2003) "Conservation International: privatizing nature, plundering biodiversity," *Seedling of Grain*, October, Online. Available at: www.grain.org/seedling/?type= 00002003 (accessed June 4, 2006).

CLAC. (2004a) "Document for discussion for the regional assembly of the Latin American and Caribbean Coordination of Fair Trade Small Producers," unpublished, Oaxaca, Mexico, August.

—— (2004b) "El precio de ser un productor certificado por FLO (El precio de la certificación)," Internal document circulated prior to the Regional Assembly of the Latin American and Caribbean Coordination of Fair Trade Small Producers, unpublished, Oaxaca, Mexico, August.

—— (2004c) "Private plantations and FLO's future," unpublished document to be discussed by the Meeting of Members and FLO Board, May.

COMPRAS. (2005) "Report, San Cristobal de las Casas," Chiapas, Mexico.

Cookson, R. (2005) "String-along or beanfeast?," *The Guardian*, September 21, Online. Available at: www.society.guardian.co.uk (accessed June 12, 2006).

FLO. (2003) "A quantum leap in the impact of fairtrade labelling. FLO's strategic plan 2003–2008," Bonn: FLO.

González, A. and Nigh, R. (2005) "Smallholder participation and certification of organic farm products in México," *Journal of Rural Studies*, 21: 449–460.

Guerrero, M. (2005) "¿Qué café tomar?," *Revista Poder y Negocios*, Mexico, August 8, 58–60.

Martínez, M.E. (2002) "Poverty alleviation through participation in fair trade coffee networks: the case of the Tzotzilotic Tzobolotic Coffee Cooperative, Chiapas, México," Report prepared for Fair Trade Research Group, Colorado State University, Online. Available at: www.colostate.edu/Depts/Sociology/FairTradeResearchGroup (accessed June 12, 2006).

Murray, D., Raynolds, L.T., and Taylor, P.L. (2003) "One cup at a time: poverty alleviation and fair trade coffee in Latin America," Fort Collins: Colorado State University, Online. Available at: www.colostate.edu/Depts/Sociology/FairTradeResearchGroup/index.html (accessed August 10, 2006).

Pérez-Grovas, V. and Cervantes, E. (2002) "Poverty alleviation through participation in fair trade coffee networks: the case of Unión Majomut, Chiapas, México," Report prepared for Fair Trade Research Group, Colorado State University, Online. Available at: www. colostate.edu/Depts/Sociology/FairTradeResearchGroup (accessed June 12, 2006).

Pérez-Grovas, V., Cervantes, E., Burstein, J., and Carlsen, L. (2002) "El café en México, Centroamérica y el Caribe. Una salida sustentable a la crisis," Mexico: Coopcafé-CNOC.

Raynolds, L. (2002) "Consumer/producer links in fair trade coffee networks," *Sociología Ruralis*, 42: 389–409.

Renard, M.C. (1999a) "Los intersticios de la globalización. Un label (Max Havelaar) para los pequeños productores de café," México: CEMCA.

—— (1999b) "The interstices of globalization: the example of fair coffee," *Sociología Ruralis*, 39: 484–501.

—— (2003) "Fair Trade: quality, market and conventions," *Journal of Rural Studies*, 19: 87–96.

—— (2005) "Quality certification regulation and power in fair trade," *Journal of Rural Studies*, 21: 419–432.

Roozen, N. and VanderHoff, F. (2002) "*La Aventura del Comercio Justo*," México: Ediciones El Atajo.

Sanz, J. and Macías, A. (2005) "Quality certification, institutions and innovations in local agrofood systems," *Journal of Rural Studies*, 21: 475–486.

Sylvander, B. (1995) "Conventions de qualité et institutions: le cas des produits spécifiques," in E. Valceschini and F. Nicolas (eds), *Agro-alimentaire: une économie de la qualité*, Paris: INRA.

Taylor, P., Murray, D., and Raynolds, L. (2005) "Keeping trade fair: governance challenges in the fair trade coffee initiative," *Sustainable Development*, 13: 199–208.

Valceschini, E. and Nicolas, F. (1995) "La dynamique économique de la qualité agro-alimentaire," in E. Valceshini and F. Nicolas (eds), *Agro-alimentaire: une économie de la qualité*, Paris: INRA.

VanderHoff, F. (2002) "Poverty alleviation through participation in fair trade coffee networks: the case of UCIRI, Oaxaca, México," Report prepared for Fair Trade Research Group, Colorado State University, Online. Available at: www.colostate.edu/Depts/Sociology/FairTradeResearchGroup (accessed June 12, 2006).

Watts, M. and Goodman, D. (1997) "Agrarian questions: global appetite, local metabolism: nature, culture, and industry in fin-de-siècle agro-food systems," in D. Goodman and M. Watts (eds), *Globalizing Food, Agrarian Questions and Global Restructuring*, London: Routledge.

Yépez, I. and Mormont, M. (2006) "Le commerce équitable face aux nouveaux défis commerciaux: évolution des dynamiques d'acteurs," Politique Scientifique Fédérale, UCL, Ulg, Belgium.

10 The making of the Fair Trade movement in the South

The Brazilian case

John Wilkinson and Gilberto Mascarenhas

Introduction

Since the beginning of the new millennium the fair trade concept has become an important theme in Brazilian popular movements and policies alike. In the 1990s, there were some Fair Trade Labelling Organization (FLO) certified producer groups, especially in orange juice, and some integrated into Alternative Trade Organizations (ATOs), especially handicrafts and tropical food products, directly articulated by Non-Governmental Organizations (NGOs) and/or religious organizations. Fair Trade, however, was not seen as a component of the varied social movements, producer organizations, civil society groups, and government policies directed at the small-farming sector and rural development.

In less than a decade, the situation has changed greatly. From the president, through to various ministries and public agencies, the fair trade concept has become incorporated into official policy discourse. It has similarly been espoused by popular movements, global, and leading national NGOs, and assimilated within corporate social responsibility objectives. It has come to prominence at a time when free trade, hawked as the panacea for development by the multilateral organizations, has been subject to repeated protests from new transnational social movements (Bologna, Seattle, Cancun, and Hong Kong). Since the turn of the century free trade has been challenged by the criteria of trade justice, adopted by the world's leading opinion-forming NGOs.

At the same time, this period has seen rapid changes within the global Fair Trade movement due to the shift to the mainstreaming of trade circuits by FLO, the most polemic of which, in the Latin American context, have been the registering of plantations, licensing of transnational corporations and introduction of certification fees. The founding of Mexico's National Labeling Initiative, Commercio Justo (see Chapter 9), opened up new strategic perspectives for Southern countries, no longer limited to the role of beneficiary producer organizations, but now also including the goal of developing national Fair Trade systems.

Brazil's burgeoning Fair Trade movement has emerged as the initiative of global NGOs, previously involved in sustainable development issues and ATO trading circuits in Brazil, together with the participation of FLO, government, and social movements. Fair Trade producer groups, for their part, owe their still incipient organization and participation to the dynamic of this movement. The Brazilian experience, therefore, presents a sharp contrast with the other country and case studies (Mexico, South Africa, and Bolivia) discussed in this section. In this chapter, we will provide a profile and analyze the dynamic of the Brazilian Fair Trade movement, taking into account both the specificities of the domestic context and Brazil's new role as a global player in agribusiness and world politics. The first section presents a succinct view of Brazil's agrofood system, policies, and participation in multilateral forums. This is followed by an appreciation of the producer organizations mobilized by different Fair Trade initiatives. We then analyze the nature and evolution of the Fair Trade movement identifying key questions raised by the Brazilian strand of the movement, which we see as central to the future of the global movement – the creation of national Fair Trade systems, certification systems, the role of the State, and South/South relations. The final section deals with the mainstreaming of Fair Trade in Brazil and the pressures this exerts on the Fair Trade movement and its producer base.

Brazil's agrofood system

The dualist interpretation of Brazil's agrofood system, where the modernized sector is geared to exports and the peasant/family farm economy provides the bulk of the domestic staples, seriously underestimates both the latter's integration into agribusiness food chains and the former's contribution to the transformation of the popular diet (Wilkinson 2004). Nevertheless, it has been on this assumption that the institutional framework of agrofood policy was consolidated in the post-dictatorship 1980s and Brazil thus has an Agricultural Ministry for the Agribusiness sector (MAPA) and an Agrarian Development Ministry (MDA).

With the adaptation of temperate climate grain crops to Brazil's low latitude savannah region in the 1970s and 1980s, some 200 million hectares were opened to cultivation and Brazil's destiny as the world's agricultural commodity supply base for the twenty-first century could already be envisaged. By 2005, Brazil was the world's leading exporter of soy, red meat, sugarcane, and coffee, was second in poultry, fourth in maize and pigs, and is coming up fast in cotton and fresh fruit (Agroanalysis 2005). In addition, it is projected to become the world's leading exporter of fish as ocean fishing gives way to fish-farming (Wilkinson et al. 2006).

The institutional preconditions for this agribusiness dominance were laid in the 1990s as Brazil lowered its tariffs and quotas, deregulated and privatized its domestic markets, and leveled the playing field for transnational capital. With vigorous internal growth and a strong influx of both foreign direct investment and short-term "volatile" capital, it seemed for a while that Brazil's growth might not depend on a positive trade balance. The end of the privatizations and a slowdown in domestic growth, however, revealed that foreign investments no longer provided the hard cash for debt repayments and the drive for an export surplus became the central priority of successive governments, including that of Lula and the Worker's Party (PT). Brazil's export surplus depended almost exclusively on agro-industrial products and the agribusiness sector assumed a dominant role in industrial and trade policy.

Today, Brazil has the world's largest agribusiness trade surplus (around US$ 40 billion), has successfully challenged the subsidies of both the United States and Europe, and has assumed leadership of the G20 group in the World Trade Organization (WTO) negotiations. Brazil's opposition to US and EU export subsidies has broad support in the South and in the Fair Trade movement. Brazil's support for market access is however challenged, internally in Brazil by groups supporting family farming, including the MDA, and externally by Fair Trade advocacy groups and the Trade Justice Movement which support food security and sovereignty and the protection of the peasant/family farming sector. Market access questions become more complicated once it is recognized that Brazil now exports more agro-industrial products to other Southern countries than to the North (Jank 2005).

In spite of the great economic and political power of Brazil's agribusiness exporting interests, the transformation of its domestic agrofood system (and that of other Southern countries) has been equally or perhaps even more important (Reardon and Berdegues 2002). Modern retailing circuits, largely transnational, now dominate the domestic food supply systems of much of the South and in Brazil account for some 65 percent of food sales. Market access now takes on another meaning as the sanitary, quality, and logistical demands of the super-market system impose severe barriers to entry for the family-farming sector. The transformation of traditional values into marketing strategies and the pressures toward social responsibility predispose the dominant agrofood players toward a (highly selective) incorporation of family farm, regional, and indigenous products. As we will see in the following section, this transformation of the domestic food supply systems of the South poses new questions for Fair Trade movements in these countries, and introduces into the South the typically Northern debates associated with "mainstreaming," corporate social responsibility, and committed consumption.

Notwithstanding the dominance of the agribusiness sector, the 1990s also saw the political consolidation of the family-farming sector in Brazil, legitimized through this sector's role in domestic food provision, employment creation, and environmental protection. The period was one of political mobilization within social movements (such as land occupations, demonstrations, etc...) and in the policy arena (in land reform measures and the National Program for Family Farming, PRONAF) as well as in the promotion of spaces for civil society partic-ipation. The impetus for the agrarian reform and PRONAF was provided by organizations emerging from the Southern family-farming sector with its strong European farming tradition. From this background would also emerge the agro-ecological and organic networks of producer organizations, together with farmer's markets and community supported agriculture which in the following decade would converge with Fair Trade and ethical and solidarity trade (Fonseca and Wilkinson 2003).

During the 1990s, the demands of the market, especially the export market, were identified with agribusiness and viewed with suspicion if not downright hostility by others. The central questions were defined around redistribution, involving the basic entitlements to land and to the status of family farming as a dynamic contributor to development with the right to special policy support. These demands were underwritten by vigorous lines of academic research and NGO activism, and were as effective as those bolstering agribusiness.

By the turn of the millennium, however, the situation was radically different. The agrarian reform sector now comprised some 600,000 families and occupied 20 million hectares (Guanziroli 2001). Five years into the PRONAF program, policy makers were now giving priority to income generating solutions, other than guaranteed State crop purchases, a measure less favored in the light of the neoliberal institutional reforms.

In this changed context, the challenges of market insertion assumed pride of place both in the traditional family farm and the agrarian reform sectors. The tensions between the options of alternative/local markets and mainstreaming were now a permanent feature of debates in the family farm movement, acquiring particular force in the case of agroecology versus organics (von der Weid and Altieri 2003). The former provided a powerful movement alternative to the "Green Revolution," but the latter offered the perspective of dynamic new markets for family farming. It was the latter, too, which began to redefine perspectives on the importance of exports, as the import dependence of Northern markets in this fast-growing sector was increasingly highlighted.

This export focus received further support from two sources. First, within the new paradigm of export-oriented growth adopted by the leading multilateral institutions, government support for the integration of the Small and Medium Enterprise sector (SME) into exports was promoted (World Bank 2002). Second, the challenges of market insertion increasingly pointed to the competitive advantage of high-value intensive crops or the development of value-added processing for the family-farming sector. The promotion of special quality products became a priority of the MDA, and export orientation was promoted by the State agency, Brazilian Support Service for Micro and Small Firms (SEBRAE) (Lummertz Silva 2003). The family farm association for the Mercosul countries also supported exports. The promotion of Fair Trade markets, whether ATO or FLO certified, and sustainable markets fit this orientation and became incorporated as policy options.

By the middle of the first decade of the new millennium, not only was a market-oriented strategy inscribed in family farm policy but the export market was also seen as a legitimate component of market insertion. To the extent that the Brazilian movement[1] and organizations[2] became more integrated into global social movements,[3] distinct positions on trade became developed which brought Brazilian groups closer to Fair Trade advocacy positions against indiscriminate market access, and for measures to protect the small-farming sector. Strategies of mainstreaming and exports live in permanent tension with the priority for alternative markets and local market development. Within both social movements and public policy, the dominant position argues that trade should be subordinated to food security and food sovereignty (Maluf 2000).

This profile of the Brazilian food system helps to situate the current elaboration of the Fair Trade movement. In addition to the tensions between the agribusiness and the family farm sectors we have shown how Fair Trade has evolved from being antithetical to the dynamic of social movements and policies directed to the family farm sector in the 1990s, to being highly convergent both with the critical thrust of Fair Trade advocacy and Trade Justice campaigns and the development of Fair Trade markets. Before moving on to analyze the current dynamics of Brazil's Fair Trade movement we consider the profile of the early entrants into Fair Trade in the 1990s.

An overview of Fair Trade initiatives in Brazil

Most political leadership associated with family farming in Brazil was unlikely in the 1990s to be sympathetic to Fair Trade initiatives due to their technological and export base. The focus of the family farming movement was on redistribution (land reform) and recognition (status of family farm), goals seen as politically prior to questions of the market, with demands directed to the State rather than the market. Furthermore key Fair Trade products were not central to the dominant social bases of the family farm movement. Brazil is the largest producer and exporter of coffee, but coffee is produced primarily by medium and large plantations, unlike in countries like Mexico where it is produced by small holders. In addition coffee production is concentrated in Minas Gerais, a region marginal to small farmer organizations and movements. While coffee is important for some Brazilian Fair Trade producer groups and is likely to become more so given the rapid growth of the North American market, its political importance to the small farmer movement remains negligible. Fair Trade's second most important commodity, bananas, is produced in Brazil almost exclusively for domestic consumption and regional markets.

Rather than the problematic of exploitative inclusion via falling prices in traditional commodities, the family farm movement has been marked by the threat of exclusion, as traditional crops are replaced by highly mechanized farming and traditional regions faced with marginalization by the scale economies of the savannah frontier. This in its turn has led to a policy emphasis on the need for diversification out of commodities, involving a greater openness to new quality markets, within which Fair Trade becomes an attractive alternative, primarily to the extent in which it incorporates a wider product range.

The Brazilian producer groups incorporated into Fair Trade during the 1990s comprise three strands. There was a Northern demand-driven initiative to develop Fair Trade orange juice for export to Europe, motivated by a concern with the use of child labor in the conventional commodity chain. This initiative was promoted by Business meets Social Development (BS&D), FLO's representative in Brazil. The orange juice initiative involves a complex and tense coordination between five producer groups (at least of the group falls within the plantation category) aligned to achieve the necessary scale. A more unlikely candidate for Fair Trade from a Brazilian perspective could hardly be imagined, since orange juice production is almost exclusively based on medium and large plantations and overwhelmingly concentrated in only one region. The ambiguous dynamic of buyer-driven value chains (Gereffi 1994) emerges clearly in this case since on the one hand it may lead to intervention in sectors which are at a tangent to, or even problematic from, the point of view of the social movements and political objectives organized around the small farmer and rural development in the country concerned. On the other hand, it may provide an opportunity for unexpected market integration of previously marginal producer groups.

The second and third strands in the development of Fair Trade markets in the 1990s have significant areas of overlap, including their concentration in the north and northeastern regions of the country. Religious (largely Italian) groups have promoted handicraft exports to Europe through ATOs as a means of generating income for traditional communities. The global visibility of the struggles of the "peoples of the forest," enhanced by Chico Mendes, promoted a spate of "sustainable development" initiatives involving both the certification of forestry management and the promotion of nontimber forestry products. In the process, there has been a convergence between sustainable and Fair Trade activities leading to the involvement of NGOs in both these areas. Given the nontraditional character of the products being promoted and the importance of handicraft production, access to international markets has been primarily based on ATO channels.

In the more favorable climate of the early years of the new millennium there was a rapid growth in the number of producer groups entering Fair Trade, both through ATO circuits and through FLO registration. By the end of 2005, 16 organizations had products certified by FLO (see Table 10.1), with a further 4 in the process of certification and 12 applying for certification. Some 15 traders dealing with Brazilian products were FLO registered. Of the certified organizations, 7 exported coffee, 5 orange juice and mangos, 2 just mangos, 1 dried bananas, and 1 brazil nuts (FLO 2005b). As noted in Table 10.2, coffee exports have expanded rapidly in recent years and by 2005 coffee emerged as the most valuable Fair Trade export with sales over US$ 2.5 million. Orange juice sales have grown much more slowly, and even declined in 2005 (see Table 10.3). Other FLO certified products play a more minor role.

The ATO sector is more difficult to outline with many more actors involved in autonomous initiatives. Probably the majority of the ATO producer organizations are involved in handicrafts with sales being conducted through trading systems which group together products from a number of different associations. There may be dozens of ATO linked handicraft associations, especially since smaller items are now being dispatched via simplified posting arrangements. Food products are more visible since they normally involve more complex logistics but there are still no agreed upon figures. Our own research identified 10 associations exporting products including honey, cachaça, hearts of palm, cashew nuts, guaraná, açai, tangarine juice, and mate tea (see Table 10.4). ATO sales are even more difficult to pin down, but appear to be on the order of US$ 600–800 thousand. ATO sales are substantially less than the FLO certified exports and are growing much less rapidly (a tendency that reflects the differential dynamics of ATO and FLO certified markets in the North).

Table 10.1 Brazilian producer organizations certified by FLO

Organization name	FLO's category[a]	Number of families	Year of FLO certification	Traded products
COMPAEB-CAPEB (Cooperative agroextrativista of producers Epitaciolândia and Brasiléia)	SP	65	2004	Brazil nut
ASSOCIAÇÃO DE PEQUENOS AGRICULTORES DE SANTANA DA VARGEM (Association of small producers of Santana de Vargem)	SP	126	2004	Coffee Arabic
ASSOCIAÇÃO DE PEQUENOS PRODUTORES RURAIS DE SAMPAIO (Association of small rural producers of Sampaio)	SP	40	2004	Coffee Arabic
COASOL (Cooperative of solidarity producers of Leroyville)	SP	46	2004	Coffee Arabic
COOCAFÉ (Cooperative of coffee producers of the region of Lajinha, Ltd.)	SP	3,000	2004	Coffee Arabic
COOPFAM (Cooperative of the small producers of Poço Fundo)	SP	130	1998	Coffee Arabic
FACI (Federation of rural community associations of Lúna and Lrupi)	SP	900	1998	Coffee Arabic organic
ACARAM (Central articulation of associations for mutual support)	SP	1,200	2003	Coffee Conillon (Robusta)
CEALNOR (Central of associations of the Litoral Norte)	SP	820	2001	Concentrated juices of orange and passion fruit
COAGROSOL (Cooperative of solidarity agropecuaristas of Itápolis)	SP	47	2001	Concentrated juices of orange, mango, lemon and passion fruit
APACO (Association of small farmers of the west of Santa Catarina)	SP	117	2001	Concentrated orange juice
ARPROCLAN (Association of representatives of orange producers and harvesters of the region of northwest of Parana)	HL	800	1998	Concentrated orange juice
ASSOCIAÇÃO DE PEQUENOS PRODUTORES RURAIS DE BATUVA (Association of the small rural producers of Batuva)	SP	23	2000	Dried bananas (raisin)
ASPPIF (Association of the producers of the Perimentro Irrigado of Formoso)	SP	37	2004	Mango
MOCÓ AGROPECUÁRIA (Moco agropecuaria)	HL	35	2004	Organic mango, dehydrated mango
ECOCITRUS (Cooperative of the ecologic farmers of the Cai Valley)	SP	43	2005	Tangerine juice

Source: FLO (2005b).

Note
a SP = Small producers; HL = Hired labor.

Table 10.2 Coffee sales by FLO certified producers

Year	Quantity (tons)			Value (US$)		
	Nonorganic	Organic	Total	Nonorganic	Organic	Total
2002	0	14	14	0	40,940	40,940
2003	297	47	344	704,217	121,072	825,290
2004	533	52	586	1,250,243	150,156	1,400,399
2005	1,128	0	1,128	2,636,714	0	2,636,714
Total	1,958	113	2,701	4,591,175	312,168	4,903,343

Source: FLO (2005b).

Table 10.3 Concentrated orange juice sales by FLO certified producers

Year	Quantity (tons)			Value (US$)		
	Nonorganic	Organic	Total	Nonorganic	Organic	Total
2002	528	0	528	633,600	0	633,600
2003	1,479	0	1,479	1,744,110	0	1,744,110
2004	1,391	135	1,526	1,660,320	204,120	1,864,440
2005	267	0	267	320,400	0	320,400
Total	3,665	135	3,800	4,358,430	204,120	4,562,550

Source: FLO (2005b).

Table 10.4 Brazilian producer organizations integrated with Northern ATOs

Organization name	Number of families	Traded products
COFRUTA (Cooperative of the fruit producers of Abaetetuba)	1,200	Assai in natural and organic
COPALJ (Cooperative of small producers agroextrativistas of Lago do Junco)	—	Babassu oil; babassu flour
COASA (Cooperative agro-industrial for export)	38	Cashew nuts
COOPERCAJU (Cooperative of artisanal beneficiaries of cashew nuts of the Rio Grande do Norte)	160	Cashew nuts
CGTSM (General council of the tribe of Sateré-Maué)	200	Guarana: powder, drink, pills, and in syrup; candies
APA (Association of alternative producers)	250	Hearts of palm
AAPI (Association of beekeepers of the micro-region of Simplicio Mendes)	730	Honey and by-products
CCA-PR/CCA-UBEM (Central of land reform of Parana)	350	Mate tea and mate cups (artcrafts)
ASSM (Association Mutirão)	—	Organic hearts of palm
ASS. QUILOMBOLAS E FAZENDA VACCARO (Association quilombolas of the Vaccaro Farm)	216	Sugar cane organic rum (Cachaça)

Source: Authors' research 2005/2006.

These figures point to the emergence of a complex and potentially conflictive relationship between the producer base of Fair Trade and the current dynamic of the movement's configuration. As we will see in greater detail in the following section, one of the most significant recent developments has been the organization of this producer base, establishing its collective identity as a Fair Trade producer, with a distinct voice in the movement. Although characterized by the heterogeneity of its various components, the movement's dominant axis could be loosely described as gravitating around the solidarity economy, ATO-style Fair Trade, and the promotion of the domestic market. The producer group, on the other hand, is likely to be increasingly focused on the demands of the Fair Trade global market and particularly FLO policy within this market.[4] Before analyzing the main features of the Fair Trade movement we will present a profile of these producer groups based on field work involving seven organizations chosen to broadly represent the product, market, and regional mix of the Fair Trade movement as a whole.

Table 10.5 provides a summary of these organizations. In most cases, these are organizations of small farmers which have been around for more than 10 years (those with more recent foundation dates were actually restructured at that time). If we consider the value of Fair Trade exports and, even more so, the percentage which the Fair Trade market occupies in total sales, it is clear that we are dealing with organizations with considerable administrative and organizational competence. The number of associates involved in Fair Trade activities is typically in the hundreds and even thousands. These associations and cooperatives tend to represent the best that family farming has achieved in their respective local contexts. The very fact of being durable associations involving significant numbers of associates is in itself exceptional.

In general, therefore, in the Brazilian case, the organizational and productive competences of these producer groups were consolidated prior to the development of specific Fair Trade initiatives and have drawn on a range of supporting actors and sources of finance. Some have been the result of, or include components of agrarian reform or were the result of specific projects. Lutheran and Catholic religious activity has been at the origin of a number of the organizations. Rural unions have also played an important leadership role. Global or national NGOs linked to international cooperation financing have often been the decisive force. As these associations become consolidated, there tends to be a multiplier effect in relation to finance, research, and organizational support. Many of these organizations now have extensive national and international networks, cooperation agreements and sources of financing.

National policies have also been increasingly important as the National Family Farming Program (PRONAF) extended its reach. All of the associations in our table were recipients of PRONAF financing which now covers a range of activities, including working capital for farming, collective infrastructure, and agro-industrial investments. The SEBRAE organization in support of small firms is increasingly active with these producer groups (Sebrae 2004). With the Lula Government, new instruments have been adopted, including the financing of harvest purchases.

Table 10.5 Characteristics of seven producer organizations linked to Fair Trade in Brazil in 2004

Product line	Orange juice		Coffee		Cashew nuts		Hearts of palm
Producer organization	Cealnor	Acaram	Faci	Coopfam	Copercaju	Coasa	Apa
Brazilian region	Northeast	North	Southeast	Southeast	Northeast	Northeast	North
Date of foundation	1997	1989	1994	1991	1991	1999	1992
Number of families	820	1,200	800	130	160	38	250
Average size of the farms (ha)	5	Variable (5–100)	10	6	50	Variable (5–30)	Variable (15–100)
Productivity (kg/ha)	14,000	600	3,000	2,400	600	400	2,000
Quantity commercialized (tons)	400	1,080	780	600	92	28	46
Organic certification	In process	No	Yes	Yes	Yes	No	No
Year of the first FT export	1999	2003	2003	2003	1991	1993 (start/stop) 2001 (restart)	2003
FT branch	FLO	FLO	FLO	FLO	ATO	ATO	ATO
FT market destination (%)	50	16	60–80[a]	60–85[a]	35	90	40
Quantity of FT exports (tons)	200	168	211	360	37	25	18
Value of FT exports (US$)	240,000	392,000	562,667	1,032,000	226,188	154,438	120,414
Main markets	Germany, Belgium, Italy, Austria, Switzerland	EU	USA, Germany, Italy, Switzerland, France, Canada	USA	Switzerland, Austria, Italy, Germany	Italy	France
Export mechanism	Direct	Trading co.	Trading co.	Trading co.	Trading co.	Direct	Direct

Source: Authors' research 2005/2006.

Note
a Export quantity depending of the quality of the product (there is no limitation for exports).

Lack of circulating capital to finance purchases, storage, and marketing costs, has always been the Achilles heel of these small cooperatives, and advanced payments systems within Fair Trade arrangements are unique in focusing on this need.

Fair Trade represents an important market for the majority of our sample, but it is in most cases a significant revenue source, and for the producers directly bene-fited is certainly very significant. The fact that the associations have in general a strong orientation to domestic markets, and often a wide range of products, many of which are not appropriate for export markets, is an important factor when con-sidering the preoccupation of the movement with developing a Brazilian Fair Trade system. A wide range of traders are involved in Fair Trade exports, both ATO and FLO, ranging from transnationals (Dunkin Donuts), leading national firms, a variety of Fair Trade traditional traders, and new style mainstream traders (Altereco). Most of the associations export to Italy, which reflects both the strength of networks developed through missionaries active in Brazil, and the importance of the role of the Italian Fair Trade organizations, CTM Altromercato and Liberomondo, for Fair Trade in Brazil.

Some organizations are certified by an internationally accredited organic certifier (e.g. the BioDynamics Institute, IBD) which for FLO-affiliated organi-zations implies double monitoring. It should be remembered that in Brazil, the family farm movement (led by Ecovida ecological producer network in the south of the country) has espoused participatory monitoring and certification, and views official certification as authoritarian, ineffectual and exclusionary (Medaets and Fonseca 2005). In fact, Brazil is currently playing a lead role in the International Federation of Organic Agricultural Movements (IFOAM) to promote participatory certification systems. The fact that almost all these organi-zations have, or intend to have official certification is testimony to their financial and organizational capacity. Pointing to the extent of overlapping certification, one producer group is simultaneously a member of the Ecovida network, certified by IBD, in the process of getting FLO certification, and audited by the trader Altereco.

In conclusion, we can say that, with the possible exception of orange juice (and this may well become true for coffee also), Fair Trade enters as an important, and sometimes crucial, complementary market for generally established producer organizations, which already sport multiple ties with supporting actors (financial, research, and technical), national and international, private and public. In some cases, however, Fair Trade networks may prove crucial both in raising the pro-ducer groups to new levels of organizational capacity and in securing further forms of support. These producer groups, however, had little or no contact with each other, a situation which was to change markedly in 2004 as outlined in the following section.

The Brazilian Fair Trade movement

The Brazilian Forum for the Articulation of Ethical and Solidarity Trade (FACES do Brasil) was created in 2002 on the initiative of 13 organizations, including national and international NGOs, representatives of government ministries and agencies, bodies linked to the rural trade union structure and alternative farmers' networks (see Table 10.6). Questions related to Fair Trade exports form part of the Forum's agenda and it includes Brazil's FLO representative, BS&D. But the central concern of the Forum and its *raison d'être* has been the development of a Brazilian national Fair Trade system. With this in mind, since 2002 it has organized a series of national and regional meetings to mobilize support for and discuss the framework of such a system. In this, it has been very much influenced by the Mexican experience and from the outset it has placed its discussions within a regional and South/South perspective, a standpoint which was reinforced in the context of its organization of a parallel

Table 10.6 Members of FACES do Brasil in 2002

Organization name	Acronym	Activity
Banco de Alimentos da Cidade de São Paulo (São Paulo City Food Bank)	SEMAB	Food safety and procurement programs
BS&D (Business and Sustainable Development)	BS&D	FLO Certification Licensee in Brazil
Federाção de Órgãos para Assistência Social e Educacional (Federation of Organs for Education and Social Assistance)	FACES	Training and education for small producers and organizations, member of the Brazilian Network of Solidarity Economy (RBSES)
Fundação Friedrich Ebert (Friederich Ebert Foundation)	ILDES	Human Rights, private/public relations
Fundação Lyndolpho Silva (Lyndolpho Silva Foundation)	FLS	Promotion of North/South FT for small producers
Instituto de Manejo e Certificação Florestal e Agrícola (Institute for Forest and Agricultural Certification and Management)	IMAFLORA	FSC's Forest and Agricultural Certification
Instituto Kairó – Ética e Atuacao Responsavel (Kairos Institute – Ethics and Responsible Behavior)	KAIROS	Education and Campaign for Responsible Consumption
Ministério do Desenvolvimento Agrário/Secretaria de Agricultura Familiar (Ministry of Agrarian Development/Secretary of Family Farming)	MDA/SAF	Regulation and public policies for family farming
Movimento Viva Rio (Viva Rio Movement)	VIVA RIO	Social inclusion of disadvantaged urban and rural people
Rede Ecovida de Agroecologia (Ecovida Network of Agroecology)	REDE ECOVIDA	Agroecology and Participative Certification
Serviço Brasileiro de Apoio às Micro e Pequenas Empresas (Brazilian Service of SME support)	SERE	Sustainable Local Development
Visao Mundial (World Vision)	VISAO MUNDIAL	Social inclusion and Trade for disadvantaged producers

Source: Faces do Brasil (2004c).

Fair Trade forum at the São Paulo, UNCTAD meeting in 2004 (Faces do Brasil 2002, 2004a,b,c).

The Friederich Ebert Foundation has financed the Forum's activities and played a leading role in its organization, together with the NGOs, World Vision and Imaflora, which work fundamentally in the north and the northeast of Brazil on rural poverty and alternative forestry strategies (Visão Mundial 2005). These organizations have been more closely related to the International Fair Trade Association (IFAT) and ATO Fair Trade circuits. An important Brazilian NGO which coordinates an extensive rural network has also played a central role and, as a member of the Brazilian Network of the Solidarity Economy, has introduced the goals of the solidarity economy movement into the Forum's discussions. These, in their turn, have been reinforced by strong international links with organizations similarly influenced by solidarity economy perspectives, such as Artisans du Monde (Artisans du Monde 2002; Faces do Brasil 2004d, 2005a).

From the outset, a public/private hybridity has predominated, involving the participation of a representative from the Ministry for Agrarian Development and one from the public agency for small and medium firms. To the extent that Fair Trade in Brazil is not conceived to be an appendix to the international movement, the issue of labeling, certification, and monitoring has raised the question of which institutional framework would guarantee the requisite authority and regulatory capacity. The government was already involved in discussions on the development of a national family farming label within the framework of the national family farm program. To the extent that Fair Trade in a Southern context is inseparable from the issue of development, the direct involvement of government bodies is not necessarily problematic. In addition, Fair Trade has defined itself more explicitly within the trajectory of the solidarity economy, whose principles already define the objectives of a special secretaryship in the government (as had similarly been the case in France during the period of the Socialist Government in the 1990s). It should also be recognized that the victory of the PT in Brazil has led to a more generalized blurring of the lines between NGOs and government.

In the course of four years of seminars, workshops, and electronic discussions the Forum has worked on the production of a consensus document, which summarizes the values, principles, and criteria considered necessary to underlie a Fair Trade movement in Brazil (Faces do Brasil 2004c, 2005a). To date, however, this has not led to the definition and elaboration of an institutional framework for Fair Trade in Brazil. In part this would seem to be a product of the heterogeneity of the Forum's members (ranging from the Brazilian FLO representative to delegates from the solidarity economy) which is polarized around the issues of mainstream versus alternative circuits, exports versus local markets, middle-class versus poor consumers, North/South versus South/South, and formal versus participatory certification schemes. On the other hand, there has been a persistent questioning of the Forum's lack of representation at the level of producer organizations (Faces do Brasil 2005b).

A major development in this respect was the autonomous organization of Fair Trade producer groups into what has become known as the Articulation of Family

Farm Organizations involved in Fair and Solidarity Trade (Ventura and Gastel 2005).[5] This group, organized by the Brazilian representative to CLAC, has expanded from 6 to over 50 members, since its formation in 2004, with branches in each of Brazil's major regions. Membership is open to organizations not yet involved, but interested, in Fair Trade as a strategy either for exports or the domestic market. This group has now become an independent actor within the Brazilian Fair Trade movement with its own program and funding (see Box 10.1).

A second shift with regard to the key components of the Brazilian Fair Trade movement has occurred at the level of federal government participation. Initially individuals from the family farm sector of the government, specialists in the question of regulation and certification, participated as members of the NGO-based Faces do Brasil Forum.[6] Since then, the situation has been inverted and the different segments of the Fair Trade movement are now organized within a working group of the Secretary for the Solidarity Economy, which has become the new forum for discussing the institutionalization of Fair Trade.[7] Faces do Brasil participates in the new forum, but at the same time has now transformed itself into an institute for the provision of technical expertise to the movement. In addition to the NGOs who formed part of Faces do Brasil, four government departments participate, together with the agency for small and medium firms. The Brazilian FLO liaison office is also a participant, although only in its capacity as a Brazilian NGO involved in Fair and Solidarity Trade. And finally the Articulation of Family Farm Organizations involved in Fair Trade represents the Fair Trade producer organizations.[8]

Within this new institutional context, Fair Trade is seen as a subcomponent of a broader promotion of the solidarity economy. In Brazil, the solidarity economy has now established itself as a significant movement (Laville et al. 2006) with emblematic, successful experiences and involves the mobilization of a considerable number of actors, both in production–consumption networks and academic circles. In 2004, the government brought together some 4,000 solidarity enterprises at a National Solidarity Fair and some 20,000 solidarity enterprises were identified in a national census carried out the following year. In addition to discussing policy support mechanisms for Fair Trade, the Working Group is debating the framework for a Brazilian national Fair Trade system. Four options

Box 10.1 Main Fair Trade proposals of the Articulation of Family Farm Organizations involved in Fair and Solidarity Trade (AOPFCJS)

A national statute for Fair and Solidarity (CJS):

- A dialogue should be established with civil society and government to promote a solidarity market and a broad debate on "fairness" in conventional trade.
- A juridical statute should be defined, aiming to protect the CJS in its several modalities against abuses and to distinguish it from conventional commercial practices.

Broader objectives than those existing for the North–South FT:

- The CJS concept should be *widened* in order to consider local, national, South–South and North–South markets.
- It is defined as a group of practices aimed at sustainable development, giving priority to food sovereignty and safety, autonomy, territorial development, and diversification.
- The impact of CJS should be extended, mainly among disadvantaged producer groups.
- CJS should be broadened to include new products and services, including those with greater value added.

Target-public:

- The CJS should give priority to disadvantaged producers; the participation of plantations and corporations in CJS does not promote the well being of small producer groups, generally represents a threat to them, and tends to distort the principles of CJS and confuse consumers.
- The CJS products should be accessible to a greater number of consumers, including through the mass distribution system, but dependence on exporters and wholesalers should be avoided.

Inclusiveness and systems of guarantee:

- The systems of guarantee (certification) should *not exclude* small organizations or those that have small revenues.
- Agroecology and participatory certification should be strengthened and the solidarity trade of agroecological products should be broadened.
- Family Farming Groups and Solidarity Economy share the same values and should seek for more cooperation and combined activities.

Autonomy, participation, and transparency:

- The CJS should promote autonomy and support producer groups to develop their capacities for participative management and commercialization.
- Participation in networks and articulations, will help the producer organizations improve their capacities
- Producers and workers should participate fully in the creation of policies and systems of guarantees as well as those related to marketing.
- Transparency and full information for producers and consumers from their CJS partners.

Source: Letter of Presentation (AOPFCJS 2005a).

are currently under discussion involving different degrees of private and public regulation, together with varying combinations of participatory and/or third-party certification.

While there may be sharp ideological differences between conceptions of the solidarity economy and those of FLO-style Fair Trade, with material interests, in the case of NGOs, and academic spaces also at stake, the heterogeneity and, at the same time, pragmatism of the producer groups often reduces what would appear to be opposed strategies, to the status of complementary options. In our research sample of firms interviewed (see Table 10.5), producer groups simultaneously export, sell on local and national markets, and are benefited by government procurement programs. They use participatory and third-party certification depending on the demands of the market, although this may be accompanied by vigorous campaigning in favor of cheaper and more self-managed certification systems. On the other hand, even the networks most committed to alternative circuits do not rule out sales through supermarkets (Rede Ecovida da Agroecologia 2000). Organics, which in many ways serve as a model for Fair Trade strategies, have prepared the way for a more pragmatic appreciation of market dynamics both as this effects exports versus domestic strategies, and popular versus middle-class markets in the domestic context. Even within the solidarity economy circuits, middle-class markets are by no means excluded, particularly in the case of handicraft production, with designer clothes and upgrade handicrafts being targeted at boutiques, but also in the case of traditional health products and dual purpose (food/cosmetics) ingredients similarly targeted at food/health stores.

Mainstream interest in a national Fair Trade system in Brazil

In the first section to this chapter, we argued that the traditional divisions between exports and domestic markets makes less sense as the transnationalization of the agrofood system has led to a convergence of both food habits and food standards under the aegis of a fast globalizing retail sector. The domestic organics market, which has grown very quickly in Brazil, would be a case in point, revealing the presence of a "global" middle-class demand pattern, influenced by health and environmental criteria. Corporate social responsibility has also accelerated with more than a thousand firms (including the retail leaders) now involved in the voluntary social and ethical auditing system set up by Ethos, a business NGO created to promote social responsibility. With the collaboration of the FLO representative, this auditing system has now incorporated Fair Trade criteria. FLO has itself endorsed the notion of a national Fair Trade system in Brazil, and, after efforts to move in this direction, would seem now to be awaiting the results of the government's deliberations.

The activities of Brazil's two leading supermarket chains are indicative of the degree to which social responsibility has become part of business strategy in Brazil. Pão-de-Açucar/Cassino, which holds 16 percent of the Brazilian market, has developed a program of procurement directed to small farmers and artisans named Caras do Brasil. Typical products are bought from small farmers, artisans, and indigenous communities with the objective, according to the firm, of promoting communities whose production process has an ecological and environmental profile by providing a market channel and special sales conditions. The Caras do Brasil program involves 305 products (90 percent food and handicrafts) from 19 Brazilian states and 72 small producers, benefiting around 13,000 people. These products are commercialized in 36 stores throughout Brazil (Angélico 2006). While the producer groups and volumes transacted are probably much smaller than in the case of Fair Trade, this program is directed to the same public as both the Fair Trade and solidarity economy. After only three years, more producer groups are now involved in this supermarket program than in the FLO and ATO Fair Trade initiatives combined.

Carrefour, which holds 12 percent of the Brazilian market, initiated a line of Guaranteed Origin products in Brazil six years ago. This program builds on the supermarket's earlier program in France and is focused on sustainable production and traceability. The Carrefour program is similar to the Ethical Trade Initiative in England (Smith and Barrientos 2005). There are now 42 Guaranteed Origin products in Brazil which are supposed to uphold social, environmental, and health criteria (be socially correct, produced by registered workers under Brazilian labor law and without child labor; visually pleasant; without chemical residues; environmentally adequate; no GMOs; and without use of feed of animal origin). The Carrefour program involves 60 suppliers in Brazil, including family farm producer groups. Under both supermarket programs, products can be exported to subsidiaries in other countries (and in the case of Carrefour even to other retail outlets), accelerating the blurring of domestic and export markets discussed at the beginning of this chapter. In 2003, Carrefour had a Brazilian export target of US$ 24 million of certified products up from US$ 11 million in 2002. As these programs become consolidated, the debate on mainstreaming so present in Northern countries, will become an increasingly central issue in Brazil. In addition to supermarkets, dedicated food health stores, with outlets in all the major urban centers, are also committing themselves to Fair Trade style trading practices.[9]

An interesting development in this direction from within the Brazilian Fair Trade movement has been the creation of the *Etica Comercio Solidario*, a trader formed through an association between the Inter-American Bank (IBD) and World Vision (one of the main promoters of the Faces do Brasil and a leading figure in the Brazilian Fair Trade movement). Investments in this initiative amount to almost US$ 2 million. Its stated objectives are the following: to promote marketing arrangements according to fair, ethical, and solidarity trade for producer organizations; to provide assistance to rural and urban organizations in this direction, and to adopt the principles defined by the Faces do Brasil. In addition to exporting, primarily to Fair Trade World Shops, *Etica* also trades on the domestic market through large-scale retail outlets and plans to set up three specialized Fair Trade shops, one of which is already in operation in Recife, in Brazil's Northeast. To date *Etica* works with 3,000 producers, largely in the Northeastern region of

Brazil. It has also developed its own detailed auditing and monitoring system by which producers receive a certificate of conformity at no charge, other than the investments necessary to achieve this status. Once accorded the certificate, the producer group is subjected to yearly auditing (AOPFCJS 2005b). This trader, which has emerged, from the leading actors of Brazil's Fair Trade movement, is also responding to the new dynamic of globalization combining exports with domestic market activities.

The most consistent effort to develop a mainstream Fair Trade market in the South is that currently being developed by Altereco in Brazil, a new style trading company, half business, half NGO, whose "CEO," Lecomte, is a frequent contributor to Fair Trade discussions (Lecomte 2004). Created in 1998 with the aim of importing and distributing Fair Trade products from Southern countries, Altereco's current commercial strategy in France is to sell Fair Trade products in leading retail chains using its own brand name and the labels of Max Havelaar and Agriculture Biologique (AB). Altereco is a member of IFAT and of the French *Platforme pour le Commerce Équitable* (Altereco 2005). Over the past five years, it has audited 100 producer organizations in 30 Southern countries, and currently has 35 cooperatives as direct partners, marketing a range of 80 products, among them coffee, tea, chocolate, rice, fruit juices, hearts of palm, quinoa, olive oil, and sugar (Altereco 2005).[10] Altereco's sales in France have increased from US$ 804 thousand in 2002 to a projected US$ 12 million in 2005. In addition, Altereco is developing products for the US market, and has already set up a subsidiary in California. Altereco's objective is to become a world brand for Fair Trade, on the basis of maximum visibility and efficiency, directly confronting the competition of conventional brands in mainstream markets (Altereco 2005).

Since 2003, Altereco has shipped hearts of palm from Brazil from one producer organization and is in the process of auditing and certifying others. In 2004, Altereco completed an analysis of potential supplies from small-farming production and the ability of the Brazilian market to absorb these products. The results pointed to a large and diversified but still disorganized supply base and a strong demand potential if produced under the quality, health, environmental, and social concerns that characterize the Fair Trade proposal (Penchèvre and Sacca 2005). The relevant consumer market is estimated at 2.5 percent or some 4.5 million people, based largely on the demand for organics. To fill this gap, Altereco has now launched its *Altereco Brazil* project.[11]

The Altereco strategy is based on the three main actors of the value chain: the producer organizations, large supermarket chains, and middle/high-class consumers. As regards the producers, the idea is to promote value added through processing, thereby generating higher price levels than those prevailing in conventional markets. With this aim, Altereco is going beyond a purely commercial relationship and is proposing the creation of a nonprofit enterprise whose shares will be divided equally among producer organizations and Altereco. In the new firm, producers and Altereco would each have 45 per cent of the capital and each be represented by two members of the administrative council; civil society actors would have 10 percent of the capital and one council representative.[12]

This proposal has been discussed with several producer organizations, receiving strong support and is now being implemented.

Altereco's marketing strategy is to begin with the two main supermarket chains Pao de Acucar/Cassino and Carrefour. Pricing is intended to offer "the best product for the best price" with consumer prices close to competitive quality products. The price differential paid to producers would be generated through the value added based on processing or through savings along the trading circuit (Altereco 2005). The Altereco proposal, although representing a wager on corporate social responsibility and responsible consumer movements, is mainly founded on the quality, innovation, and appeal of marketed products sold at prices close to those of conventional quality products.

Conclusions

In Brazil the Fair Trade movement has not grown organically out of the increasing organization and demands for participation of producer groups integrated into global ATO or FLO handicraft and food chains. Nor were these producer groups central to the broader social and political movement, which emerged around the defense and the strengthening of the family farm model. Rather, Fair Trade was promoted as a movement in Brazil by national and global NGOs involved in sustainable rural development who constructed a broad coalition, involving a range of actors associated with alternative production networks, responsible consumption, the Government Family Farm Ministry, FLO, and the solidarity economy movement.

At its outset the goal was to create a national Fair Trade system in Brazil, inspired by the Mexican model, at a time when the trajectory of FLO was coming under increasing criticism (around issues of mainstreaming, plantation registration, and certification fees). The network affiliations of these NGOs and their promotion of strategies based on nontraditional crops (mostly not registered by FLO) led to a greater identification with IFAT and ATO global trading circuits and funding bodies.

Government involvement was a feature of the Fair Trade movement from its outset and seen as unproblematic to the extent that Fair Trade was understood as a policy for social inclusion, and a strategy for family-farming/sustainable development. With the Lula government this involvement has intensified and has strengthened the solidarity economy axis of the Fair Trade movement. As we have seen, solidarity economy priorities converge with the traditional anti-agribusiness and anti-export oriented agriculture emphasis of the family farm movement and the emphasis on local markets and food security and food sovereignty.

In the first half of the new millennium, both ATO and especially FLO Fair Trade initiatives have accelerated. In Brazil, we now see the separate organization of Fair Trade producer groups within the movement. Integrated into the broader Latin American producer base of Fair Trade, this development has reinforced opposition to FLO policies on plantation registration and paid certification and has reinforced the joint organization of Fair Trade and solidarity economy producer organizations. On the other hand, the greater presence of these producer groups has introduced a marketing pragmatism, which tends to temper more ideological polarizations. As we have seen in our sample, producer groups see export and domestic markets, niche/mainstream and solidarity markets as complementary and have a similar approach to certification demands.

Given the differential expansion of FLO/mainstream Fair Trade markets as compared with ATO networks – both globally and in the domestic context – combined with retail strategies of global sourcing, an increasing accommodation to mainstreaming in the Brazilian Fair Trade movement would seem likely. Such a tendency would also correspond to the profile of the certified producer groups which situates them among the best organized segments of the Brazilian family-farming sector. Corporate social responsibility initiatives and the emergence of new style traders geared to domestic market opportunities would reinforce this trend.

At the same time, the greater space for social policies related to the partial reflux of neoliberal solutions, increases demand for basic foodstuffs and provides new market opportunities for products not contemplated in mainstream Fair Trade markets, reinforcing the development and solidarity economy character of Fair Trade in Brazil. At the ideological level, the recent decision to accept Nestlé on the Fair Trade register in Britain is sharpening the divide between ATOs and FLO. These developments, together with the consolidation of national Fair Trade systems in the Global South will tend to shift the traditional polarization between ATO and FLO strategies, to a more nuanced and permanently monitored discrimination among different mainstream options.

Notes

1 Most notably the MST – the Brazilian Landless Movement – and Ecovida – Brazil's most important agroecological network of producer and consumer organizations which has developed the alternative participatory certification scheme.
2 The principal ones being: CUT – Central Trade Union Organization linked to the Workers Party; CONTAG – National Confederation of Agricultural Workers (both family farm and rural labor); FETRAF – Family Farm Federation.
3 MAELA – Latin American Agroecological Movement; through Campesina – a global peasant movement with strong bases in Latin America and Asia together with international solidarity economy networks.
4 A qualifying factor here would be the importance of domestic sales for these producer organizations. Estimates based on information gathered from these organizations would suggest that sales to the domestic market are worth double those to Fair Trade export markets.
5 This was facilitated by the MDA's organization of a National Symposium on Experiences of Family Farm Producer Organizations in Export Markets, and provides a good example of the synergies between public and private initiatives, in addition to highlighting the importance of Government resources (human and financial).
6 The fact that a Government department is considered a founder member of an NGO reflects the fuzzy frontier between social movement and social policies. The global policy network literature analyzes this emergence of hybrid forms of governance. Given the ambiguity of this situation Brazilian government representatives later assumed the status of invited participants.

7 In addition to being an accepted arena for articulating actions related to social inclusion and development, this government body also has networking resources. Yet a change in government or even in the political composition of the government could quickly reveal the fragility of this arrangement (as demonstrated by the experience of the solidarity economy in the French Socialist Government in the 1990s).

8 With the multiplication and differentiation of the actors involved, the name which characterizes the movement has also suffered evolution. Beginning as Solidarity and Ethical Trade with Faces do Brasil, SEBRAE, along with various other Latin American organizations, has preferred the international designation, Fair Trade, whereas the organization representing producer groups has opted for Fair and Solidarity Trade. To accommodate this evolution, Faces do Brasil now refers to Fair, Ethical and Solidarity Trade (CJES) or the Brazilian System for Fair, Ethical and Solidarity Trade (SBCJES).

9 See Mundo Verde's official site.

10 Altereco has developed a monitoring and evaluation system in partnership with PriceWaterhouse Coopers called Fair Trade Audit 200 (FTA 200), whereby producer organizations are evaluated according to economic, social, and environmental criteria on the basis of 150 indicators. The final result is based on an average with economic criteria weighing 40 percent, environmental 10 percent and social, 50 percent. The system is both educative and diagnostic, allowing audited organizations to identify their weakness and strengths.

11 In 2005, Altereco also launched this project in France with the objective of attracting financial backing.

12 Communication at Altereco meeting in Rio on November 19, 2005.

References

Agroanalysis. (2005) Rio de Janeiro, FGV 25, 3.

Altereco. (2005) Seminário Altereco Brasil, Rio de Janeiro, November 19, unpublished.

Angélico, F. (2006) *Pequenos artesãos ganham chance nos grandes centros*, Online. Available at: www.pnud.orgl (accessed December 1, 2006).

Aopfcjs. (2005a) "Articulação de organizações de produtores familiares para o comércio justo e solidário," *Relatório da Reunião de Articuladores*, São Paulo, 14 p, unpublished.

—— (2005b) *Seminário Construçãodo Sistema Nacional de Comércio Justo e Solidário*, São Paulo, 10 p, unpublished.

Artisans du Monde. (2002) *Resultados dos Estudos de Impacto Junto aos Produtores do Hemisfério Sul da Ação Comércio Justo Desenvolvida há 25 Anos por Artisans du Monde*, Paris: Artisans du Monde.

Faces do Brasil. (2002) "Perspectivas para a consolidação de um mercado consumidor brasileiro: relatório síntese," *II Seminário Internacional de Comércio Justo e Solidário*, São Paulo, unpublished.

—— (2004a) *Simpósio Comércio Ético e Solidário: Desenvolvimento Sustentável na Prática*, São Paulo, unpublished.

—— (2004b) *Reunião Estratégica do Comércio Ético e Solidário*, São Paulo, unpublished.

—— (2004c) *Valores, Princípios e Critérios de Comércio Ético e Solidário do Brasil*, Online. Available at: www.facesdobrasil.org.br (accessed November 11, 2005).

—— (2004d) *Seminário Internacional*, São Paulo, August 24, 2004.

——(2005a) *Sistema Brasileiro de Comércio Ético e Solidário* (SBCES), Online. Available at: www.facesdobrasil.org.br (accessed November 18, 2005).

—— (2005b) *Elementos Para Discussão e Construção Conjunta de um Sistema Brasileiro de Comércio Ético e Solidário*, Online. Available at: www.facesdobrasil.org.br (accessed November 15, 2005).

FLO (Fair Trade Labelling Organizations International). (2005a) *Flo-Cert: Central Inspection Plan*, Online. Available at: www.fairtrade.net (accessed November 12, 2005).
—— (2005b) "FLO presentation at Biofach Brazil," Rio de Janeiro: BSD, unpublished data.
Fonseca de Albuquerque, M.F. and Wilkinson, J. (2003) "As oportunidades e os desafios da agricultura orgânica," in M.F. Albuquerque, D.M. de Lima, and J. Wilkinson (eds), *Inovação nas Tradições da Agricultura Familiar*, Brasilia: CNPq, Palalelo 15.
Forum Brasileiro de Economia Solidária. (2005) "A trajetória da Economia Solidária no Brasil: do Fórum Social Mundial ao Fórum Brasileiro de Economia Solidária," Informe da Economia Solidária no Brasil, Porto Alegre, unpublished.
Gereffi, G. (1994) "The organization of buyer driven global commodity chains: how US retailers shape overseas production networks," in G. Gereffi and M. Korzeniewicz (eds), *Commodity Chains and Global Capitalism*, London: Praeger.
GT-PCCS. (2005) "Relatório da Reunião do Sub-Grupo 'Sistema de Comércio Ético e Solidário' do GT de Produção," Comercialização e Consumo, Brasília, unpublished.
Guanziroli, C. (2001) *Agricultura Familiar e Reforma Agrária no Século XXI*, Rio de Janeiro: Garamond.
Jank, M. (2005) "Inserção do Brasil no comercio internacional agrícola e expansão dos fluxos comerciais Sul-Sul," ICONE, September 21, 2005.
Lagente, S. (2005) *Panorama du Commerce Équitable au Brésil*, Campinas: CIRAD.
Laville, J.-L., Magnen, J.-P., De França Filho, G.C., and Medeiros, A. (2006) *Action Publique et Économie Solidaire*, Érès, Paris.
Lecomte, T. (2004) *Le Commerce Équitable*, Paris: Eirolles Practiques.
Lummertz Silva, V. (2003) "O Sebrae e a agricultura familiar," in M.F. Albuquerque de Lima, D.M. de Linam, and J. Wilkinson (eds), *Inovação nas Tradições da Agricultura Familiar*, Brasilia: CNPq, Palalelo 15.
Maluf, R.S. (2000) *Consumo de Alimentos no Brasil: Traços Gerais e Ações Públicas Locais de Segurança Alimentar*, São Paulo: Polis.
Medaets, J.P. and Fonseca, M.F. (2005) *Produção Orgânica: Regulamentação Nacional e Internacional*, Brasília: NEAD.
Penchevère, S. and Sacca, J. (2005) *Oportunités du Marché Brésilien pour Altereco: Vers un Commerce Équitable Sud-Sud*, Rio de Janeiro, Altereco, unpublished.
Pistelli, R. and Zerbini, F. (2003) "A comercialização no contexto do comércio ético e solidário," in C.L. de França (ed.), *Comércio Ético e Solidário no Brasil*, São Paulo: Fundação Friedrich Ebert/ILDES.
Raynolds, L. (2002) "Forging new consumer/producer links in fair trade coffee networks," *Sociologia Ruralis*, 42: 404–424.
Reardon, T. and Berdegue, J. (2002) "The rapid rise of supermarkets in Latin America," *Development Policy Review*, 20: 371–388.
Rede Ecovida de Agroecologia. (2000) *Normas de Organização e Funcionamento*, Lages, Brazil, unpublished.
Renard, M.C. (2004) "Entre la equidad y el mercado: el comercio justo," International Rural Sociological Association, World Congress, Trondheim, July 25–29.
Santos, L. (2003b) "Rede ecovida de agroecologia e certificação participativa em rede: uma experiência de organização e certificação alternativa junto à agricultura ecológica familiar no Sul do Brasil," in C.L. França (ed.), *Comércio Ético e Solidário no Brasil*, São Paulo, Fundação Friedrich Ebert/ILDES.
Sebrae. (2004) *Comércio Justo: Pesquisa Mundial*, Brasília: Sebrae.

Silva, E. (2003) "O sistema brasileiro de comércio ético e solidário como agente de segurança alimentar," in C.L. de França (ed.), *Comércio Ético e Solidário no Brasil*, São Paulo: Fundação Friedrich Ebert/ILDES.

Smith, S. and Barrientos, S. (2005) "Fair trade and ethical trade: are there moves towards convergences?," *Sustainable Development*, 13: 190–198.

Ventura, L. and Gastel, M. (2005) *Rumo a um Sistema Nacional de Comércio Ético e Solidário no Brasil – Proposta para Desenhar o Processo de Construção: Subsídios para Discussão*, Rio de Janeiro, unpublished.

Visão Mundial. (2005) Online. Available at: www.eticabrasil.com.br (accessed June 14, 2005).

Von der Weid, J.M. and Altieri, M. (2003) "Perspectivas de manejo de recursos naturais com base agroecologica para agricultores de baixa renda no século XXI," in D.M. Albuquerque Lima and J. Wilkinson (eds), *Inovação nas Tradições da Agricultura Familiar*, Rio de Janeiro: CNPq/Paralelo 15.

Wilkinson, J. (2004) "The food processing industry, globalization and developing countries," *Journal of Agricultural and Development Economics*, 1: 184–201.

Wilkinson, J., Rocha, R., and Fuertes, P. (2006) *The Traditional Fishing Sector in Developing Countries and the Transnationalization of Retail and Food Services*, Rome: FAO.

World Bank. (2002) *Globalization, Growth and Poverty: Building an Inclusive World Economy*, Oxford: Oxford University Press.

11 Fair Trade and quinoa from the southern Bolivian Altiplano

Zina Cáceres, Aurélie Carimentrand, and John Wilkinson

Introduction

Murdoch et al. (2000) suggest that transformations in the nature of food demand have led to the incorporation of new territories and groups of producers who did not participate in the technically based production systems typical of the Fordist period. This has been the case for Bolivian peasants who grow "*Real Blanca*" quinoa, a specialty product whose characteristics can only be obtained when grown in the agricultural areas of Oruro and Potosí in Bolivia. Previously marginalized production systems have been transformed into sources of added value. Complementary marketing strategies based now on red and black quinoa varieties are opening up similar opportunities to other Andean regions and producers.

This chapter discusses the response of the actors in the Andean quinoa value chain to the growth in international markets for this traditional subsistence crop. Our historical account is largely based on the rich testimony of founder members of Bolivia's National Association of Quinoa Producers (ANAPQUI), bolstered via the analytical and impact literature dedicated to quinoa and supplemented by our own field research interviews. In analyzing the dynamics of the emerging Fair Trade market for quinoa, we argue that attention should be given particularly to the heterogeneity of the actors within Fair Trade which leads to differing organizational structures and differing returns along the quinoa value chain, particularly for farmers and their producer organizations.[1]

Most discussions on tensions within Fair Trade have focused on the polarization between alternative and mainstream strategies. We show that there are in addition marked variations within each of these strategies leading to different outcomes for Andean quinoa producers. To understand the dynamic of Fair Trade for the quinoa sector, therefore, we will advance beyond the above polarization and analyze the specific strategies of each of the lead firms in the value chain. To this end we develop a typology of these leading firms, highlighting the different ways in which they influence the organization of quinoa producers and the returns accruing to participation in the emerging organic and Fair Trade markets.

Quinoa, unlike other Fair Trade crops such as coffee and cocoa, is not a traditional export product. This makes the case of quinoa somewhat unique. The Andean grain differs from other commodities explored in this book in several ways.

(1) It is a crop with strong connections to the food safety and sovereignty of Andean peasants. (2) Quinoa's price is set in local rural markets by intermediaries rather than internationally. (3) Producers of quinoa were marginalized via the deterioration of city–countryside exchange and domestic production rather than by insertion into global commodity chains. (4) Quinoa's exceptional nutritional qualities were recognized before integration into the circuits of fair/solidarity trade, and its commercialization was accompanied by organic qualification. (5) The initial processing of quinoa is done locally prior to entering the global market. (6) Quinoa has joined FLO's relatively new group of certified products where the setting of a fair price is quite complex.

This chapter begins with a brief history of the changing position of Andean quinoa. We analyze the early links between quinoa producers and European alternative and Fair Trade markets which led to the adoption of new quality criteria for quinoa, including organic production. The increase in demand for quinoa in the 1990s attracted new actors (particularly French retailers) to what was now becoming a global value chain involving novel patterns of coordination and control. We discuss the subsequent emergence of Fair Trade certification and other brand initiatives which have created new expectations among quinoa producers. We then present a typology of different value chain strategies, identifying the consequences in each case for producer organization and participation. The chapter concludes with an indication of the challenges posed by current patterns of Fair Trade market insertion.

The historical evolution of quinoa and marginalization of Andean peasant agriculture

Quinoa is one of the range of crops planted by peasants in the high mountains of South America, particularly Bolivia, Peru, and Ecuador.[2] The production of quinoa in these three Andean countries amounts to 52,900 metric tons in a planted area of 70,400 hectares (FAOSTAT 2005). It is one of the few crops that grows at the highest Andean ecological levels and is particularly resistant to the harsh local climate. There are a large number of varieties of quinoa depending on ecotype, topography, and human intervention. The small round quinoa grain is covered with a bitter substance called saponin which needs to be removed before exporting (FAO 1999).[3]

With the modernization of the agrofood system beginning in the middle of the twentieth century, quinoa, like other traditional Andean grains, legumes, roots, and tubers underwent severe contraction in both consumption and area planted, as traditional eating habits were substituted by Western wheat-based habits (Hellin and Higman 2001; Repo-Carrasco 1992). During this time quinoa acquired a negative reputation among urban consumers as a food of the poor and Indians (Salis 1985). Post World War II economic policies in Peru and Bolivia provoked unequal regional growth, further aggravating the erosion of the peasant economy (Gonzales de Olarte 1994). As a result, the cultivation and consumption of quinoa, as well as other Andean crops, became ever more restricted to marginal peasant agricultural zones. In 1970 the three Andean countries together produced only 17,747 metric tons of quinoa (FAOSTAT 2005). This represented a sharp decline from the volume produced 20 years previously in Peru (where 42,500 metric tons of quinoa was produced and annual per capita consumption was 4.56 kgs).[4]

Quinoa has rich nutritional properties due to the extraordinary quality of its protein, with a high amino acid content superior to wheat, oats, and maize. Of special importance is the presence of lysine, an element more commonly found in meat than in vegetables. In the 1980s, studies by the FAO, the American Academy of Sciences, and the National Administration of Space and Aeronautics (NASA) classified quinoa as a "complete" food important for food safety. Quinoa's adoption by NASA as food for astronauts heightened the grain's positive image (Schlick and Bubenheim 1996).[5] Local public research institutions began to systematize the traditional knowledge of the uses and customs of quinoa among the peasants, and publicize the multiple properties of quinoa as not only nutritional but also health promoting since it is free of fats and gluten. Quinoa's qualities are so polyvalent that it also became an exotic alternative for vegetarian consumers, leading an English company to produce a quinoa-based meat substitute, *Quinova*,[6] and a Spanish company to produce quinoa milk.[7] A French company has developed as many as 33 products from the basic grain (including noodles, cookies, quinoa rice cake, and beer).[8] Quinoa adjusted well to the new forms of food "qualification" which became incorporated into consumers' purchasing decisions due to concerns about social questions, the preservation of the environment and health (Cáceres 2005; Fonte 2002).

Of the 70,000 quinoa producers in Bolivia's northern Altiplano, 80 percent are farmers with very limited economic resources practicing subsistence agriculture on no more than one-third of a hectare (Brenes et al. 2001). These producers use between 70 and 85 percent of their quinoa crop for household consumption; the rest is sold. By contrast, for the 15,000 producers in the southern Altiplano region, the average production area for quinoa is between 3 and 10 hectares, with 60 percent of the harvest going to market (PROINPA 2004). The majority of quinoa exports come from this region, generally with organic certification. These exports represent between 9 and 17 percent of Bolivia's total volume.[9]

Traditionally, peasant producers kept most of their quinoa for their own consumption, selling a part in rural markets and reserving some for seeds. Part of the quinoa is also used for bartering within and between communities (FAO 2003). On the southern Bolivian Altiplano, the rural market of Challapata represents the quinoa "Wall Street,"[10] where the price of quinoa is set every week. Quinoa traditionally reached the urban consumer in bulk with little care being taken over selection or cleaning. There was very limited quality control and almost no public health control. The market was dominated, as we observed in our visit there in 2004, by the logic of supply and demand, with about a dozen buyers and the peasant as price taker. In the 1970s the price paid to the quinoa producer was equivalent to one third the price of imported wheat (Ayaviri et al. 1999). Purchased in small quantities from peasant producers, quinoa was collected and consolidated by wholesalers who monopolized its distribution. For the marginalized quinoa producers this was basically the only commercial path between the peasant communities of the Andes and the urban consumer (Egoavil 1983; Egoavil et al. 1978) although the State tried to foster more direct links between peasants and markets (ADEX 1996).

The emergence of a quinoa network based on peasant organizations, alternative trade, and international technical cooperation[11]

During the 1970s small producer organizations were created, known as OECAs (Peasant Economic Organizations), with the purpose of marketing through alternatives to the existing intermediaries. At the same time, in the North the alternative trade organizations (ATOs) gathered strength. The creation of a network linking the OECAs and the Fair Trade organizations provided a promising outlet for the production of organized peasants, while financial support from the International Technical Cooperation Program (ITC) allowed for the construction of a quinoa processing plant (Ayaviri et al. 1999).[12]

The first organization of quinoa growing peasants in Bolivia was the OECA "*Operación Tierra*" Union of Agricultural Cooperatives (CECAOT), comprising 14 cooperatives from the Nor Lípez province in Potosí. This federation of community-based cooperatives emerged from earlier programs of agricultural mechanization promoted by Belgian missionaries. Each cooperative corresponded to a community and more than 500 families were affiliated with the union. At the time, however, the cooperative idea was foreign to quinoa producers. Further initiatives were also launched at this time to counter the deteriorating conditions of the quinoa market. The First National Meeting of Quinoa Producers was held in the city of Oruro, focusing on the production, industrialization, and marketing of quinoa and on peasant participation in these processes. At the same time, CECAOT promoted the first Quinoa Festival. This was followed by the creation of the Quinoa Defense Committee at the provincial level, whose objective was to prevent the sale of quinoa at prices below the cost of production and to create controls to enforce this among producers (Ayaviri et al. 1999).

In 1983 CECAOT received the first contract for 200 tons of quinoa from the Quinoa Corporation in the United States (IICA/PNUD 1991). That same year the National Association of Quinoa Producers (*Asociación Nacional de Productores de Quinua* – ANAPQUI) was founded as the result of a division between CECAOT members with regard to the creation of a national association proposed by the Belgian volunteers. This new peasant organization consisted initially of 150 producers from the departments of La Paz, Oruro, and Potosí, with support from the Central Union of Peasant Workers (*Central Sindical Única de Trabajadores Campesinos* – CSUTCB).[13] Support from the ITC was also intensified during this period, financing the entire process of converting quinoa producers into agro-business operators (through bilateral network programs of the United Nations and the European Community), and promoting popular education programs. The following decade saw the construction of quinoa processing plants with significant funding from the United Nations. Through collective action, the organized peasants were able to upgrade from the agricultural to the primary processing stage. The introduction of organics also intensified the reorganization of the quinoa chain, with impacts upstream in addition to new downstream relations (Cáceres and Carimentrand 2004a; Laguna et al. 2006).

It was in this favorable context that connections with the Fair Trade movement, particularly ATOs, were created. GEPA, a German ATO composed of religious institutions, played a fundamental role in the creation of Fair Trade linking small producers from the South to consumers from the North (GEPA 2005). GEPA centralized demand for quinoa from European ATOs, thereby reducing the costs to Fair Trade importers interested in distributing quinoa. In 1989, the first contracts were closed between ANAPQUI and GEPA.

GEPA was responsible for the decision to combine social and ecological quality criteria and stimulated ANAPQUI to produce organic quinoa to increase exports to the European solidarity market (Laguna 2002b). We can say, therefore, that a new stage in the partnership between quinoa producers and the solidarity market was thus initiated based on long-term commercial relations, distribution in European World Shops, payment of a fair price, funding for agricultural campaigns, and the establishment of contacts with other purchasers. This new "partnership" consolidated the expansion of quinoa, increasing exports and allowing this product to break out of the confines of the regional Andean market, becoming transformed into what we have described as a global value chain (Cáceres and Carimentrand 2004a). Organic conversion of quinoa in the Bolivian Altiplano was also influenced by market studies carried out by the Inter-American Institute for Cooperation on Agriculture in partnership with the Bolivian Ministry of Agriculture (IICA/PNUD 1991). These confirmed the potential for growth in European organic markets and the qualification of the "*Real Blanca*" quinoa grain as the one accepted by consumers in the North. In this way the OECA/ATO/CTI network laid the foundations for the transformation of a peasant agriculture producing for its own consumption and for rural markets into an export-orientated agriculture, generating better producer prices (Cáceres and Carimentrand 2004; Laguna et al. 2006).

Peasant *upgrading* and the construction of "organic" quality in the quinoa global chain

The 1990s were characterized by an extensive process of organic conversion carried out by the Bolivian peasant organizations linked to Fair Trade, not only in quinoa, but also cocoa and coffee. At the same time, the entry of the new actors, CECAOT and ANAPQUI, into mechanized primary processing, represented a pioneer upgrading experience for producer organizations within the quinoa chain allowing greater control of production, primary processing, and direct contact with international traders (Cáceres 2005).

The United Nations supported the consolidation of the agro-industrial phase through the construction of production plants undertaken by ANAPQUI.

Six plants were built, of which two are still in operation in La Paz and Challapata, with the others now forming part of the logistics and grain reception network. This "excess" of processing plants was a response to local pressure from ANAPQUI association members (Ayaviri et al. 1999). The relations between the ANAPQUI members were in part based on trust, family ties, and friendship, constituting in Granovetter's (1973) terms "strong ties" among the quinoa growing peasants, which can also be identified according to the values of the "domestic world" in the terminology of the French convention approach (see Chapter 3). Nevertheless, these did not always act in synergy with the business profile of the OECAs and the commercial dynamic of the new quinoa markets, including the Fair Trade market.

In 1992 the Quinoa Natural Production Program (PROQUINAT) was initiated. This resulted in the reorganization of planting areas through the introduction of new production systems to achieve organic quality for the "*Real Blanca*" variety of quinoa. The initiative was implemented in Oruro and Potosí as a response to global market demand, especially the European Fair Trade market. This program was responsible for introducing organic production methods and the standards and certification procedures of Northern importer countries (Ayaviri et al. 1999; Laguna 2002b). The latter consolidated a pattern of buyer-driven governance (Gereffi 1999) in which quality is adjusted, and with this the organization and coordination of the quinoa chain, to the demands of the purchaser, in this case, GEPA. This program promoted soil conservation and the introduction of equipment and machinery. Attracted in part by a contract covering the whole year-long crop cycle, 845 producers joined the program. Numerous problems emerged in the program due to the limited knowledge of organic agriculture and the lack of staff to carry out internal controls. With the adoption of organic practices, quinoa was transformed into a "credence good" validated through submission to certification and inspection processes (Carimentrand and Ballet 2004; Sauvée and Valceschini 2004). In practice, control was limited to one annual scheduled inspection and one unannounced visit by "third party experts" in addition to the internal controls of the peasant organizations. Lack of continuous monitoring in certain cases led to opportunistic behavior, such as the use of prohibited agrochemicals.[14]

Organic conversion was accompanied by a mobilization of producer organizations leading, with the support of the International Cooperation Program, to the creation of the Association of Bolivian Ecological Producers (AOPEB). This organization was responsible for the development of Bolivian norms of organic production based on European Union Regulations and IFOAM's basic standards (Cáceres and Carimentrand 2004b; Laguna et al. 2006).

Nevertheless, the high costs of external certification and inspection incurred in the first shipments of organic cocoa stimulated the peasant organizations to look for another alternative – the creation of local certification. The first Bolivian certifier, Bolicert, was created with the active participation of producer organizations, such as ANAPQUI and AOPEB, completing the institutional framework for the new organic quality of quinoa (Ayaviri et al. 1999).

New structures of governance: peasant economic organizations vs. private quinoa companies[15]

The quinoa global value chain received an important initial boost from the US market, which at one stage absorbed up to 60 percent of legal exports. This support was later reversed in favor of the European market based largely on an increased demand for organic quinoa. During the second half of the 1990s international organic quinoa prices rose, oscillating between US$ 1,200 and US$ 1,600 per ton (FTDA Altiplano-CEP 2002). Until the first half of the 1990s the peasant organizations had an almost absolute monopoly over quinoa exports. In 1998 these groups obtained their greatest share of the market. As demonstrated in Table 11.1, ANAPQUI held a market share of 57 percent, while CECAOT reached 21 percent. Together they were responsible for almost four-fifths of total quinoa exports.

A comparison of the official data presented in Table 11.1 and the dates of entry/ creation of new firms from our questionnaires suggests that the growth in quinoa demand and favorable prices did not, however, translate into a strengthening of the position of peasant organizations in the market. On the contrary, to the entrance of new Bolivian and Franco-Bolivian private companies. Furthermore, international trade and quality requirements for the markets in the North created new entry barriers which resulted in ANAPQUI losing its position in various markets.

The entry of new private companies in the upstream segment of the quinoa chain also consolidated the "contract model" between individual peasant producers and agro-industrial companies, establishing a functional division of labor whereby peasants were limited to their agricultural function and subject to "selection" according to quality requirements. These contracts between now nonorganized quinoa producers and private enterprises cover: duration (generally a year with

Table 11.1 Bolivia: evolution of top 10 quinoa exporting firms' market share, 1995–2003

Firms	1995	1996	1997	1998	1999	2000	2001	2002	2003
CECAOT	5.7	3.0	15.5	20.8	18.3	10.6	14.0	15.4	8.1
SAITE	3.9	12.5	21.6	13.7	17.4	18.2	11.9	11.9	5.3
ANAPQUI	42.1	41.6	43.2	56.5	39.1	21.1	23.5	24.5	25.1
CORONILLA							0.1	0.1	0.3
ANDEAN					3.6	14.6	9.7	8.8	7.3
JATARIY			3.1	8.7	11.0	28.5	26.7	24.6	25.2
QUINOA-BOL					10.0	6.6	8.2	13.5	11.0
IRUPANA								0.9	3.1
QUINOA FOOD								13.3	
TIERRA									0.7
Subtotal	51.7	57.1	83.4	99.8	99.4	99.7	93.9	99.5	99.2
Other	48.3	42.9	16.6	0.2	0.6	0.3	6.1	0.5	0.8
Total	100.0	100.0	100.0	100.0	100.0	100.0	100.0	100.0	100.0

Source: SIVEX (2004).

the possibility of renewal); price (set in relation to the Challapata market); pre-financing (for organic certificate and technical assistance); and organic monitoring and inspection (Cáceres and Carimentrand 2004a; Laguna et al. 2006).

The entry of new companies was also the result of vertical integration strategies by the French distributors of organic products, EURO-NAT and Markal, who financed the creation of quinoa processing subsidiaries JATARIY and QUINOA-BOL on the Bolivian Altiplano (Laguna 2002b). This more business orientation ran counter to what had been achieved by the associative model of producers supported by the Fair Trade movement, and its initial impact was an important loss of market share by the Peasant Organizations.[16] Furthermore, the increase in quinoa supplies caused a decline in international prices.

One of the most important recent actors to have entered the quinoa chain is the new private company SELEME, a local trading company that has very quickly won a significant market. In 2003 it was responsible for 13 percent of legal Bolivian exports of quinoa, directed especially at the US organic market, in addition to opening up new markets, such as Israel. This company has organized itself both downstream, that is, by contacting Quinoa Food SA a new quinoa processing company, and upstream with quinoa producers and suppliers including the Salinas de Garci Mendoza Processing Plant. This latter plant, in contrast with ANAPQUI and CECAOT, was not able to establish solid relations with traders and worked on a sub-contracting basis with farmers.[17]

Our interviews confirmed that the Peasant Organizations were very vulnerable to the entry of new companies because they were not able to fully meet the demand of Northern organic markets. Their shipments suffered from quality problems (presence of impurities, or inadequate elimination of the *saponina*), in addition to difficulties related to the frequency and punctuality of their shipments. Lack of experience regarding the management of foreign trade also led to high broker costs, straining their already precarious administration. Despite this, international demand for quinoa was very promising both in the Fair Trade and the organic markets.

The French network that connects the companies of the EURO-NAT holding company,[18] EURO-NAT S.A and JATARIY S.R.L, the French humanitarian NGO *Point d'Appui*, the certification company Ecocert Int., and the supermarket chain Carrefour is representative of these new trends. EURO-NAT S.A and *Point d'Appui* began an intense marketing campaign to stimulate the demand for quinoa in France using the Priméal brand (Barthelet 2001). Quality problems with quinoa from ANAPQUI were the reason alleged for the creation in 1996 of JATARIY,[19] which stored and processed quinoa for the EURO-NAT distributor in the Bolivian city of Oruro.

With the creation of the EURO-NAT holding company in 1999, another governance structure emerged upstream in the quinoa chain, dominated by a vertical coordination by the Northern part of the chain via an organic product distributor. JATARIY benefited from a fully equipped plant with a self-contained production circuit and it established its quinoa supply using the contract model. The intense marketing carried out in France was very beneficial to JATARIY, resulting in

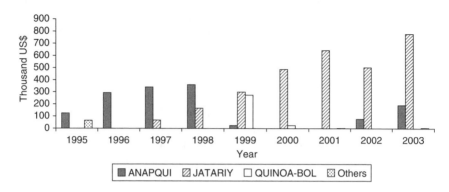

Figure 11.1 Bolivia: quinoa exports to French market, 1995–2003.

Source: SIVEX (2004) – La Paz Aduana Nacional – Development Ministry, La Paz Bolivia.

a sharp growth in its quinoa exports, which at the same time displaced ANAPQUI in this market. This inverse relationship between the exports of ANAPQUI, and JATARIY, can be seen in the graph Figure 11.1.

Downstream in the French segment of the chain, a large global player entered the Bolivian *real* quinoa global value chain, the supermarket Carrefour, which signed a five year contract with the EURO-NAT holding company network and JATARIY in 2004.[20] After working with Bolicert, JATARIY decided to move to the international French certifier Ecocert Int., alleging lack of confidence in the Bolivian certifier. In partnership with four other French companies specializing in the transformation and distribution of organic products, EURO-NAT established the private fairly traded brand, "Bio-équitable," also certified by Ecocert.

Quinoa in the new Fair Trade phase: private brands and the FLO seal

In the new Fair Trade phase, quinoa sold by the ATO GEPA encountered competition from the private, "Bio-équitable," Carrefour "Bio" (latter named Carrefour "Agir Bio") and "Hand in Hand" brands.[21] Until this period, the Peasant Organizations had only operated with the organic label on boxes distributed by GEPA, or with no distinguishing label on the shipments sent to the United States. The Bolivian organic *real* quinoa processed by JATARIY was distributed in organic product shops with the "Bio-équitable" label causing confusion for consumers who had difficulty distinguishing it from ATO organic quinoa, distributed in World Shops and sharing the same shelves in organic product shops.[22]

In 2004 the FLO document *Fair Trade Criteria For Quinoa* (FLO 2004) was published outlining criteria relating to social and economic development, environmental protection, working conditions (both on the farm and in the processing plants), and marketing. The minimum Fair Trade price for quinoa in Bolivia, Ecuador, and Peru was fixed at US$ 861 per ton for farm-gate non-desaponified organic and US$ 711 for conventional quinoa, with a Fair Trade social premium of US$ 85 per ton. The setting of this minimum price introduces an important change in the dynamic of the quinoa chain, decoupling payments from the volatile Challapata market. In addition to establishing a fair price, the marketing criteria include the creation of long-term contracts and the possibility of pre-financing for producer organizations. FLO criteria for the certification of Bolivian quinoa require that producers be small, organized growers.

The authors carried out interviews in 2005 to evaluate perceptions in the quinoa chain, especially those of the peasant producer organizations, regarding the new FLO certification. This certification process began in 2003 and the first producer organization to adopt the FLO seal was CECAOT in 2005 for its organic quinoa. In 2004, FLO told private companies that if they bought quinoa from organized producers they could be included in Fair Trade certification. In the case of the FLO label, the Peasant Organizations had exclusivity since a private small producer organization, the Salinas de Garci Mendoza Processing Plant was excluded from the first contacts because it had been created as a joint stock company.[23]

Up to the date of our interviews in October/November 2005, contacts with the new FLO system for quinoa were made directly between the Peasant Organizations and FLO's representatives and consultants, without any evidence of other public or local municipal institution involvement. By contrast, the initial promotion of organic quinoa had been based on broad ranging collective action which developed into an institutional network and included the implementation of public policies. Local actors appear to have had little participation in the elaboration of FLO's quinoa certification.

Initial expectations regarding the new FLO certification system have been very positive and the Peasant Organizations are optimistic that it "could result in economic benefits"[24] increasing the market share of Fair Trade outlets, thereby leading to higher prices than those currently prevailing in Northern organic markets. One of the Peasant Organizations interviewed stated that 70 percent of total certified exports went to what they call the "commercial market." This category is used to designate the organic market, since it is dominated by the logic of supply and demand, and is often characterized by low prices. Nevertheless, organic prices are superior to local and regional market prices (one Peasant Organization reported receiving US$ 1,000 per ton for organic quinoa). The remaining 30 percent of certified exports go to the ATO solidarity trade, although the Peasant Organizations complain that this market, in contrast with FLO, is also vulnerable as regards price and volume.

Despite the optimism regarding FLO certification, only a little over a dozen tons were sold at the new FLO price in 2005, failing to cover Peasant Organization losses in the organic market. FLO quinoa faces competition within the Fair Trade sector since importers continue to favor the cheapest quinoa, responding to the logic of the commercial world.[25]

One Peasant Organization that was interviewed argued that the minimum FLO price set in advance above the market price offered the promise of stability, something that quinoa producers are unused to. However, the insertion of quinoa in the global market, even through Fair Trade, did not eliminate the tensions and pressures of the mercantile and industrial world. The ATO Fair Trade market offers higher prices than the organic market, but it too lacks stability and volumes tend to fluctuate.

The Peasant Organizations did not consider the FLO certification process an obstacle and argued that the know-how gained from the organic certification process simplified the task. Nevertheless, problems with updating Bolivian public registry statutes have delayed FLO certification, since FLO has requested that the Bolivian State be the guarantor of Peasant Organization records to ensure transparency. The new certification conditions have already made a qualitative difference in the conditions of plant processing workers. These have now to be formally contracted with the right to social benefits and work stability, which has led to a consequent reduction in casual labor. The workers are responsible for organizing themselves into a trade union. The Peasant Organizations are concerned, however, that extra social charges will be added to their costs and that they will have to deal with the demands of a potential new actor, the trade union.

The directors of the Peasant Organizations all stressed that the additional part of the FLO price would be divided equally between all their active members to avoid discrimination or ill feeling. The question of the premium is more delicate, since the directors have more economic concerns and would like the premium to be used for the costs of technical assistance to ensure organic certification of the quinoa. The older associates, however, propose that this premium be used for a life insurance and/or retirement system. Other members want the premium to be used for university education grants for their children. Thus, we can observe a tension between the social demands of the members and the economic priorities of the organizations' leadership.

Different Fair Trade organizational models and implications for the participation of Andean quinoa producers

Oppenheim (2005), in a widely commented article, criticized the profit margins of importers and supermarkets in marketing Fair Trade products, especially for bananas and coffee. This article raises the question: How much of what the consumer pays for a Fair Trade certified product really reaches the producer? The retail price can be broken down among the different actors in the quinoa value chain. In Tables 11.2 and 11.3, constructed on the basis of data collected in our interviews, we compare price distribution in the "Bio-équitable" and the "Peasant Organization-ATO" models. We also contrast these with the newly established FLO price (though FLO price distribution data is not yet available).

In addition, we compare these models with the recent intervention of Alter Eco and conclude the section with a brief discussion of the very different principles governing the Fair Trade initiative of ANDINES in relation to quinoa in Ecuador.

The private brand "bio-équitable" – individual producer model

In the "Bio-équitable" model, the contracts signed by producers and JATARIY take the Challapata market price and add an extra 20 percent. Large-scale merchants control this price which varies depending on supply and demand and is particularly influenced by the informal Peruvian market in El Desaguadero, on the frontier between Peru and Bolivia, the destination of approximately 50 percent of nonregistered (contraband) exports to Peru (Laguna 2002b). The reference price in Challapata was 150 *bolivianos* per quintal of quinoa (US$ 19.50) for the 2003–2004 season.[26] Thus the JATARIY price is only 17 percent higher than the Challapata price, not the promised 20 percent. A half kilo box of Priméal Bio-équitable quinoa grain from EURO-NAT costs consumers 1.98 euros (US$ 4.92/kg) in the French shopping chain Biocoop. The same quinoa is sold in Carrefour supermarkets under the "Carrefour Agir Bio" brand for 1.95 euros. Based on this data the Bolivian producer receives 10 percent of the price paid by the French consumers. Furthermore, this percentage is the maximum

Table 11.2 French market: price distribution for the private brand Bio-Équitable Fair Trade model (2004)

	Quinoa Bolivian price (bolivianos)[a] quintal[c]	Price in US$[b] Quintal[c]	kg	Consumer price distribution (%)
Quinoa consumer price Bio-Équitable priméal (1)			4.92	100
Price to Bolivian producer	175	22.7	0.49	10
Challapata market price	150	19.5	0.42	
FOB price (ton) received by JATARIY (2)		1,200	1.20	24
Difference (1–2) = northern margin			3.72	76

Source: Authors' research 2005/2006.

Notes
a US$ 1 = 7.7 bolivianos.
b 1 Euro = US$ 1.2433.
c 1 quintal = 46.5 kgs.

price for producers contracted by JATARIY, since they do not belong to the company and have no right to a share in the values generated by the transformation processes.

The ATO – peasant producer organization model

The Peasant Organizations aim to pay a higher price than that quoted on the quinoa *Wall Street*, Challapata, but this latter is still used as a reference by the producer organization. In 2004, the price of a half kilo box of washed quinoa grain from ANAPQUI sold by the French ATO *Artisans du Monde* was 2.46 euros (US$ 6.12/kg), while the producers of this association received 8.2 percent of the price paid by the French consumer in World Shops. The price paid to the producer by this model is both relatively and absolutely higher than that of the private fair trade brand, as well as being 20 percent above the Challapata price. Given that they also process the product, Peasant Organization members are paid both for their agricultural activities and their participation in the transformation and direct sale of quinoa to importers. Depending both on the degree of democracy and the business ability of its management, this model offers more opportunities for increased earnings. Opportunities exist also for further value added as in the production of quinoa noodles although to date ANAPQUI's experience with producing quinoa noodles for GEPA has not been good.[27] Finally, it is worth noting that the price paid by ATOs per ton of quinoa FOB is also higher than the price of the previous mode.

Table 11.3 French market: price distribution for the ATO importer Fair Trade model (2004)

	Quinoa Bolivian price (bolivianos)[a] quintal[c]	Price in US$[b] Quintal[c]	kg	Consumer price distribution (%)
Quinoa consumer price Artisans du monde (3)			6.12	100
Price to Bolivian producer	180	23.4	0.50	8.2
Challapata market price	150	19.5	0.42	
FOB price (ton) received by OECA (4)		1,300	1.30	21
Difference (3–4) = northern margin			4.82	79

Source: Authors' research 2005/2006.

Notes
a US$ 1 = 7.7 bolivianos.
b 1 Euro = US$ 1.2433.
c 1 quintal = 46.5 kgs.

FLO-label – producer organization model

The FLO minimum price for quinoa is set at 47 percent above the Challapata reference price. If we add the 10 percent premium per quintal of organic quinoa sold through the FLO system this price is 62 percent higher than that obtained by producers in the Challapata market. Furthermore, the FOB price paid per ton of quinoa is the highest, with the minimum being set at US$ 1,400. In France, the Monoprix and Leclerc supermarkets have recently begun to stock quinoa from the CECAOT Peasant Organization with the "Max Havelaar" label, sold under the "Jardin Bio-équitable" brand by Naturenvie SAS. Of the three types of "fair price," the FLO Fair Trade model is clearly the highest in relation to the local market price of Challapata.

The ATO and FLO prices are much higher than the international organic price. These higher prices compensate for the fluctuations of the organic market and function as a "subsidy" on the part of Fair Trade to cover the costs in maintaining the quality criteria for all organic quinoa exports. The prices paid by organic markets oscillate between US$ 900 and US$ 1,200 per ton, lower than those established for ATO Fair Trade, where the FOB price in 2004 oscillated between US$ 1,300 and US$ 1,350 per ton[28] and lower still than those promised by Fair Trade under the FLO label, where the price set for 2005 was US$ 1,400 per ton, plus the premium offered to producer associations.[29]

The Alter Eco brand – producer organization hybrid model

Alter Eco (AE) is a private company specializing in fairly traded and organic products selling principally through large-scale retail. It was created in France as a Fair Trade importer in 1999, and three years later it affiliated to EFTA and the same year launched a new transversal brand covering 13 products including quinoa. AE currently deals with more than 70 different foodstuffs: coffee, tea, rice, sugar, fruit, cacao, olive oil, and many others. Its objective is to become the leading brand in the emerging market for fairly traded products (Lecomte 2004) and to date it has been able to meet the demands of the European market and achieve significant commercial penetration. According to Lecomte (2004), AE works with the Leclerc, Cora, Monoprix and, more recently, Carrefour, supermarkets, and in France its products are available in 400 supermarket and 200 hypermarket stores. AE has now expanded to the United States and is in the process of opening a branch in Brazil. In 2004 it began to sell quinoa from the ANAPQUI Peasant Organization with its own packaging and using the AE brand. After buying quinoa from Solidar' Monde (the French partner of GEPA), it decided to establish direct relations with ANAPQUI in Bolivia, as well as establishing contacts with another Peasant Organization. AE emphasizes the importance of continued market innovation and is currently promoting the red quinoa variety (Lecomte 2004).

Alter Eco works with a system of "premiums" to establish quinoa prices. Alter Eco (2004) explains the characteristics of these premiums which when added together define the final price of quinoa. In the case of Bolivian quinoa, premiums are given for organic quality and for the classification of the type of producer. Since 2005 the premium corresponding to the certification requirements of the FLO seal has not been paid, because the ANAPQUI has not completed relevant local processes. In Cora supermarkets, a 500 gr box of AE quinoa is sold for 2.59 euros, higher than both other models for which we have data. We have insufficient data to calculate the margins for this model in 2004 but according to Alter Eco (2005), the percentage paid to the producer organization as a proportion of the turnover was 35.7 percent, which (if true) would be considerably higher than the other models discussed.

The Andines-Ratinpak-ERPE – an alternative network model

An Ecuadorian network questions the insertion of small producers in international trade altogether. This network was created by the French cooperative ANDINES with the producers of the *Fundación Escuelas Radiofónicas Populares de Ecuador* (ERPE – the Popular Radio Schools Foundation) in Chimborazo. This initiative developed on the basis of a "local correspondent" modality, that is, a third party charged with controlling the quality and quantity delivered by producer organizations and responsible for transport and exports. ANDINES' local correspondent is the Ecuadorian association Ratinpak, based in Quito, which in addition to organic quinoa handles other fairly traded products imported by ANDINES (including sugar, green beans, and dried mushrooms). Like the producers from the southern Bolivian Altiplano, the Ecuadorian producers in the ERPE program converted to organic agriculture, though they have not converted to monoculture. They grow on average less than one hectare of quinoa. In 2004 ANDINES imported 17 metric tons of the 120 metric tons produced by ERPE. According to figures published by ANDINES, the Ecuadorian producer receives a price of US$ 0.71/kg, that is, US$ 33.20 per quintal, a price lower than the minimum price set by FLO, though this represents 15 percent of the price paid by consumers and is higher in relative terms than three of the models discussed earlier (FLO, Bio-équitable, ATO). The sales strategy is also different, being directed at institutional markets, in this case catering, providing food for the staff of the French electric company. According to ANDINES: "The principal objective for all the partners is food sovereignty and economic and political self-determination. This does not involve either... economic dependency, participating in the plundering of wealth, encouraging monoculture or cultivation aimed at export, nor at competing with European products" (ANDINES 2005).

Conclusions

In our introduction, we situated quinoa within a more general tendency noted by Murdoch et al. (2000) for previously marginalized products and regions to be valorized as new quality criteria begin to determine agrofood market dynamics. Our analysis draws attention to the scope of this adjustment. Quinoa exports to new high-quality markets, as we have seen, increased sharply in the 1990s and between 2001 and 2004 export earnings jumped from US$ 1.6 billion to US$ 44.2 billion (CEPROBOL-IICD 2005). During this period there was also a large-scale conversion to organic production. In many respects, therefore, we are dealing with a success story, with market opportunities expected to continue to expand based on mounting exports of black and red, as well as *"Real Blanca"* quinoa varieties and the widening spectrum of quinoa consumer products. The commercial success of the quinoa global value chain, however, has its costs. The rapid growth of quinoa exports may be undermining the sustainability of production, due to agroecological changes (including the rise of mechanized monoculture production, of soil and nutrient erosion, and of shifting cultivation from hillsides to the flat lowlands) as well as social changes (including shifting migration patterns) (Felix 2004; Hellin and Higman 2001; Laguna 2000, 2002a; PROINPA 2004; Ramos 2000).[30] Vancauteren (2005) argues that the rise of Fair Trade in quinoa fuels these unsustainable tendencies since FLO standards do not take into account the diversity of quinoa production systems and producer economic situations and may favor unsustainable production systems in the "pampa" region, indirectly contributing to the desertification of the southern Bolivian Altiplano.

Our analysis suggests that there are no unilinear conclusions to be drawn on the contribution of Fair Trade either to the acceleration or the mitigation of these broader social and agroecological tendencies. As regards the impact on collective organization, we find that Fair Trade has for years been accompanied in some cases with community development projects and that these links will now be built into FLO-based contracts through the payment of social premiums. Measures to strengthen traditional communities should also receive a boost from Fair Trade in so far as the FLO model bases itself firmly on producer organizations. The opening of non-FLO certified mainstream Fair Trade markets for quinoa, however, appears to be promoting supply contracts with individual producers and may thus weaken collective responses. This may not always be the case however, as for example AE has committed itself to working with producer organizations.

The sustainability of the North-South quinoa Fair Trade model can also be questioned from the angle of consumption. Krautstein (n.d.) argues that Fair Trade groups are in danger of putting at risk the food security of poor Altiplano peasants by mobilizing their resources to satisfy the affluent middle-class market in the North. While this argument may be oversimplified, concerns over the impacts of rising exports for local food security find an echo within the Fair Trade movement itself, as we have seen in the case of the ANDINES' initiative in Ecuador. This caution regarding the North/South axis of Fair Trade and the preference for linking traditional production systems to local and regional markets appears common across the Fair Trade movement in the South (as reflected also in Chapters 8 and 10 of this volume). In a parallel fashion AE is also actively promoting the Southern market, although directed in this case to the emerging middle class in these countries.

Above all, what our analysis has highlighted is the variability of initiatives within Fair Trade itself. In the case of quinoa, this involves multiple patterns of coordination between the actors in the value chain which leads to different organizational structures upstream and equally different marketing strategies downstream. The very dynamism of the quinoa market and changing North-South relations (including the growth of Latin American quinoa markets) suggests that this heterogeneity will tend to be a permanent feature of the Fair Trade quinoa value chain.

Notes

1 Our analysis is situated within the global value chain literature discussed in Chapter 3.
2 Quinoa is also produced in Chile, Argentina, and Colombia and has been introduced in the United States (Colorado), Canada (Saskatchewan), Europe, and recently Brazil (in the central savannah region).
3 For technical details as regards this crop see also the work of a range of Andean and international institutions and researchers covering more than a dozen volumes included in the CD Rom "Cultivos Andinos," www.rlc.fao.org
4 Peru's annual per capita quinoa consumption fell from 6 to 2 kgs between the mid-1940s and 1972, while consumption of imported and subsidized cereals such as rice and wheat jumped from 14–23 kgs to 24–31 kgs (Salis 1985). By the middle of the 1990s, Peruvian average quinoa consumption had fallen to closer to 0.5 kg per person annually (ADEX 1996). Bolivian quinoa consumption shows a similar decline. Annual per capita consumption in 1991 was 9.6 kgs in Oruro and 4.9 kgs in Potosi, far below the intake of rice and noodles (100 kgs in Oruro and 62.5 kgs in Potosi) (FDTA-Altiplano-CEP 2002; PROINPA 2004).
5 In the United States, a spiritual quality has been attributed to quinoa as a food favoring meditation (Wood 1985).
6 See for example http://www.quinova.co.uk
7 See for example http://www.nutriops.com
8 See for example http://www.euro-nat.com
9 Bolivian exports of certified organic quinoa in 2004 reached 4,266 metric tons, practically double the 2,133 tons exported in 2001 (FAOSTAT 2005).
10 Expression used by a Bolivian businessman.
11 Discussion of the emergence of the producer organizations in the following section draws heavily on Ayaviri et al. (1999), an account of ANAPQUI by founder members, one of a number of such accounts from different Latin American countries edited by the World Bank and the Indigenous Fund.
12 Interview with ANAPQUI President in Challapata, 2004.
13 ANAPQUI is currently the largest association of quinoa producers bringing together seven regional associations and 1,000 members.
14 Interview with ANAPQUI President.
15 The information and interpretations included in this section draw on interviews carried out in 2004 by two of the authors.
16 The dominance of the mercantile over the domestic world in the case of the South/North trade for organic products is highlighted by Raynolds (2004).
17 Information based on interviews with two managers of private quinoa firms, 2004.
18 EURO-NAT was created in 1999 and includes: EURO-NAT S.A (cereal storage, preparation of muesli, and distribution of organic products), BIOLAND S.A.R.L (distribution of organic products), TERRITOIRE S.A.R.L (preparation of organic biscuits), NICOLAS S.A.S (preparation of organic noodles), JATARIY S.R.L (storage and processing of quinoa, preparation of expanded quinoa), and S.C.I EUROPRIM.
19 Personal interview with the manager of EURO-NAT and Perréol, 2004.

20 Information based on interview with JATARIY director.
21 "Hand in Hand" is the private fair trade brand of Rapunzel.
22 In France, depending on the organic product shop, one or more quinoa grain references can be found, with competition existing mainly between the quinoa from JATARIY, sold under both the Priméal brand, and the Bio-équitable label, the quinoa from Quinuabol, sold under the Markal brand and the quinoa from ANAPQUI imported by GEPA and distributed in France by Solidar' Monde, the French platform of Artisans du Monde World Shops. Quinoa from Anapqui is now marketed with the Solidar' Monde label.
23 Personal interviews with a representative from IRUPANA, the commercial partner of PPQSM. October 2005, Rio de Janeiro – La Paz, Bolivia.
24 Interviews carried out in October 2005.
25 The French convention approach is discussed in Chapter 3 and also in Cáceres and Carimentrand (2004a,b) and Cáceres (2005).
26 The price, however, in Challapata is very unstable, and after rising strongly in 2004 due to drought and frost, it fell sharply in June 2005, threatening peasants with insolvency.
27 This applies at least in quinoa noodle exports to Northern markets; they appear to be more successful in the case of Brazilian exports.
28 Interview with ANAPQUI.
29 The Peruvian experience of the NGO network – Centro Pastoral Urbano Rural – El Altiplano SAC – APROAL Association of the Altiplano Producers – provides a counterpoint to the Bolivian approach to financing the organic quality of quinoa. Here, the costs of technical assistance and organic certification are shared between the NGOs and the Peruvian member producers. Low interest loans are available to producers and compensation is available for harvest failures. Monoculture is avoided and synergies are established with the traditional small producer risk diversification strategies including crop rotation and animal husbandry (Carimentrand 2006).
30 The registration of a patent for quinoa in the United States threatened the sustainability of Andean exports, provoking a strong response coordinated by specialists from PROINPA, ANAPQUI, and the NGO RAFI leading to the rejection of the quinoa patent claim. This collective action then led to the promotion of a Geographical Indication standard for *real* quinoa financed by the Inter-American Development Bank. However, the implementation and regulation of this mechanism has been delayed due to lack of suitable experts on this issue in Bolivia.

References

ADEX (1996) "Quinoa: estudio de la demanda," ADEX, USAID-MSP, ASO-COSUDE ESAN, Lima, Peru.
ALTERECO (2004) "Small change, big difference!" Activity Report, 2003.
—— (2005) *Rapport d'Activité 2005*, Online. Available at: www.altereco.com/PDF/ rapport-d-activité-2005-alter-eco-pdf (accessed October 3, 2006).
ANDINES (2005) *La Quinoa Biologique d'Equateur, Dossier filière 2003–2005*, Andines Scop, Ile Saint Denis, France.
Ayaviri, G., Choque, N., and Panamá, G. (1999) "La historia de nuestra organización asociación nacional de productores de quinua," in T. Carrasco, D. Iturralde, and J. Uquillas (eds), *Doce Experiencias de Desarrollo Indígena en América Latina*, Foundation for the Development of the Indigenous Peoples of Latin American and the Caribbean.
Barthelet, L. (2001) Le quinoa bio Priméal, une expérience de commerce équitable réussie. *Aventure*, 93, Guilde Européenne du Raid, Paris.
Brenes, E., Crespo, F., and Madrigal, K. (2001) "El cluster de quinua en Bolívia: *Diagnóstico competitivo y recomendaciones estratégicas*," INCAE-CAF, September 2001.

Cáceres, Z. (2005) "Quinoa: a tradição frente ao desafio dos novos mercados de qualidade," unpublished thesis, CPDA-UFRRJ, Rio de Janeiro, Brazil.

Cáceres, Z. and Carimentrand, A. (2004a) "La quinua, del altiplano andino hasta el consumidor europeo: la construcción de cadenas de productos orgánicos y del comercio justo," paper presented at International ARTE Congress: *Rural Agro-industry and Land*, December 1–4, 2004, Toluca, Mexico.

—— (2004b) "Globalisation et agriculture biologique: la filière quinoa biologique en Bolivie," *Actes du Colloque International AIEA2, Développement durable et globalisation dans l'agroalimentaire*, August 23–24, 2004, Québec, Canada.

Carimentrand, A. (2006) "Production de quinoa biologique pour l'exportation et durabilité des moyens d'existence en milieu rural: l'expérience péruvienne," paper presented at International ALTER Congress, October 18–21, 2006, Baeza, Spain.

Carimentrand, A. and Ballet, J. (2004) "Le commerce équitable entre éthique de la consommation et signes de qualité," paper presented at International ARTE Congress: *Rural Agro-Industry and Land*, December 1–4, Toluca, Mexico.

CEPROBOL-IICD (2005) *Quinoa y Derivados, Perfil Sectorial*, La Paz, Bolivia, Online. Available at: www.ceprobol.gov.bo (accessed March 11, 2005).

Egoavil, M. (1983) "Comercialização de la quinua en el altiplano Peruano," UNMSM, Andean Rural History Seminar, Lima, Peru.

Egoavil, M., Reinoso, J., and Torres, H. (1978) *Costos y Margenes de Comercialização de la Quinua*, Simón Bolívar Fund Project, Ministry of Agriculture.

FAO (Food and Agriculture Organization) (2003) *'Cultivos Andinos' – Aspectos económicos de la producción de quinoa*, Online. Available at: www.fao.org (accessed October 9, 2003).

FAOSTAT (2005) *Statistics per Product: Quinoa*, Online. Available at: www.fao.org (accessed January 15, 2005).

Félix, D. (2004) *Diagnostic agraire de la Province Daniel campos, Bolivie. Le développement de la filière quinoa et ses conséquences sur l'équilibre du système agraire des Aymaras de la marca Llica-Tahua*, Agro Montpellier, CNEARC and CICDA-VSF.

FLO (Fairtrade Labelling Organizations International) (2004) *Criterios de comercio justo para la quinua*, June 2004.

Fonte, M. (2002) "Food systems, consumption models and risk perception in late modernity," working paper, University of Naples Federico II, Naples, Italy.

FTDA Altiplano-CEP (2002) "Propección de demandas de la cadena productiva de la quinua en Bolivia," La Paz, Bolivia, July 2002.

GEPA (2005) *De la Idea de Acción a la Casa del Comercio Justo*, Online. Available at: www.gepa3.de (accessed November 15, 2005).

Gereffi, G. (1999) "A commodity chains framework for analysing global industries," unpublished, Duke University, Online. Available at: www.ids.ac.uk/ids/global/pdfs/gereffi.pdf (accessed November 9, 2004).

Gonzáles de Olarte, E. (1994) *En las Fronteras del Mercado, Economía Política del Campesinado en el Perú*, Institute of Peruvian Studies, Lima, Peru.

Granovetter, M. (1973) "The strength of weak ties," *American Journal of Sociology*, 78: 1360–1380.

Healy, K. (2001) *Llamas, Weaving and Organic Chocolate: Multicultural Grassroots Development in the Andes and Amazon of Bolivia*, Indiana: University of Notre Dame.

Hellin, J. and Higman, S. (2001) *Quinoa and Rural Livelihoods in Bolivia, Peru and Ecuador*, Oxford, Oxfam.

IICA/PNUD (1991) "Estudio de market y comercialización de la quinua real de Bolivia," Proyecto BOL/C01/Procesamiento de Quinoa. Study Bulletin, La Paz, Bolivia.

Krautstein, H. (n.d.) *Quinoa Das Korn aus den Anden.* Online. Available at: www.naturkost.de/cgi-bin/drucken/printer.pl?file=//aktuell/sk9807e2.htm (accessed June 20, 2006).

Laguna, P. (2000) "El impacto de la exportación colectiva de quinoa en los sistemas productivos y modos de vida del Altiplano Boliviano," Mimeo, La Paz, Bolivia.

—— (2002a) *Capital Social o Caja de Pandora? Contestación y Deformación de Acción Colectiva en Comunidades y Organizaciones Económicas Campesinas de Cara a la Mercantilización de la Quinua.* Online, Available at: www.FondoMinkaChorlavi.org (accessed February 12, 2004).

—— (2002b) "Competitividad, externalidades e internalidades, un reto para las organizaciones económicas campesinas: la inserción de la Asociación Nacional de Productores de Quinua en el mercado mundial de la quinua," *Debate Agrario*, 34, CEPES, Lima, Peru.

Laguna, P., Cáceres, Z., and Carimentrand, A. (2006) "Del Altiplano sur Boliviano hasta el mercado global: coordinación y estructura de gobernancia de la cadena de valor de la quinoa organica y del comercio justo," *Agroalimentaria*, 11(22): 29–40, Mérida.

Lecomte, T. (2004) *Le Commerce Equitable*, Paris: Ed. Eyrolles – Pratique.

Murdoch, J., Marsden, T., and Banks, J. (2000) "Quality, nature, and embeddedness: some theoretical considerations in the context of the food sector," *Economic Geography*, 76: 107–125.

Oppenheim, P. (2005) "Fairtrade fat cats," *The Spectator*, November 5, 2005.

Perreol, D. (2004) *Une Graine Sacrée: Le Quinoa*, Paris: JML.

PROINPA (2004) *Estudio de los Impactos Social, Ambiental y Económico de los Procesadores de Quinua Boliviana*, Proinpa Foundation, La Paz, Bolivia.

Ramos, N. (2000) "La quinua, el grano de oro de los incas, Anapqui una experiencia de desarrollo y manejo sostenible," *Review AOPEB No. 5*, La Paz, Bolivia.

Raynolds, L.T. (2004) "The globalization of organic agro-food networks," *World Development*, 32: 725–743.

Repo-Carrasco, R. (1992) *Cultivos Andinos y la Alimentación Infantil*, Comisión de Coordinación de Tecnologia Andina, CCTA, Lima, Online. Available at: www.lostiempos.com/oh/16-01-05/act.htm (accessed July 5, 2006).

Sakamoto, S. and Peric, Y. (2002) "Proyecto de mejoramiento del proceso industrial y comercialización de quinua," Informe Final MAGDER-JICA.

Salis, A. (1985) *Cultivos Andinos. Alternativa Alimentaria Popular?*, Bartolomé de las Casas Center, CEDEP-AYLLU, Cusco.

Sauvée, L. and Valceschini, E. (2004) "Agro-alimentaire: la qualité au coeur des relations entre agriculture, indusriels et distributeurs," *Déméter 2004, Économie et Stratégies Agricoles*, Paris: Armand Colin.

Schlick, G. and Bubenheim, D. (1996) "Quinoa: Candidate Crop for NASA's Controlled Ecological Life Support Systems," Online. Available at: www.hort.purdue.edu/newcrop/proceedings1996/V3–632.html (accessed November 9, 2004).

SIVEX (2004) "Estadisticas sobre la quinua 1995–2003," unpublished report, Aduana Nacional-Viceministerio de Industria, Comercio y Exportaciones – Ministerio de Desarrollo de Bolivia, La Paz, Bolivia.

Vancauteren, D. (2005) *AVSF: Encore un effort pour accompagner l'entrée de la paysannerie dans le système capitaliste*, final report, AVSF.

Wood, R. (1985) "Tell of a food surviver: quinoa," *East West Journal*, April, Boulder, Colorado.

12 Reconstructing fairness

Fair Trade conventions and worker empowerment in South African horticulture

Sandra Kruger and Andries du Toit

Introduction

There has been a dramatic increase in the number of large South African commercial farms, particularly fruit farms certified by the Fair Trade Labelling Organizations (FLO) since 2002. This has presented both FLO and its South African partners with important new political and strategic dilemmas which can not be resolved by simply appealing to established practice and precedent. The economic and political challenges arising out of the expansion of Fair Trade into South African plantation agriculture has forced FLO and its partners to reinvent and reimagine fairness, developing new answers to the question of what would constitute "fair" trade in the South African context. These debates have resulted in a complex process of convention setting, culminating in the Fair Trade Fresh Fruit and Empowerment Consultation Forum.

That this consultation happened at all, and how it happened, suggests that there is much to be learned about Fair Trade convention setting and mainstreaming processes. This chapter considers the negotiations and network formation between South African stakeholders and FLO, and describes the complex trade-offs and risks that confronted the negotiators. It should be noted that this chapter is in large part an exercise in self-reflection. One of the authors of this chapter, Sandra Kruger, became over time intimately involved in the negotiations. The story of the South African Fair Trade convention setting process is a story, inter alia, of the disproportionate influence of a small handful of fortuitously positioned individuals – and this raises important questions about power and the construction of agency in the convention setting process.

The chapter starts with a sketch of the events leading up to the convention setting process. This is followed by an account of the historical conditions of Fair Trade's entry into South Africa and how the particular trajectory of the convention setting process was shaped first by the history of social change in South Africa and second by the strategic realignment and organizational change within FLO. This sets the scene for a discussion of the substantive content – and the underlying dynamics – of the consultation process itself. The chapter closes with an evaluation of the partnership and the convention setting process and a discussion of some of the key lessons learned about the convention setting process.

The expansion of FLO into South African horticulture: new questions and dilemmas

Alternative trade organizations (ATOs) were active in South Africa years before the formation of FLO. Shortly after South Africa's first democratic elections Traidcraft (United Kingdom) and Fair Trade Assistance (Netherlands) started sourcing a limited range of mostly processed products – pickles, jams, crafts, and wine – from small producers or community-based projects. The range of Fair Trade products expanded with the introduction in 2002 of FLO certified Rooibos tea produced by a small-farmer cooperative in the Northern Cape. The certification of this group was supported by the Environmental Monitoring Group (EMG), a Cape Town based NGO working with the cooperative.

Initially Fair Trade wine was exported through alternative trading channels, and was sourced in particular from the Citrusdal Cellars in the Western Cape. When FLO became active in South Africa these farms became certified in accordance with newly developed wine standards.[1] However, one certified producer, Lebanon Fruit Farm Trust, had a number of features setting it apart from other Fair Trade wine producers. While the Citrusdal producers were "traditional" (white-owned, commercial) wine farms which had managed to comply with Fair Trade *labor* standards, the Lebanon Fruit Farm Trust had a much more developed "social" component. It was well known in the Western Cape not only as a progressive employer, but also as a land reform and worker empowerment project. It was the majority owner of the Thandi wine brand, one of the most successful "social" wine brands in the South African wine industry (Merten 2004). Even before the farm was FLO certified, Capespan, the largest fruit exporter in South Africa, had entered into an agreement with the Lebanon Fruit Farm Trust to expand the Thandi brand to include fresh fruit from empowerment and land reform projects. They had also decided that all projects participating in the Thandi project would be FLO certified in order to have the benefit both of an external monitor and a premium which could insure the sustainability of these projects. In 2003, FLO certified five fruit farms producing a variety of citrus, deciduous, and table grapes as part of the Thandi project. Other large-scale producers and exporters of varying sizes followed suit soon thereafter. Fairtrade Foundation launched the Thandi brand in UK supermarkets in 2003. In July 2003, Thandi citrus was launched as the first Fair Trade citrus in the United Kingdom in Co-op and Tesco stores (Fairtrade Foundation 2003a). This was followed in November 2003 with the launch of the first Fair Trade grapes and apples in March 2004 (Fairtrade Foundation 2003b). Thandi wine has also done well in the UK market, and sales have more than doubled since the adoption of the Fair Trade Mark in 2003.

Spurred by rising demand[2] in the United Kingdom and Europe for South African Fair Trade products, the number of certified producers rose rapidly. By May 2004, there were 18 FLO certified wine, fruit, and tea producers in South Africa and by May 2005 this number had almost doubled (Figure 12.1). This growth also led to a change in the profile of Fair Trade certified producers. Three out of the 42 producers certified by mid-2005 were small farmer cooperatives – two

Number of producers per product group

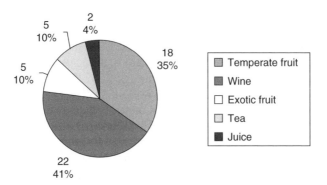

Figure 12.1 Product composition of FLO certified farms in South Africa, November 2005.

Source: FTSA (2006).

producing Rooibos tea and one producing raisins, with an average of 3–4 hectares of land. The other 39 FLO certified farms were plantations or large commercial farms dependent on hired labor. These farms varied in size depending on region and type of product, ranging from 50 to 100 hectares for wine farms, and 50–300 hectares for citrus and other temperate fruit (including table grapes). There is growing demand for Fair Trade wine in Germany, especially for Fair Trade Organic wine. There are established markets for Rooibos tea in Europe (especially Germany, the Netherlands, and the Scandinavian countries), the United States and Canada, and a growing demand in the United Kingdom.

This rapid growth, unmatched by any other Fair Trade producing country, was hotly contested. One key issue is the domination of South African Fair Trade by large commercial – and usually still substantially white-owned – farms. This led to challenges from those who argue that the Fair Trade movement and FLO should favor small, black producers. Other national initiatives were particularly vocal, seeing the certification of South African commercial farming as threatening the inclusion of small producers into new fresh fruit lines. They also objected because, far from being a poor or underdeveloped country, South Africa is a middle-income country with a sophisticated human resource and technical infra-structure and export capacity. These objections carried additional weight because South Africa, after all, had until 1994 been the subject of a boycott led by some of the same interest groups that had supported the Fair Trade movement. There was thus significant opposition to accepting FLO's expansion into South Africa.

The South African participants in Fair Trade, on the other hand, were concerned about very different issues. These arose from the deeply unequal and thoroughly racialized nature of South African society – especially the highly unequal and racially skewed distribution of land. Activists argued that although South African labor and employment legislation was in line with International Labor

Organization (ILO) Conventions, these conventions did not constitute an adequate response to the challenge of transforming South African agriculture. Labor market reform on its own, they believed, could not change the underlying inequality of land ownership and the unequal distribution of wealth in the rural economy of South Africa. While the normalization of exploitation under the apparent "fairness" of liberal labor laws might be politically acceptable in Europe, questions of political economy and distribution could still be politically explosive in South Africa. It might be possible to think that "fair is fair" regardless of the context from a universalizing and normalizing perspective of Eurocentric modernity. But activists and others argued that the South African realities showed that locally appropriate answers had to be found to the question of what fairness actually meant in any particular delimited social and historical context. If all plantations had to do to be certified for Fair Trade was to conform to fairly standardized labor requirements, Fair Trade could very easily end up legitimizing the racial and material legacy of slavery, colonialism, and Apartheid. It was indeed, a strange situation. Country partners were criticizing the certification of South African producers because they believed this would dilute the political purpose and social justice aims of Fair Trade – while South African labor activists were critical of Fair Trade standards themselves, arguing that these would dilute the potential for equitable change in South Africa.

Two pressing questions confronted FLO in its quest for wine and fruit suppliers in South Africa. First, how could South Africa be accommodated in the FLO system, and could a solution be found to the plantation impasse? Second, how can FLO and Fair Trade generally contribute to "genuine transformation" in South Africa? The rest of the chapter will unpack the underlying issues, tensions, and politics of these two questions by describing the convention setting process between FLO and their South African "partners."

The history and political economy of Fair Trade conventions in South Africa

The resolution of these debates was shaped by the underlying political economy of Fair Trade in South Africa. To understand what was at stake, it is important to understand what motivated and enabled South African producers and exporters to become involved in Fair Trade. Why was Fair Trade suddenly so attractive to a growing number of producers?

De- and reregulation in South African horticulture and viticulture

Part of the answer lies in the history of South African agriculture and the central role played by the white-landed elite. This wealthy social class formed the core of the "commercial" South African agricultural sector throughout Apartheid. The development of both the wine and fruit industries was shaped by the political power of this group, and by the growth of an elaborate regulatory apparatus which helped to stabilize production and control (particularly in the wine industry) by this tiny elite. By the mid-1980s this protective apparatus was already experiencing growing pressure – a pressure that became irresistible after 1994 following the takeover of a democratic government unsympathetic to sectional white interests.

The new government had accepted a broadly neoliberal framework for the transformation of the South African agricultural sector. This framework called for the deregulation of agriculture and the dismantling and privatization of the state institutions which had hitherto controlled production and export. Agricultural reform had complex consequences. On the one hand, deregulation opened up producer access to international markets. Many saw important opportunities in getting access to prime European markets. For those who could differentiate their product and find their way into these markets the rewards were, for a time, significant.

On the other hand, deregulation also meant that pressures and risks increased. The liberalization of access to overseas markets happened at the same time as two important global trends in agrofood commodity systems (see Chapter 3). The first was the consolidation of buyer-driven supply chains in agrofood commodities in key Northern markets, especially the United Kingdom and Europe. The second was increasing levels of competition from other wine and fruit-producing countries, particularly from Latin America. In South Africa market deregulation was accompanied by increasing levels of labor and social regulation (see du Toit and Ewert 2005; Hamman and Ewert 1999). These contradictory pressures meant that the new opportunities for producers had ambiguous results for workers. While some producers were able to benefit substantially from increased export opportunities, many fruit and wine producers responded to a more unforgiving environment by adopting strategies that passed on costs and risk to workers (Barrientos 2002; du Toit and Ewert 2005).

The complex politics of agrofood reregulation and labor market restructuring were further complicated by the unique dynamics of South African land reform and black empowerment. In 1993, the ANC, heavily influenced by the World Bank, adopted a market-based land reform policy focused on the development of small-scale farming. The market-led nature of this policy imposed heavy constraints on the capacity of the State to effect major reforms (Hamman and Ewert 1999). These limits were particularly constricting in the Western Cape, where high market prices for land militated against the outright transfer of productive land to black ownership. Instead land reform in the Western Cape was pursued mostly in the form of farm worker equity share initiatives (Hamman and Ewert 1999). These projects involved complex schemes whereby the State helped black farm workers to buy shares in white-owned farms or in new partnerships with their employers or others. While equity share projects offered a pathway toward farm worker ownership, considerable challenges were raised by the highly competitive environment of modern-day fruit and wine production and by the capital-, labor- and management-intensive nature of the sector. Equity share projects were difficult to implement in practice and there were major obstacles to their long-term viability. There were also considerable social risks involved.

The farms involved were after all, steeped in the history and practices of more than 300 years of racist and authoritarian paternalism. Converting formal share ownership by workers into real power involved a complex political struggle, the outcome of which was far from certain. Though it is unfair and simplistic to represent farm worker equity share schemes *simply* as processes whereby white plantation owners continued and consolidated control, it should be clear that the presence of an equity share scheme could not by itself guarantee progressive labor relations and social formations.

These projects were therefore often fragile, internally contested, and controversial (Selva 2005). Those that supported and engaged in them were always to some extent involved in an enterprise the social value and eventual fate of which remained uncertain. To make matters even more complicated, such enterprises sought a special place in the market, and often attempted to achieve this by trading on their "social content." Although there have been both successes and failures (Mayson 2003), it was far from clear whether equity share schemes could in fact challenge the deeply entrenched and racialized inequities inherited from three centuries of colonialism, slavery, and Apartheid.

At the same time it was clear that a decisive investment in equity sharing projects offered significant benefits both to farm workers and white owners. Workers often stood to gain both materially and from opportunities for greater participation and voice in management. And in the often loaded context of South African politics, an explicit identification with land reform, transformation, democracy, and change became for white farm owners an attractive way not only of forestalling Zimbabwe-style pressure on white farmers and gaining political credibility with the new government, but also of positioning themselves within the market, signaling that they were part of the "new South Africa" not the old, and suggesting to consumers that the "Madiba magic" – the "feel-good factor" associated with the "miraculous" transition to democracy – could be linked with a product previously associated with labor conditions verging on slavery.

These factors significantly shaped certification itself as a site and stake of engagement and contestation. There were distinct advantages to differentiating oneself from the rump of white-owned and commercial agriculture, and persuading consumers that by buying the products of a "social" project they are participating, vicariously, in South African democratization and change. As more and more players crowded into this niche – often relying more on advertising puffery than any real verifiable claims – there were increasing incentives for those competing in this market to raise the bar and to buy into certification systems like those pushed by the Ethical Trading Initiative and FLO. With the strengthening Rand and increased competition in the mainstream, the supermarket wine and fruit business became more and more of a blood sport. Consequently many progressive plantations that had previously regarded Fair Trade as marginal and irrelevant became increasingly interested in certification.

At the same time, political developments raised the stakes and complicated the politics of land reform and "social" marketing. While land reform continued to be a key policy issue in the public domain – at least rhetorically if not in the budget[3] – it gradually began to be overshadowed and sometimes swallowed by the increasingly hegemonic discourse of Black Economic Empowerment (BEE). BEE was a national ideological and economic project reaching across all sectors. While BEE was considered integral to the transformation and reconciliation of South African economy and society, it was also quite controversial. Critics of BEE argued that it enriched a few black individuals who could be considered to already be empowered while the majority of black and previously disadvantaged individuals remained disadvantaged (Cronin 2004; Rumney 2004; Tabane 2004). This criticism and the need for broader empowerment and poverty alleviation led to the formulation of the Broad Based Black Economic Empowerment Act in 2003 (BBBEE). In 2004, the Department of Agriculture announced an "Agri-BEE" framework document (NDA 2004) that encompasses the principles of broad-based empowerment. This framework document for agriculture focused not only on ownership, but on management, procurement, and capacity building. Since 2003, a veritable "empowerment" industry developed – in many cases borrowing from and elaborating on vocabularies and social technologies of "scoring" and "auditing" that have come to dominate the discourse of corporate social responsibility (see Blowfield 1999).

While land reform remained fundamental to the project of transforming the rural landscape, the requirements and targets of BEE increased the urgency for change. The specific targets set by BEE frameworks defined the parameters in which land reform and empowerment projects are pursued. This created a window for creative social and commercial partners to generate solutions which satisfied government policy and maintained the commercial sustainability of agricultural enterprises.

FLO and the tensions of expansion into South Africa

The specific political context of change in South Africa thus raised complex issues for FLO. Above all, it created the ironical situation that given the deeply entrenched inequalities in South Africa and the pressure for real social change, a cookie-cutter implementation of standard Fair Trade principles could be argued to be conservative and inequitable in impact. Fair Trade activists – many of whom were weaned on the verities of the Outspan boycott[4] – were forced to realize that if producers in South Africa were to be certified according to FLO's generic hired labor standards, large numbers of mainline commercial farms in South Africa – all of them built on the legacy of land expropriation, forced labor, and the legacy of racism – would formally be eligible for certification.

This created some strange scenarios. For one thing, extending unchanged FLO criteria to South Africa would *undermine* the incentive for transformation in the agricultural sector. For another it would result in volumes that would not be easily absorbed by the Fair Trade market. So unless something was done, Fair Trade roll-out in South Africa could undermine the "niche" status of Fair Trade products and put pressure on premiums – and at the same time it could also work to normalize and legitimize the unequal racial power relations inherited from colonial settlement and Apartheid. The question, then, was how Fair Trade could be implemented in South Africa in order to promote the objectives of social and economic change, and at the same time maintain the integrity of the international Fair Trade system.

It is important to understand that FLO's entry into this complex and socially contested market happened at a critical juncture in its own growth, and an important historical moment in the development of the Fair Trade movement. These pressures had led to a hotly contested "plantation debate": a debate over how – and whether – plantations should be included in the Fair Trade system. Within this debate, the "extreme and exceptional" (Bernstein 1996) character of South African agrarian history posed new questions and hitherto unconsidered possibilities for FLO and the movement. The expansion of FLO into a political and agrarian context, quite unlike those in which the plantation debate had first arisen, presented the participants with something of a crisis – a moment of undecidability (Laclau 1990) in which existing frameworks and principles of legitimation did not provide a clear way forward. This provided an important opportunity: a moment in which it was both possible and necessary to reimagine and rearticulate the underlying principle of "fairness" and how it could be applied to South African conditions.

Reconstructing fairness

Interventions from the South

The first major step in the convention shift was taken by the Thandi project. In addition to requiring that land reform and empowerment projects within the Thandi project were FLO certified, Thandi set additional *internal* criteria, standards, and timelines. These set specific benchmarks for participation and ownership (25 percent minimum)[5] as well as criteria relating to skills development and capacity building (Capespan 2003). The internal criteria were agreed upon with FLO, but not applied to other Fair Trade applicants from South Africa. This raised the question of how FLO should interpret and perhaps "define" empowerment in South Africa more broadly – but also provided an example of how this could be achieved.

While these deliberations were underway within FLO, applications from South Africa were rapidly increasing from all types and sizes of farms. These applications were sometimes driven by the producers themselves, but many were also initiated by exporting agents seeking Fair Trade products either to satisfy an existing demand or to add to the products already offered. This led to concerns among existing producers about the size and potential growth of the Fair Trade market, especially with the inclusion of a variety of exporters and producers with no internal guidelines or benchmarks for empowerment. This not only raised policy questions within FLO, but also practical challenges for its external certifying body FLO-Cert, which could not keep up with assessing, processing, and inspecting these applications.[6]

FLO also benefited from the fact that in South Africa two simultaneous, and in many ways dissimilar, proposals for producer support had developed concurrently and independently of one another. One was developed by EMG, the NGO that had originally supported Heiveld Rooibos tea cooperative. This proposal embodied a stance fairly hostile to the certification of plantations. The other was developed by Hamman & Schumann,[7] a land reform and rural development consultancy closely tied to the Thandi project. This proposal saw worker empowerment within commercial agriculture as an entirely legitimate candidate for Fair Trade certification. After an initial standoff, the two organizations agreed to join efforts and "collect" potentially interested individuals and organizations to form the Fair Trade Producer Support Network (FTPSN).

The first network meeting was attended by a variety of actors interested in the development of Fair Trade in South Africa. There were 12 participants representing 9 organizations, including NGOs, academics,[8] consultants, and trade associations. Some of these organizations had been directly involved with FLO certified projects, or were doing specific research into Fair Trade. Others were interested in how Fair Trade could promote the specific interests of their target or beneficiary groups, for example, women seasonal workers. Needless to say, there were many links already existing within the group through political, professional, or social relationships.

A number of key issues were raised in this meeting, in particular the domination of the Fair Trade movement by Northern stakeholders. It was argued that a Southern perspective on Fair Trade was needed. In the South African context the need to include the priorities of BEE in this interpretation was deemed to be critical. However, it was noted that there was a lack of dialog between Fair Trade producers, who tended to operate in isolation of one another. Although the initial purpose of the network as proposed by FLO was to provide services to FLO certified producers the discussions dominating the network forced it into a more political position, focusing its attentions on standards, policy, and advocacy.

Various positions were articulated in the workshop, including concern about the unqualified certification of plantations. Some argued that by certifying plantations the Fair Trade movement was moving away from its political beginnings. Others argued that there were other groups – seasonal women workers for example – who should benefit from Fair Trade, and that cleaving to a traditional "small farmer" vision of Fair Trade would exclude them. Although some in the group remained skeptical about whether this constituted real agrarian transformation, it was accepted as an option. Another concern which was raised related to the reorganization of FLO into separate standards and certification organizations, and how the charging of a certification fee raised the barrier to entry, especially for small producers.

While there were many different perspectives represented in the network and some points of contention, consensus was reached regarding the need to engage FLO in consultations about land reform and empowerment and the certification of commercial farms in South Africa, and also the need to form a networking platform for Fair Trade producers. A task team was appointed to pursue these objectives. This team specifically included an NGO representative, a consultant and a researcher primarily because of their direct involvement with FLO certified producers, their established contacts with FLO and knowledge of the Fair Trade system.

A window of opportunity for the task team to engage with FLO representatives arose shortly afterwards at a FLO training meeting in Grabouw in the Western Cape, where the members of the task team articulated the concerns of the network about the "unqualified" certification of large commercial farms in South Africa and suggested that FLO place a moratorium on certifications in South Africa until local stakeholders were consulted. In response to these discussions the FLO representative circulated a document outlining empowerment in South Africa. The focus of the document was limited to legislation on employment equity and did not reflect the crucial requirements of BEE and the specific objectives of the transfer of ownership at the center of the South African policy debate. On the basis of their knowledge of land reform and Black Economic Empowerment, the task team members prepared an alternative and more comprehensive analysis of the frameworks regulating land reform and empowerment in South Africa (Hamman and Kruger 2004). This document helped FLO realize that it did not fully understand the South African context and that it needed to consult more broadly. In order to facilitate this FLO decided in May 2004 to hold the "Fair Trade Fresh Fruit and Empowerment Consultation Forum" not in Bonn, as originally proposed, but in Grabouw, in the center of the South African deciduous fruit producing region. The forum was hosted by FLO and the Fairtrade Foundation (United Kingdom) and attended by a variety of international and South African stakeholders.

Two key issues stand out here. One is that the decision by FLO to shift the site of its consultation to South Africa was a major step. FLO was putting up significant and substantial issues for negotiation. The purpose of the Forum was to discuss how empowerment and the development needs in South Africa should be interpreted, and to discuss the Fair Trade pricing for fresh fruit with all the relevant stakeholders. This was the first time that FLO had engaged in such a process of consultation (FLO 2004c). In other words, FLO had opened itself to negotiating the basic conditions of "fair" production and trade outside the comforts of its existing standards.

The second issue is the highly contingent nature of these developments. The decision to shift consultations geographically to the South and to negotiate the content of Fair Trade criteria with potential role players was neither historically inevitable nor the result of a carefully thought out game plan. It arose "in the heat of battle" out of very particular interventions by individuals reacting to a complex and unstable strategic situation. The story of the backstage events that led to and accompanied the "Fairtrade Fresh Fruit and Empowerment Consultation Forum" highlights something that is often passed over in accounts of the development of Fair Trade and other regulatory schemes – the centrality (despite – or perhaps because of – all the institutional paraphernalia of technical research and broad-based consultation) of individual actions and personal influence. While it is true that the development of Fair Trade conventions for South Africa was the result of a wide-ranging process of consultation, often couched in the language of democratic decision making, it is also true that many of the key and decisive interventions lay in the hands of a small group of technical experts, NGO staffers, and consultants. It is worth observing that this is of course far from unusual; despite the rhetoric of transparency, consultation, and democracy that character- izes the self-description of both the Fair Trade movement and initiatives like the Ethical Trading Initiative, *all* these processes are marked by the disproportionate role of individual actors. In the final paragraphs of this chapter, we will return to this phenomenon and explore its theoretical and practical implications.

Negotiating the outcome: participants, mediators, and underlying tensions

The "Consultation Forum" was the result of social and market forces. Members of the producer support network interested and involved in FLO certified farms and with close links to other Fair Trade organizations were in a powerful position to forge direct links with individuals in FLO. The exponential surge in interest in Fair Trade certification in South Africa from producers and exporters meant that FLO certified exporters and producers had established contacts through personal visits to their buyers and national initiatives in the North, and had also raised con- cerns about the rapid growth of Fair Trade in South Africa. These relationships, especially the policy links forged between the members of the network and FLO, enabled the formulation of a broad agenda for the forum: both empowerment and price setting for fresh fruit.

The participants who attended the forum were motivated by very different agendas derived to some extent from their position in the supply chain, their different class and cultural backgrounds, and different experiences of Fair Trade. In addition, these differences and historically entrenched relationships of power made it more difficult for some to participate. At the same time, support organi- zations had forged important relationships with some of the worker and small farmers bodies. These intermediaries, who identified themselves as part of the political left, were able to "take up" and render audible the voices of more marginalized groups. The combination of these factors created a particularly uneven terrain to battle out issues of apparently common interest – the inter- pretation of empowerment in South Africa.

A number of critical questions were raised in the process of negotiating the conventions. What are the dimensions of empowerment in the South African context? How should they be included in the FLO system of standards and certi- fication? How can stakeholders coordinate communications with FLO about Fair Trade policy? How can producers better track the market? Who should have access to the Fair Trade market, and how should this access be governed?

Both FLO and the National Initiatives, especially the UK Fairtrade Foundation (the largest market for Fair Trade fruit from South Africa) had an interest in the consensual solution of the South African situation. FLO opened the forum with an exercise in "setting things straight," that is, reporting on the recent division of standards, producer support, and certification functions. The focus of the presentations was on both the opportunities and challenges that this process of streamlining presented. On the one hand, the rationalized systems of policy, standards, and certification have the effect of locking one into a decision: once a standard has been set all applicants will be equally assessed against these standards. On the other hand, it was made clear that this would not exclude the possibility of giving a context/country specific meaning to development in terms of the FLO standard "Fair Trade adds development potential to..." (FLO 2004a).

Large commercial producers argued that the inclusion of empowerment was "raising the bar." Those producers who were not certified, especially those who had empowerment projects in the pipeline, suggested that Fair Trade could be better used to facilitate the entry of their empowerment projects rather than reward those that were already empowered. In turn those that were already certified (and who had the most to lose from competition) cautioned against "overestimating the Fair Trade market." They argued the number of entrants would need to be limited if the benefits of Fair Trade were to be maintained. The producers were quite vocal about their respective positions regarding empowerment and Fair Trade. The level of empowerment was hotly debated – is 25 percent worker interest in a farm sufficient? Should Fair Trade be limited to farms where workers have a 75 percent interest?

The small-scale farmers were vastly outnumbered by the large-scale/plantation farmers. However, they were proactively supported by NGO's who reminded the other participants of the more basic challenges facing small farmers, and the importance of including these concerns in the otherwise technical deliberations. Nevertheless, in discussion groups the small-scale farmers bemoaned the fact that they were derogatorily referred to as small when they actually consider themselves to be commercial farmers.

The exporters on the other hand were more measured in their approach to Fair Trade – constantly cautioning against "expecting too much from the Fair Trade market." Some of the exporters argued for "raising the bar" even higher – though what exactly this would mean for worker empowerment standards was unclear. The exporters' biggest concern was convincing the other stakeholders, including their clients and critical social partners, that a lower price and premium would enable more absorption in the market.

These questions were framed by the FLO standards as well as by the targets and timelines of BBBEE. Although the government departments did not occupy the center stage at the forum, their motivation to align with Fair Trade stemmed from the potential of leveraging external support and monitoring systems in the implementation of national policies. The strategic position of government policy derived from the fact that the concept of BBBEE had been defined and officially adopted and as such also framed the convention setting process.

While technical challenges of aligning FLO standards with BBBEE requirements and their political implications had been debated within the local producer support network, the majority of the certified producers (large and small scale) were still unfamiliar with the FLO system. Their main motivations were the expectation of a fair price on an agreed volume to a specific market, and a professional service from their exporter and FLO. Importantly, they also expected FLO's understanding of their specific context and conditions and were able to articulate their expectations along with those of their workers.

Workers and small producers were more marginalized. Other than the Thandi producers and workers who by that time already had sporadic contact with other role players, most Fair Trade producers were isolated from one another. This isolation in some cases fostered "urban legends" about the benefits of Fair Trade. In most cases workers were not knowledgeable about the principles and systems of Fair Trade. While they knew that they were the intended beneficiaries, they were not clear about what this meant, and many came to the forum with the perception that FLO was a charity. While commercial farmers, consultants, and exporters in the forum were touting the importance of capacity building and skills development and the need for broad-based ownership and decision making, workers were conspicuously silent.

Two key points are central here. The first is the high degree of *apparent consensus* in the discourse that dominated the convention setting exercise, and the remarkable convergence around, for example, the need to secure the interests of poor and black people who had hitherto been marginalized. The second is that this apparent consensus masked a great degree of contestation and disagreement. This does not mean that the broadly shared commitment to worker empowerment was merely rhetoric or lip service. Rather it should be recognized that the forum was a site of discursive contestation about the very meaning of "fairness," "land reform," "transformation," "empowerment," and other key terms. A wide variety of different options were open, none of which were inevitable, and much depended on the course of events at the forum.

Although some "answers" were found, these "answers" remained incomplete and contested. With respect to empowerment it was decided, on the basis of stakeholder group inputs, to "lift" the standard to include a 25 percent minimum interest of workers in the agricultural enterprise, worker participation on all levels of operational management and an auditable skills development and capacity-building program. Hamman, who has a background in law, led the process of formulating the standards which were adopted by FLO as guidance for South Africa (FLO 2004b).

Stakeholders elected a local coordinator to be contracted by FLO to facilitate communications between South African stakeholders and FLO and to investigate the possibility of establishing a South African National Initiative. While the South African national initiative was being developed, the coordinator would serve as a central contact point for FLO as well as for South African producers and applicants. Although he had been nominated by the forum the legitimacy and scope of this position was limited by a number of factors. First, while he was mandated by South African stakeholders, he was contracted by FLO. Second, his contract was limited to specific functions which were far more narrowly defined than the expectations created by the forum. Though formed and formalized under a "common" purpose, the partnership between FLO and South African stakeholders remained narrow and fragile.

On the whole, the forum seemed to be a success. Role players coming from very different positions had "gotten to yes," reaching agreement on a new set of locally sensitive conventions based on the principles of BEE. The moment of crisis in the existing and expanding set of Fair Trade conventions had stimulated the organization of stakeholder groups in South Africa to leverage their collective political power and influence the outcome of a "new" set of conventions. But the shifting terrain of conventions was far from stable. The outcome of the convention setting process, while representing something of an advance for Southern partners, also included some important ambiguities and new risks.

Implications for Fair Trade in South Africa

Having discussed the contingent nature of the convention setting process, it is necessary to reflect on what was "resolved" by this process, and what remains contested and open for negotiation. The shift in the convention setting process had important implications for Fair Trade in South Africa as well as for FLO. The conceptualization of empowerment in the context of commercial or plantation agriculture created new incentives for white commercial farmers to engage the concepts of BEE, including transformation of ownership, and the distribution of wealth. Time frames have been set out for certified producers to comply with the new standards, and new applicants are now to be certified on the basis of empowerment criteria.

The adoption of empowerment guidelines in South Africa has important implications for the plantation debate internationally, especially in the African and European national initiatives. While FLO's expansion in South Africa is contentious, the inclusion of plantations in other countries where the labor standards are lower is no less contentious. The South African case has provided FLO with an example of how plantations can be included in the Fair Trade system in a way that maintains the political objective of changing power relationships. The process of negotiating these conventions, however, can not be understood outside the very distinctive and particular local context of South African agricultural restructuring, land reform, and social change. South African exceptionalism and the ability of role players to invoke the moral legitimacy and urgency of land reform and BEE gave importance to the need to adapt the operations and systems of FLO. But the adaptation of these systems is rooted in a "new" understanding of "fairness" in the South African context.

Perhaps more important than the model itself is the light that this process has shone on the possibilities for reinterpreting fairness. While opening a window of opportunity for other Southern partners to engage in similar negotiations to redefine "fairness," this unexplored territory poses considerable risks for FLO in maintaining the uniformity of the "guarantee" that it provides. The value of the Fair Trade "brand" rests on its ability to invoke meanings associated with freedom from moral taint. The reinterpretation of the political and social values of Fair Trade to suit "new conditions" is to some extent a testament to the ingenuity and flexibility of the participants in the process, but there are also substantial risks involved. The business arrangements legitimized by FLO certification in South Africa are themselves highly ambiguous. The integrity of the brand and the essence of its value both rely on the socioeconomic and development benefits to marginalized producers and workers in the South. The risk remains that the "stories" from the South will be reduced to a marketing strategy for large-scale producers "to have an edge" in the market, rather than a sincere commitment to social transformation.

What do these changing conventions actually mean for the beneficiaries of Fair Trade? There will always be winners and losers and the interests of the poorest and most marginalized will not necessarily be addressed through voluntary regulation (du Toit 2001). One of the dangers is the creation of "islands of wealth" in impoverished communities. Another is the possibility of public exposure of the coercion of workers or other forms of mismanagement of the Fair Trade standards. These risks remain. It has also been argued (Raynolds et al. 2004) that the indirect benefits of Fair Trade in terms of democratic organization of producers and capacity building are longer lasting than the direct monetary benefit of the premium generated by the Fair Trade label. But that is, of course, only if real democratic organization occurs – an outcome which is far from guaranteed even in the most progressive farm worker equity schemes. Here, much depends on the quality of support given to farm worker bodies in the reorganization process.

The debates around Fair Trade have created the impetus for organizing the beneficiaries of Fair Trade. In particular two worker and small farmer groups have been organized over the past year, both with the help and support of inter-mediaries. The more formalized of the two, the Association for Fairness in Trade is a membership organization for the beneficiaries of Fair Trade. Membership is limited to workers and small farmers, but not limited to those that are FLO certified. The second group, the Black Employees Empowerment Forum is a more diverse forum for land reform and empowerment beneficiaries, some of whom are also FLO certified. Within these groups workers and small farmers are able to share their experiences and articulate common concerns, but the success of these groups remains dependent on the facilitation of social actors who are able to articulate and defend these "beneficiary" interests.

In addition, the "champions" of a national Fair Trade organization in South Africa face not only the internal challenges of inclusion, transparency, and legitimacy, but also the broader political challenges of building relationships and partnerships with other Fair Trade producers in Africa. One of the main objectives of the national initiative envisaged by the consultation forum was the promotion of the market for Fair Trade products within South Africa. In part this is intended to build solidarity with other African producers by facilitating South/South trade, and thus also "soften" the blow of the rapid inclusion of South Africa into the FLO system. Many of these challenges now face Fair Trade South Africa, a trust which was formed in May 2005 at the second South African stakeholder forum.[9] The newly elected Fair Trade South Africa Board of Trustees consists of two small-scale farmers, two workers, two large-scale farmers, two exporters, and two NGO's representing various stakeholders other than the government. What role will this structure play in Africa, and what will the impact be if the majority of Fair Trade producers in Africa are South African? How will these structures represent the interests of workers and producers and protect the integrity of the Fair Trade brand? Those stakeholders marginalized by the process or threatened by the outcome will continue to challenge the legitimacy of these institutions. Here, too, outcomes are far from inevitable and there are a variety of interests at stake.

Conclusion: power, knowledge, and the reinterpretation of fairness

The events that led up to the development of an appropriate Fair Trade convention for South African fruit and wine producers highlight some important theoretical points about convention setting itself. It requires a reconsideration of the way these processes are presented by participants in the Fair Trade movement. According to the most prevalent self-understanding, the negotiation of Fair Trade conventions is a complex but essentially transparent one involving give and take, in which participants find a suitable compromise between divergent national and sectoral interests, technical requirements and realities, commercial imperatives and civic norms. According to this vision the challenge is to come up with a set of workable regulations that can be reconciled with the concept of "fairness."

That is clearly part of the reality, but it is a sanitized account that passes all too easily over the complex underlying politics of the convention setting process. In these concluding paragraphs we make some general observations about the "infrastructure" of fairness – the sometimes disavowed processes and social technologies that underpin the construction of "Fair Trade."

It is important to consider the ambiguous political force of the concept of "fairness" that is so central to the discursive and institutional formations and operations of the Fair Trade movement. The point is not simply that the concept of fairness is open ended and available for reinterpretation, but rather that there are very particular issues at stake in the processes that determine what constitutes "fairness." These tensions issue partly from the Fair Trade movement's identity as a project that exists, as Baratt Brown pointed out, "within and against the market" (Barrat Brown 1993). The prospect continually exists that Fair Trade, far from being a way of challenging the power imbalances between North and South, can function as a way of commodifying political concern and deflecting challenge, renormalizing consumption and legitimizing a "kinder, gentler" food regime that is perhaps more paternalistic and less nakedly exploitative.

Such a co-optation of the Fair Trade movement is of course far from inevitable. Much depends on the debates and contests that accompany the expansion of the Fair Trade movement. While the outcomes of these contests are not predetermined, it must be pointed out that they happen on an uneven playing field. The processes and institutional formations within which they happen, and the social technologies of power and knowledge on which they depend, create a context that sets limits on what can and can not happen.

Perhaps the most important phenomenon to highlight, then, is the adoption by the Fair Trade movement of the social technologies and grammars of labeling, branding, auditing, and standards. This embodies a move away from an explicitly ideological, situational, and political articulation of fairness as *solidarity*, and toward a much more liberal notion that fairness can be operationalized and contained within a set of *conventions* that can be impartially and objectively adjudicated. As in the case of the Ethical Trading Initiative, the operationalization of "fairness" in the context of globalized agrofood regimes creates a tension. On the one hand, the success and power of the FLO label depends on the perceived moral clarity and simplicity of the concept of "fairness" – a concept that is assumed to be self-evident, universally and acontextually valid, and expounded in a few simple slogans or assurances on a product label. On the other hand, it is evident that fairness is never simply fairness, and that it requires reinterpretation and rearticulation to insure that it is operationalized in locally appropriate ways on the ground.

This means that it is important to look very closely at the ways in which fairness is interpreted and reinterpreted as the Fair Trade movement expands into new contexts. FLO's ability to expand into new markets while still presenting its operations as "fair" depends on a hidden infrastructure: a spatially distributed social technology of power and knowledge which allows for the backstage *and* onstage creation of consensus around the rearticulation of principles such as fairness. Consultative processes and the setting of industrial, regional, and sector-specific codes allow for complex processes of mediation and translation, and for the political management of the disjuncture between the universality and simplicity of "fairness" and the political and technical diversity of the particular localities within which that "fairness" is practiced.

From this perspective, what matters is not only the substantive issues and interests that are negotiated and the tradeoffs that are made, but also the way in which these spaces are places where the meaning of fairness, transformation, and change are redefined. In the South African case, the crucial process was one where fairness in fruit and wine production came to be understood in relation to the concepts of land reform and black empowerment – an understanding very different from those that previously governed its assessment of plantation agriculture.

It is in this context we need to analyze the particular forms of agency and power mobilized by the individuals involved in these events. The ability of Kruger, Hamman, EMG, and their colleagues to impact FLO's consultation was not simply the result of technical argument and logical persuasion, nor of the mobilization of authentic voices from the ground. Clearly the ability to engage technically and in detail with FLO documents made a big difference, but it is also important to note that this engagement happened at a moment in FLO's history in which its own interpretive and ideological narratives were internally in crisis, and many otherwise settled issues were up for contestation. The considerable power of these agents within the network was also shaped by their identity as activists in the South African white left, and their ability to link a high degree of training – and the significant confidence as "speaking subjects" that this gave them – to their political capital and their ability to mobilize the political authority invoked by institutional and NGO links. In addition, they were able to draw on the symbolic capital and leverage created by South Africa's political history and the legitimacy of the aims of South African land reform and transformation within the broader moral universe of the Fair Trade movement.

These factors played a large part in creating a space in which it was possible to rearticulate what "fairness" might mean. It is true that this process resulted in conventions more sensitive to the interests of South African workers, and that it entrenched a more robust "empowerment" agenda than FLO's existing plantation criteria allowed. But this worker-friendly outcome was not the direct result of worker participation. Those who participated in the convention setting process did not meet on an even playing field. Some (FLO representatives, commercial producers, exporters, and NGO's) had a capacity to "read" the technical aspects *and* to intervene forcefully, while others – ironically, the impoverished and marginalized farm workers whose existence justified the entire process – were much less able to speak and act effectively and powerfully in this demanding context. Ultimately, while the outcome can be argued to be friendly to the concerns of producers and workers, the reality is that farm workers had a "voice" in the process only through the mediation of other actors on whom they were dependent. The worker-friendly outcome was the result of the ability of technical experts and ideological brokers to engage creatively with worker inputs, supporting their articulation and allowing their translation into technical FLO requirements.

What are the implications for Fair Trade as a political project? If it is true that the convention setting process involves consultation and negotiation mainly among an elite of technical experts and politically powerful ideological brokers, the notion that Fair Trade works in a direct and simple way to empower workers and producers needs to be taken with a pinch of salt. It is true that all these events are part of a process of development. Since the formation of Fair Trade South Africa, workers have done a lot more organizing. But it is certainly the case that more work needs to be done to understand the often hidden workings of the disregarded mechanisms that underpin the process whereby the Fair Trade movement imagines – and reimagines – the political content of "fairness" in a changing world.

Notes

1 Chile also entered the Fair Trade wine market in this time.
2 Part of the application process for producers to become FLO certified is to prove that there is an existing market for their Fair Trade product – some confirmation that there is a buyer for the product. This does not, however, require a fixed contract on volumes and prices.
3 According to Cousins (2004) never more than 0.5 percent of the National Budget has been allocated to land reform over the past 10 years.
4 The boycott of South African fruit organized by the Dutch organization Boycott Outspan Aktie played a key role in focusing early international solidarity work with the antiapartheid movement (Jackson 2004).

5 According to BEE definitions, a company with 25 percent + 1 black ownership is considered to be "black-empowered," while a company with 50 percent + 1 is considered a "black-owned."
6 FLO Cert has subsequently appointed a certifications coordinator in South Africa.
7 Kruger, one of the authors of this chapter, was interned at this consultancy at this time.
8 Both authors of this chapter attended the first Fair Trade producer support network meeting in January 2004.
9 The objectives of this institution have essentially remained consistent with those identified at its inception the year before and include: the promotion of Fair Trade labeling in South Africa; the promotion of social and economic development among the beneficiary community; the provision of producer support to Fair Trade certified producers; liaison with the African Fair Trade Network, National Initiatives, Fairtrade Labelling Organization (FLO e.V. and FLO-Cert); and to develop the market for Fair Trade certified products in South Africa (Fairtrade South Africa Trust 2005).

References

Barrat Brown, M. (1993) *Fair Trade*, London: Zed Books.
Barrientos, S. (2002) "Mapping codes through the value chain – from researcher to detective," in R. Jenkins, R. Pearson, and G. Seyfang (eds), *Corporate Responsibility and Ethical Trade: Codes of Conduct in the Global Economy*, London: Earthscan.
Bernstein, H. (1996) "South Africa's agrarian question: extreme and exceptional," in H. Bernstein (ed.), *The Agrarian Question in South Africa*, London: Frank Cass.
Blowfield, M. (1999) "Ethical trade: a review of developments and issues," *Third World Quarterly*, 20: 753–770.
Capespan. (2003) "Thandi criteria," unpublished internal document.
Cousins, B. (2004) "Grounding democracy: the politics of land in post apartheid South Africa," *Mail & Guardian*, November 26, Online. Available at: www.mg.co.za (accessed April 14, 2005).
Cronin, J. (2004) "BEE-llionaires and wanna-BEEs," *Mail & Guardian*, October 15–21, Online. Available at: www.mg.co.za (accessed April 14, 2005).
du Toit, A. and Ewert, J. (2001) "Can ethical trade help South African farm workers? Private sector self-regulation, export agriculture and equitable change in the Western Cape," unpublished research report for the Centre for Rural Legal Studies, Stellenbosch.
du Toit, A. and Ewert, J. (2005) "A deepening divide in the countryside: restructuring and rural livelihoods in the South African wine industry," *Journal of Southern African Studies*, 31: 315–332.
Fairtrade Foundation. (2003a) *Fair Trade Oranges are Launched*, Press Release, July 21, Online. Available at: www.fairtrade.org.uk/pr210703 (accessed April 12, 2005).
—— (2003b) *Thandi Fair Trade Partnership brings the First Fair Trade Grapes from South Africa to the UK*, Press Release, November 19, Online. Available at: www.fairtrade.org.uk/pr191103 (accessed April 12, 2005).
Fairtrade South Africa Trust. (2005) *Deed of Trust of the Fairtrade South Africa Trust*, Online. Available at: www.fairtrade.org.za/FTSAConference/Documents/FAIRTRADE%20SOUTH%20AFRICA%20TRUST%20(2).doc (accessed July 10, 2006).
FLO (Fairtrade Labelling Organizations International). (2004a) *Generic Standards for Hired Labor Situations*, Online. Available at: www.fairtrade.net/sites/standards/hl.html (accessed November 17, 2004).
—— (2004b) *Guidance Document for Fairtrade Labeling: Standards Guidance for South Africa*, Online. Available at: www.fairtrade.net/sites/standards/hl.html (accessed October 15, 2004).

—— (2004c) *The Fairtrade Fresh Fruit and Empowerment Consultation Forum, Grabouw, South Africa May 24–25 2004 Report*, Online. Available at: www.fairtrade.org.za/ Documents/Consultation per cent20Forum per cent202004 per cent20report.doc (accessed April 14, 2005).

FTSA (Fairtrade South Africa). (2006) *Producers and Traders*, Online. Available at: www.fairtrade.org.za/ (accessed July 10, 2006).

Hamman, J.N. and Ewert, J. (1999) "A historical irony in the making? State private sector and land reform in the South African wine industry," *Development South Africa*, 16: 315–332.

Hamman, J.N. and Kruger, S. (2004) "Guidelines for FLO's empowerment strategy in South Africa," unpublished discussion document.

Jackson, P. (2004) "Local consumption cultures in a globalizing world," *Transactions/ Institute of British Geographers*, 29: 165–178.

Laclau, E. (1990) *New Reflections on the Revolution of our Time*, London: Verso.

Mayson, D. (2003) "Joint ventures," *Evaluating Land and Agrarian Reform in South Africa Series*, no. 7. Cape Town: Programme for Land and Agrarian Studies, University of the Western Cape.

Merten, M. (2004) "Grape expectations," *Mail & Guardian*, July 23–29, Online. Available at: www.mg.co.za (accessed April 14, 2005).

NDA (National Department of Agriculture). (2004) "AgriBEE Broad-Based Black Economic Empowerment framework for agriculture," unpublished consultation document.

Raynolds, L.T., Murray, D., and Taylor, P.L. (2004) "Fair trade coffee: building producer capacity via global networks," *Journal of International Development*, 16: 1109–1121.

Rumney, R. (2004) "How broad-based is BEE?," *Mail & Guardian*, July 23–29, Online. Available at: www.mg.co.za (accessed April 14, 2005).

Selva, M. (2005) "Good intentions that withered on the vine," in *The Sunday Independent*, February 20, Online. Available at: www.mg.co.za (accessed April 14, 2005).

Tabane, R. (2004) "Ending elitism," *Mail & Guardian*, August 13–19, 2004.

Part IV

Fair Trade as an emerging global movement

13 Fair Trade

Contemporary challenges and future prospects

Laura T. Raynolds and Douglas L. Murray

Introduction

Fair Trade has emerged over recent years as a powerful critique of conventional global inequalities and a promising initiative supporting alternative globalization ideas, practices, and institutions grounded in social justice and ecological sustainability. Fair Trade has become a key rallying cry around the world for efforts challenging the negative impacts of conventional international trade. It has simultaneously become a market generating US$ 1.5 billion per year incorporating numerous commodities and thousands of producers, consumers, and distributors in the Global North and South. Fair Trade's recent success has been rooted in its ability to combine visionary goals with practical engagements in fair and sustainable trade within and beyond the agrofood sector. But as demonstrated in this volume, the dramatic growth in Fair Trade since 2000 has fueled a number of challenges which threaten to unravel this promising initiative unless its vision and practice can be realigned.

The key challenges facing Fair Trade arise from the inherent contradictions embedded within this initiative between movement and market priorities. Fair Trade seeks to operate simultaneously against the market, campaigning for changes in conventional trade practices and challenging North/South inequalities, and within the market, creating more egalitarian trade between Northern consumers and Southern producers (see Raynolds 2000, 2002). As outlined in Chapter 2, this contradictory focus is historically rooted and remains central to the definition and institutions of Fair Trade (FINE 2003). Analytically this divide can be understood (as suggested in Chapter 3) as being between alternative *civic/domestic* conventions rooted in trust, place attachment, and social benefits and conventional *industrial/market* norms, practices, and institutions ruled by price and efficiency. Conflicts between these divergent conventions emerge repeatedly in the studies presented in this volume, though they take somewhat varied forms. These tensions are characterized by different authors as being between (1) a *social, movement*, or *development* orientation that sees Fair Trade as an avenue for fundamentally transforming conventional market values and institutions based on social justice concerns and (2) a *commercial, market*, or *corporate reform* orientation that sees Fair Trade as an avenue for regulating social and environmental standards, but that largely upholds the values and institutions of the market. As Chapter 3 proposes, Fair Trade's conflicting orientations reflect the contemporary merging of economic and noneconomic actors and activities and the shift of movement efforts from social critique to the co-construction of market parameters.

Fair Trade's recent growth is heightening movement/market tensions. As the research reported in this book suggests, Fair Trade's engagement in a growing range of commodity areas, production and distribution arrangements, and social and political contexts is accentuating the divide between divergent groups and strategies. Though Fair Trade groups are positioned along a continuum, they fall increasingly into opposing camps comprised of transformers or regulators, radicals or reformers (see also Bisaillon et al. 2006). The cases explored in this volume reveal heated debates across this divide spawned by Fair Trade's rapid expansion. The key question is: Is Fair Trade's dramatic recent growth a sign of success? More specifically, is Fair Trade effectively reshaping historically unequal market relations through the integration of alternative norms of social justice and sustainability or has Fair Trade's transformative agenda been eroded by the market forces it initially set out to transform? Put more bluntly, have Fair Trade ideals of changing the world been forgotten in the pursuit of commercial success?

The path-breaking studies in this volume illuminate the impacts of Fair Trade's market success on its movement commitments in a range of settings across the Global North and South. To synthesize these insights, this chapter considers the four central challenges confronting Fair Trade identified in Chapter 1, specifically those arising from the following: (1) the mainstreaming of Fair Trade distribution, (2) the increasing scale and complexity of Fair Trade production, (3) the challenges of Fair Trade governance, and (4) Fair Trade's shifting movement location. Each of the chapters in this book shed light on these arenas of contestation in particular contexts; their collective insights increase our understanding of the nature and future prospects of Fair Trade and of the challenges of transforming globalization.

The mainstreaming of Fair Trade distribution

Fair Trade has shifted historically from the domain of small mission-driven Alternative Trade Organizations (ATOs) working to further development and social justice goals into the domain of large transnational corporate traders, branders, and retailers seeking to position themselves in increasingly differentiated markets. The mainstreaming of Fair Trade has been made possible by the growth of the FLO international certification system and national labeling initiatives which promote the sale of certified products in conventional supermarkets. The move of Fair Trade from the confines of ATOs catering to dedicated consumers into conventional distribution channels oriented to mainstream consumers has fueled Fair Trade certified sales, but it has required the engagement of a host of large operators whose commitment to Fair Trade principles is open to question. While some see the mainstreaming of Fair Trade as an indication of this initiative's success in reshaping conventional market relations, others argue that this reflects nothing more than mainstream corporate efforts to profit from Fair Trade products.

FLO and its national affiliates, such as TransFair USA and the Fairtrade Foundation, have labored with great success to maximize certified sales volumes in order to maximize the number of producers and workers benefiting from Fair Trade. FLO affiliates are sometimes critiqued for pursuing Fair Trade volumes as an "end in itself" or for promoting Northern commercial interests at the expense of Southern development concerns. Though these groups have not forsaken producer interests, they support a narrow development agenda based on integrating producers into fairer export markets. FLO and its affiliates seek to grow the market for the benefit of producers, but their efforts are often channeled by market demands to open up new commodity areas or forge more dependable sourcing arrangements. This tendency is demonstrated for example in FLO and the Fairtrade Foundation's efforts to certify South African horticultural products for the UK market and TransFair USA's efforts to certify transnational corporate bananas for the US market. The studies in this volume find that FLO and its affiliates are primarily engaged in promoting Fair Trade's market position, leaving the movement agenda of transforming North/South inequalities largely to ATOs and allied NGOs.

The rapid rise of Fair Trade labeled commodities in mainstream markets often overshadows the continued importance of mission-driven ATOs in distribution as well as advocacy. As the UK and US case studies report, ATOs and other alternative branders and traders remain critical in Fair Trade handicrafts, coffee, and chocolate, and even in some fresh produce areas like bananas. These enterprises are concerned about the growing role of large corporate distributors who may be able to underprice and undercut more socially oriented Fair Trade firms. Given the historical and contemporary importance of these alternative businesses in promoting Fair Trade, questions are raised regarding the need to align Fair Trade labeling fees and support in accordance with commitment levels. The clearest conflict is seen in the US coffee sector, where some 100 percent Fair Trade firms have given up their certification labels due to what they see as TransFair USA's lack of recognition and favoring of large corporate competitors, like Procter & Gamble or Starbucks, which certify only a minor share of their output.

The book's chapters on Fair Trade in the Global North find that even within mainstream corporations, commitment to Fair Trade varies. These studies point to the importance of "mission-oriented" firms – firms that fall somewhere between mission-driven ATOs and profit-driven corporations – in bolstering Fair Trade markets. Some corporate retailers and branders, such as Wild Oats and Green Mountain Coffee Roasters (GMCR) in the United States and the Co-op Supermarket in the United Kingdom, have made significant Fair Trade commitments, selling certified items as the dominant or even exclusive option within particular commodity lines. In these cases there is an affinity between company and Fair Trade principles, based on the strong corporate social responsibility focus of GMCR and Wild Oats and the cooperative movement lineage of the Co-op.

Yet commercial considerations remain strong and Fair Trade items are held to the same exacting quality standards, time tables, and pricing rules as other products.

The mainstreaming of Fair Trade is also engaging corporate partners with little visible commitment to social justice principles, such as the Tesco supermarket chain in the United Kingdom or the transnational banana corporations being courted by TransFair USA. These corporations remain committed to maximizing profits, which in current differentiated markets may involve sales of certified Fair Trade products. Fears regarding the potential dilution of Fair Trade principles by firms seeking only "clean washing" appear most justified in these contexts. The increasing certification of products controlled by some of the world's largest corporations strains FLO's regulatory capacity and may undermine the integrity of standards and procedures. It also strains the credulity of consumers that corporations like Nestlé or Chiquita, infamous for their exploitative practices in the Global South, might be considered to engage in "fair trade."

The chapters in this volume suggest that the challenges of maintaining Fair Trade principles in mainstream distribution channels are greatly accentuated in "buyer-driven" commodity networks controlled by powerful retailers and branders. As Barrientos and Smith demonstrate, dominant UK retailers are not regulated under the FLO system even when they are selling Fair Trade products in their own brand lines. These retailers dictate conditions in Fair Trade supply chains much like they do in other product areas. Dominant supermarkets maximize profits in Fair Trade sales by curtailing supply costs – shifting risks to suppliers, juggling suppliers, and lowering prices – and by charging high retail mark ups. The power of dominant buyers, whether retailers or branders, is heightened in fresh produce circuits which must be tightly controlled to insure undamaged and timely deliveries. As Raynolds demonstrates, the rigorous demands of sourcing Fair Trade bananas for the US market have undermined the operations of some small alternative importers and created an opening for bananas sourced by vertically integrated transnational corporate branders. While dominant retailers and branders clearly have the power to undermine Fair Trade conditions within their sourcing networks, FLO and its national affiliates do not have solid standards or procedures to regulate these enterprise practices.

The mainstreaming of Fair Trade distribution has greatly heightened the contradictions between movement and market priorities. Within mainstream channels Fair Trade products, practices, and enterprises are under constant pressure to conform to dominant market rules. Bolstering Fair Trade norms of social justice and sustainability within the mainstream is rendered more complex by the wide variety of enterprises involved. Commitment to Fair Trade clearly varies and it would be naïve to simply assume that mainstream distributors will prioritize ethical principles over profits. In this context, proposals for acknowledging and supporting enterprises that demonstrate strong commitment to Fair Trade may make sense. FLO certification systems need to be strengthened and extended within the realm of distribution given the power of dominant corporate branders and retailers to dictate supply conditions. While FLO has recently tightened the oversight of importers and exporters, if the regulation of branders and retailers is not similarly augmented it will become increasingly difficult to insure that growing Fair Trade markets really foster more equal trade relations and better returns for producers and workers.

The increasing scale and complexity of Fair Trade production

The recent rapid growth of Fair Trade has involved an expansion in the range of commodities, complexity of production arrangements, and types of enterprises entering the FLO system. Fair Trade has incorporated increasingly large production units to meet rising quality and quantity demands. This in turn has increased the number of producers and workers involved in Fair Trade. Yet this expansion has fueled heated debates, particularly over FLO certification of plantations. While some argue that Fair Trade's recent growth demonstrates its ability to transform wage labor as well as small farmer enterprises and broaden the distribution of benefits, others assert that this process is fueling the integration of fundamentally unjust operations into Fair Trade networks and reinforcing North/South inequalities.

The Fair Trade model in the agrofood sector grew out of the certification of coffee produced by small farmers. This model proposed that egalitarian North/ South trade links could be created by eliminating middlemen, providing better and secure prices, supporting farmer cooperatives, and fostering development in impoverished communities. This concept of Fair Trade is relatively simple and quite compelling to producers and consumers alike. Yet Fair Trade production on the ground is much more complex even within the small farm sector. In some fresh produce items like bananas, exporting is so complicated that intermediary firms are often essential to getting quality fruit to market. Fair Trade prices are intended to cover production costs and a decent standard of living for farmers, but producer prices are hard to establish and maintain, with persistent debate even over the price of the core commodity coffee. Although strengthening farmer cooperatives is a key facet of Fair Trade, entry into certified networks requires significant collective capacity as evidenced in the case of the Mexican coffee associations that pioneered Fair Trade as well as recently certified producer organizations in Brazil. Given these complexities, some question whether Fair Trade is able to truly engage disadvantaged producers or guarantee substantial benefits. Others question whether exports should be promoted at all, particularly as in the case of quinoa when exports of nutritious traditional crops may undermine local food security.

The chapters in Part III of this book all find that recent market trends are eroding the small farmer base of Fair Trade in the Global South. The increasing quality and volume requirements of major distributors bolster the position of larger, more commercially oriented, producers as is well demonstrated among Fair Trade coffee growers in Mexico and quinoa growers in Bolivia. In the Brazilian orange juice sector, exacting quality standards, blend requirements, and the demand for large continuous supplies have dramatically increased the share of

Fair Trade exports originating from large capital-intensive enterprises. Fair Trade producers across commodity areas are also increasingly expected to acquire costly organic certification. While producers have long been encouraged to shift to organic cultivation, organic certification has generally been funded by Fair Trade premiums. Now organic certification, like other quality requirements, operate may as a barrier to entry for small disadvantaged producers. Given these constraints, it is perhaps not surprising that social movement groups in Brazil and other parts of Latin America question the fit of Fair Trade with their small farmer and rural development priorities.

Northern market demand for Fair Trade product diversity, as well as quality and volume, is dramatically increasing FLO certification of plantation enterprises. The fastest growing Fair Trade products are newly certified fresh fruits and vegetables which are rarely produced by small farmers. Though FLO has certified hired labor enterprises for years, the escalating number and size of these enterprises has heightened debates over the applicability of the Fair Trade strategy in these situations. FLO requirements for hired labor firms parallel those for small farmers in guaranteeing prices, bolstering worker organizations, and providing social premiums. They also include International Labor Organization based labor standards. While improving labor standards, providing social premiums, and supporting unions can certainly improve the conditions of hired workers, it is not necessarily clear how in this regard Fair Trade differs from other union, corporate social responsibility, and ethical trade measures. What makes Fair Trade unique is its emphasis on trade criteria: its price guarantees and long-term trade relations. Yet within a hired labor context, how can the benefits of more egalitarian trade be accrued by workers, rather than estate owners?

The extension of certification into South African horticultural crops has required the renegotiation of FLO hired labor standards to address this question, as outlined in Chapter 12. Within this context, FLO's basic standards would have permitted the certification of almost any enterprise, despite their embodiment of the historical exclusion of blacks from land ownership. New country-specific FLO standards were devised to foster black worker empowerment within Fair Trade networks. FLO's new South African standards address the question of how trade equity can benefit hired workers by requiring that workers in certified enterprises have at least a 25 percent ownership share. Without downplaying the challenges of empowering black workers in this deeply divided country, we suggest that this case provides a provocative model for Fair Trade plantation certification.

The Latin American and Caribbean Coordination of Fair Trade Small Producers (CLAC) argues that only when plantations are converted into worker-owned collectives will they provide the same transformative potential as exists within small farmer cooperatives. Though the argument that workers must have a share in Fair Trade production units if they are to benefit from more egalitarian trade is well taken, CLAC's stance is best understood in light of their overall objection to FLO certification of plantations in the region. As outlined in Chapter 9, CLAC asserts that the very existence of small farmers is threatened if they are forced to compete with large plantations within Fair Trade. While perhaps overstated, the current competition within Fair Trade banana networks between small and large producers, which will be greatly exacerbated if TNC banana plantations are certified, lends support to this argument.

The rising quality and quantity requirements of Northern markets are shifting the profile of Fair Trade producers and accentuating the contradictions between market and movement forces. The ascendance of market priorities in Fair Trade certified networks is fostering the expansion of more commercially oriented small-scale producers and plantations. Yet movement priorities are being voiced in the diverse proposals to protect the spaces of small-scale production and require worker ownership in large estates. Maintaining Fair Trade's small farmer base may be critical for communicating the Fair Trade concept as well as for protecting producers. Fair Trade may also be used as a compelling strategy to support disadvantaged workers. But for Fair Trade to go beyond other labor standard initiatives and, as its mandate suggests, use trade as a vehicle for empowerment, certified enterprises must integrate some form of worker shareholding.

The challenges of Fair Trade governance

Fair Trade's internal governance challenges have increased greatly over recent years with the rapid expansion in certified products, markets, producer types, and production regions. The internal politics of Fair Trade have become more contentious with the integration of diverse and at times competing stakeholders. New Northern ATO alliances and Southern producer groups (like CLAC) are consolidating critiques focused largely on the FLO certification system. Interesting parallels are emerging between these critiques which may moderate North/South divisions. Recent modifications in the FLO certification system – such as changes in political representation on the FLO Board of Directors – address the rising complexity of Fair Trade governance, but they have done little to stem discontent.

FLO certification priorities have come under substantial attack over recent years, particularly by Southern producer groups. FLO and its national affiliates are broadly criticized for advancing commercial over development interests. This is elaborated most clearly in the case study of South Africa where FLO's commercial interest in generating supplies of certified products for European markets was challenged by local stakeholders insistent on linking certification to local development priorities. The plantation certification issue is often seen in a similar light, particularly by Latin American producers politically committed to supporting the small farm sector. In a move intended to validate the position of small producers in Fair Trade, CLAC has recently launched a small farmer symbol. From these diverse vantage points a common critique is emerging challenging the legitimacy of pursuing rising Fair Trade certified volumes divorced from local empowerment and development concerns.

Two ongoing debates illuminate contentions over North/South power asymmetries within FLO institutions and practices. The first revolves around a broad questioning of a Fair Trade partnership which hinges on the regulation and monitoring of "fairness" within Southern producer relations, but largely ignores the unfair practices of Northern distributors. Though not new, this concern has been heightened in recent years by the mounting control of dominant corporate retailers and branders over Fair Trade networks. A common agenda is emerging from Southern producer groups and Northern ATOs regarding the need to repudiate distributor practices which undermine Fair Trade principles. The second debate revolves around the more specific introduction of FLO certification fees for producer groups. As suggested by Renard and Pérez-Grovas the key conflict here is over the limited participation of Southern producers in developing the new fee structure. Yet while CLAC and other producer groups are united in their critique of FLO's decision-making process, there is less agreement regarding the acceptability of shifting certification costs to producers and the most appropriate distribution of these costs among producers.

Current conflicts over who establishes Fair Trade certification standards and procedures and how they are upheld reveal strong North/South and market/ movement divisions. FLO's formal standards and certification rules have been created largely by Northern labeling organizations. Rigorous standards and audit rules facilitate the acceptance of Fair Trade products in mainstream markets, yet they are in many ways antithetical to the relations of trust that Fair Trade seeks to foster. Northern ATOs challenge FLO's industrial style standards and audit procedures arguing for a less bureaucratic approach. As studies in this volume reveal, FLO certification requirements may act as barriers to entry and mechanism of control for Southern producers. Wilkinson and Mascarenhas report that the introduction of participatory certification systems has become a key component of the new Fair Trade agenda emerging in Brazil and other parts of Latin America. Given FLO's commitment to tightening regulatory procedures in line with ISO standards, these issues are likely to remain hotly debated.

Critical new governance challenges are arising from Fair Trade's incorporation of large middle-income countries committed to balancing traditional South to North exports with domestic and South to South Fair Trade circuits. As noted in Chapter 8, the development of these new trade circuits is a key component of the Southern Fair Trade agenda. Comercio Justo was established a number of years ago in Mexico to create a domestic market and limit export dependence. This group is still negotiating FLO membership, since it has argued that rather than applying FLO's general rules, it should be able to employ its own country-specific standards, certification procedures, and plantation restrictions. South Africa has already created country-specific Fair Trade criteria and is beginning to develop a domestic market model. As demonstrated in Chapter 10, in Brazil the goal of developing national as well as continental markets for Fair Trade products has been one of the few common priorities across an otherwise disparate movement. Ongoing discussions suggest that a Brazilian national initiative would align local producer development concerns with broader solidarity economy commitments, thus incorporating issues such as fair pricing for low-income consumers and food sovereignty into Fair Trade standards and procedures.

The growth and shifting composition of Fair Trade networks are significantly complicating internal governance issues while simultaneously creating provocative new alignments in Fair Trade visions. A new Southern agenda is being defined which parallels in many ways the agenda of Northern ATOs. This Southern agenda emerges from (1) a unified critique of FLO standards and procedures, (2) a shared interest in creating new domestic and South/South Fair Trade circuits, and (3) a common commitment to developing certification systems in accordance with local development priorities. While we may be seeing the formation of a broadly unified alternative vision of Fair Trade, local development concerns generate significantly different proposals regarding Fair Trade practice. These differences are visible in divergent commitments to small holder vs. estate production, formal vs. informal certification, and consumer vs. producer pricing priorities. Negotiating these diverse interests will generate significant governance challenges for Fair Trade into the future.

Fair Trade's shifting movement location

Some of the most important debates over the nature and future of Fair Trade relate to the location of this initiative within larger social movement efforts and shifting State/economy/civil society boundaries. As this volume demonstrates, the social movement location of Fair Trade is shaped via the persistent tensions between ATO and FLO certified systems and by widening social, political, and economic engagements with Fair Trade. Ongoing negotiations are breaking down entrenched market/movement and North/South divisions within Fair Trade, fueling a more complex, though potentially more significant, challenge to conventional globalization.

Fair Trade has traditionally been defined by the competing visions of the more market-oriented and ascendant FLO certification system and the more movement-oriented and less dynamic ATO sector consolidated largely by IFAT. Tensions between these two perspectives have emerged throughout this book. In the Global North these tensions define debates over mainstreaming and opposing views on whether corporate distributors are advancing Fair Trade or hijacking the movement. In the global South these tensions configure disagreements regarding the commercialization of Fair Trade export production and the need to prioritize local development concerns. Despite these cleavages there are some signs that the FLO and IFAT wings of the movement are creating some common ground through their joint advocacy under the FINE umbrella. In a national context, TransFair USA is pursuing a rapprochement with movement allies (in the wake of conflicts over the planned certification of TNC bananas) since it realizes that it can not maintain the legitimacy or popular support of Fair Trade on its own.

One of the major forces bringing the FLO and IFAT strands of Fair Trade together appears to be the heightened engagement with broader social actors. As the chapters in Part II suggest, one of the most critical forces shaping the location of Fair Trade in the Global North is the broad-based rise in popular concern over issues of trade equity and sustainability. This mounting interest has energized new social movements that bolster Fair Trade's political agenda and has fueled the dramatic rise in conscientious purchasing which bolsters Fair

Trade's economic activities. The chapters in Part III suggest that Fair Trade in the Global South is positioning itself within a field of activity defined by powerful social movements focused on issues such as agrarian reform, food sovereignty, cooperative movements, and solidarity economy. Again important political and economic spaces are being created for Fair Trade.

The shifting location of Fair Trade relates not only to its position within the terrain of social movements but also to its position within changing State/civil society relations. State engagement with Fair Trade is evidenced most clearly in the Global South. In Brazil, Fair Trade is firmly positioned within the official policy arena with substantial producer and network support being provided by State offices charged with fostering agrarian reform, small and medium enterprises, and the solidarity economy. In South Africa, Fair Trade has been tied to official Black Economic Empowerment policies, again developing a synergistic relationship between Fair Trade and State institutions. These State alliances are important in the allocation of political resources and they may unite or divide the FLO certified and ATO wings of the Fair Trade movement.

Major economic institutions are also increasing their engagement in the terrain of Fair Trade. There is a rise across the Global North and South in new labels, certifications, and corporate responsibility measures which highlight ethical and sustainability issues. For example, quinoa from producer associations in Bolivia is being sold in France under ATO, private ethical brand, and Fair Trade labels. In Brazil a new NGO/corporate ethical trade label and direct procurement programs are taking off. While this growth could be seen as an indication of the power of Fair Trade ideas and practices to reshape conventional business practices, this trend may conversely reflect moves by conventional business to appropriate the language and markets of Fair Trade. FLO and ATO strands of the Fair Trade movement are working together to ward off this potential threat by defining common guidelines for "real" Fair Trade within the FINE network and jointly opposing new corporate controlled Fair Trade "lite" or "look alike" initiatives.

Perhaps the most significant recent change in Fair Trade's movement location derives from this initiative's engagement in the transnational terrain of alternative globalization. Fair Trade has emerged as a key focal point for this much broader movement due to its conceptual and practical appeal. The Fair Trade concept captures the complex mediation of local/global and social/ecological concerns espoused by the varied groups united under the alternative globalization umbrella. In a movement too often mired in critique, this initiative presents a practical guide for converting trade justice ideas into practice. Support for Fair Trade has clearly been enhanced by the increasing engagement of major Fair Trade organizations in multilateral policy arenas. Fair Trade groups in the Global South have played important roles in a number of recent multilateral venues, often in conjunction with other Southern movements. FLO and its national affiliates have generally left the advocacy goals of Fair Trade to ATOs and allied NGOs, but this is changing based on the increasing activity of the FINE alliance. Within FINE, labeling and ATO organizations have worked together, preparing a joint position statement for the 2005 WTO Ministerial Meetings which might be seen as the first iteration of a global Fair Trade political platform.

Fragmentation or constructive reformulation?

Fair Trade is undeniably at an important juncture. Inherent tensions between Fair Trade's movement goals of transforming conventional trade and erasing North/ South inequalities and its market goals of promoting more egalitarian commodity chains have been heightened by recent expansion. A clear divide has emerged between Fair Trade movement and market ideas, practices, and institutions. Some suggest that Fair Trade will likely cleave in two along this fault line, but this is unlikely due in part to the complex insertion of the Global South. Southern actors are increasingly shaping the nature and direction of Fair Trade. While significant North/South differences remain they do not map easily onto the market/movement divide. Market priorities are typically attributed to the North and movement priorities to the South, but important segments of the initiative align differently. We could see a fragmentation of Fair Trade, but this does not appear imminent.

We propose instead that we can see the beginning contours of a constructive reformulation of Fair Trade. Fair Trade emerged from a social movement commitment to challenge global inequalities. While over the past decade efforts to expand Fair Trade markets and product supplies have been dominant, this focus may be reaching its limits as suggested by mounting conflicts around the world. Further commercialization of Fair Trade would essentially involve the absorption of the movement by the market. More likely is that commercial inroads will continue to be contested since they threaten the viability and legitimacy of Fair Trade. Rather than spelling the demise of Fair Trade, we see current tensions and debates as fueling the next wave of social movement reformulation of Fair Trade ideas and practices.

As we have outlined in this chapter the constructive reformulation of Fair Trade will be required on a number of key fronts. Within Northern markets the key challenge appears to be the mounting power of retailers and branders to undermine Fair Trade conditions within their supply chains unless these enterprises are required to uphold Fair Trade principles. In Southern production regions, the key challenge stems from Fair Trade's expansion into plantations where workers can not be guaranteed to benefit from more egalitarian trade unless they are granted ownership shares. In the arena of internal governance the insertion of Southern groups and interests remains the key priority. Lastly in its social movement location, Fair Trade will need to continue its political engagement in the ongoing effort to promote an alternative globalization agenda.

The constructive reformulation of Fair Trade as a global movement is already underway. It is beginning with the widespread rejection of the idea that Fair Trade's recent market growth should be seen as an unqualified sign of success. It is evident in the strong and repeated reassertion of Fair Trade movement priorities by ATOs, allied NGOs, and people around the world. It is even visible in the tentative moves of FLO and its national initiatives to rekindle political commitments and build new movement alliances. This constructive reformulation must work to realign Fair Trade vision and practice to continue the ongoing task of transforming globalization to bolster the rights of people and places around the world.

References

Bisaillon, V., Gendron, C., and Turcotte, M.F. (2006) "Fair trade and the solidarity economy: the challenges ahead," Montreal: Ecole des Sciences de la Gestion, University of Montreal.

FINE. (2003) *What is FINE?* Online. Available at: www.rafiusa.org/programs/Bangkok%20 proceedings/12What%20is%20FINE.pdf (accessed May 17, 2006).

Raynolds, L.T. (2000) "Re-embedding global agriculture: the international organic and fair trade movements," *Agriculture and Human Values*, 17: 297–309.

—— (2002) "Consumer/producer links in fair trade coffee networks," *Sociologia Ruralis*, 42: 404–424.

Index